50 MORE TIPS & TRICKS FOR DYNAMICS AX 2012

BY MURRAY FIFE

Preface

What You Need For This Guide

All the examples shown in this blueprint were done with the Microsoft Dynamics AX 2012 virtual machine image that was downloaded from the Microsoft CustomerSource or PartnerSource site. If you don't have your own installation of Microsoft Dynamics AX 2012, you can also use the images found on the Microsoft Learning Download Center or deployed through Lifecycle Services. The following list of software from the virtual image was leveraged within this guide:

Microsoft Dynamics AX 2012 R3

Even though all the preceding software was used during the development and testing of the recipes in this book, they may also work on earlier versions of the software with minor tweaks and adjustments, and should also work on later versions without any changes.

Errata

Although we have taken every care to ensure the accuracy of our content, mistakes do happen. If you find a mistake in one of our books—maybe a mistake in the text or the code—we would be grateful if you would report this to us. By doing so, you can save other readers from frustration and help us improve subsequent versions of this book. If you find any errata, please report them by emailing editor@dynamicsaxcompanions.com.

Piracy

Piracy of copyright material on the Internet is an ongoing problem across all media. If you come across any illegal copies of our works, in any form, on the Internet, please provide us with the location address or website name immediately so that we can pursue a remedy.

Please contact us at legal@dynamicsaxcompanions.com with a link to the suspected pirated material.

We appreciate your help in protecting our authors, and our ability to bring you valuable content.

Questions

You can contact us at help@dynamicsaxcompanions.com if you are having a problem with any aspect of the book, and we will do our best to address it.

Table Of Contents

FUNCTIONAL TRICKS (Ctd)

335   OFFICE TRICKS

389   WORKFLOW TRICKS

INTRODUCTION

Dynamics AX is chock full of features that you can implement at the module level, but the true power of the product comes from the boat load of smaller features that are built into the user interface, the modules themselves. Also you can make Dynamics AX even more powerful by taking advantage of the other foundation products such as SharePoint and Office. The real trick is to know that these capabilities are there, and that is what this book is aimed to do.

In this third volume in the Tips & Tricks series we have compiled 50 more tips that you can take advantage of within Dynamics AX 2012 ranging from tips on how you can tune your desktop client, to features within the Dynamics AX application that you may want to start taking advantage of, to creative ways to integrate with Office, and even tweaks and configurations that the system administrator could use to extend out and control the Dynamics AX processes.

Even the most seasoned Dynamics AX user or administrator should find a new tip or trick here that will make them look like a rock star.

DESKTOP CLIENT TIPS

You don't have to go very far within Dynamics AX to start finding features that can make your work a little easier because the desktop client itself is jam packed with features. You can tweak how the client looks so that you can see just the information that you want to see, and you can also use inbuilt shortcuts within the client to make finding information and getting around the system even easier.

Setting Forms To Automatically Open In Edit Mode

There are those people that are casual users of Dynamics AX that look through the data and occasionally update it, and there are those that are always updating and tweaking the data in the system. If you are in the latter of the two groups, then you probably hate going into a form and having to click on the Edit button so that you can change the data. It may be one click, but if you are doing it thousands of times a day, then this quickly starts becoming a chore. Luckily there is a simple option that you can change that will make it so that every time you go into a form, it will automatically start in edit mode.

With all the spare time that you just got, what on earth will you do with yourself.

Setting Forms To Automatically Open In Edit Mode

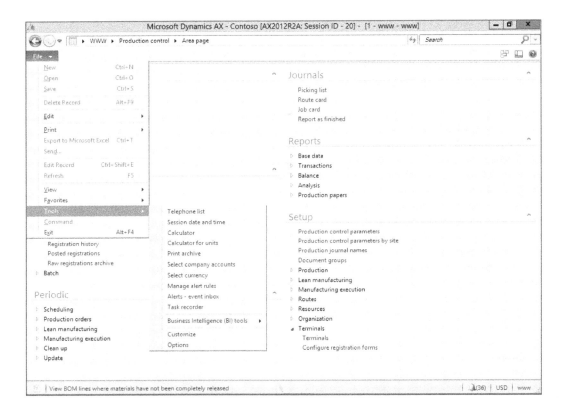

Click on the Files menu, select the Tools submenu, and then click on the Options menu item.

Setting Forms To Automatically Open In Edit Mode

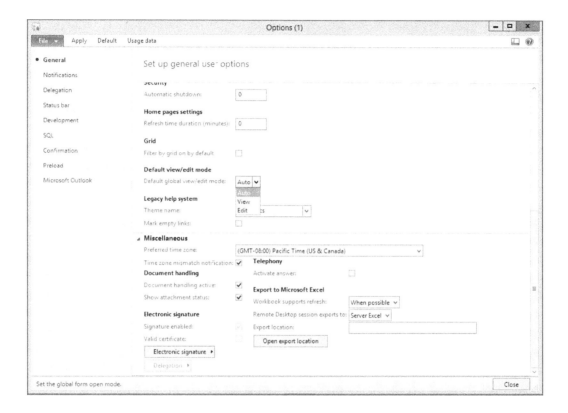

Within the General options, open up the Interface Options tab and change the Default Global View/Edit Mode to Edit.

When you are done, just click the Close button to exit the form.

Setting Forms To Automatically Open In Edit Mode

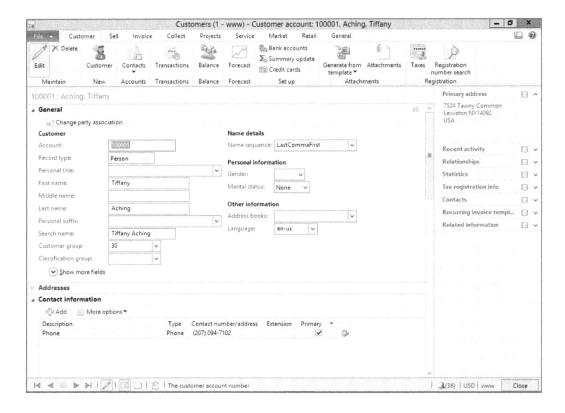

Now whenever you open up a form, you will be in edit mode automatically and you don't even have to click on the Edit button in the ribbon bar.

Create Open Ended Filters By Using Ranges With No Beginning Or End

Everyone knows that you can use the ".." to search for ranges of records when you filter out your data, but it becomes even more useful when you skip either the beginning or end filter selection because then you can create a filter for everything before, or everything after a certain value.

It's like creating your own version of the Neverending (or Neverbegginning) story.

Create Open Ended Filters By Using Ranges With No Beginning Or End

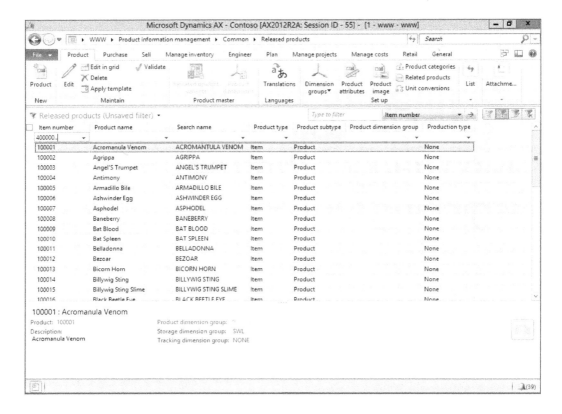

If you create a filter with a beginning value but no end value (like "400000..") then you will see everything from that record on in the system.

Create Open Ended Filters By Using Ranges With No Beginning Or End

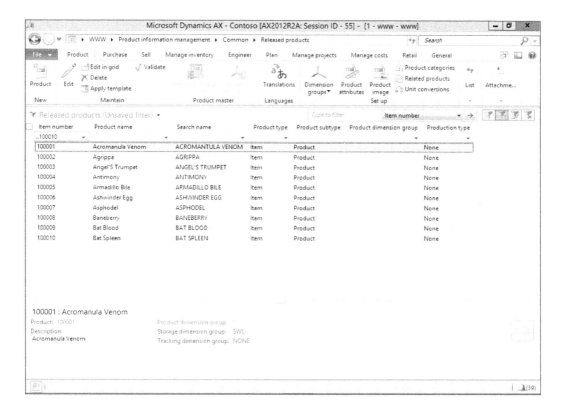

If you create a filter with a end value but no beginning value (like "..100010") then you will see everything up until that record on in the system.

Change The Default Language Within The Rich Client

Dynamics AX is truly a multi-lingual system, and switching the language that the client uses is just a matter of changing the an option.

It's like having your very own Babel Fish in your ear.

Change The Default Language Within The Rich Client

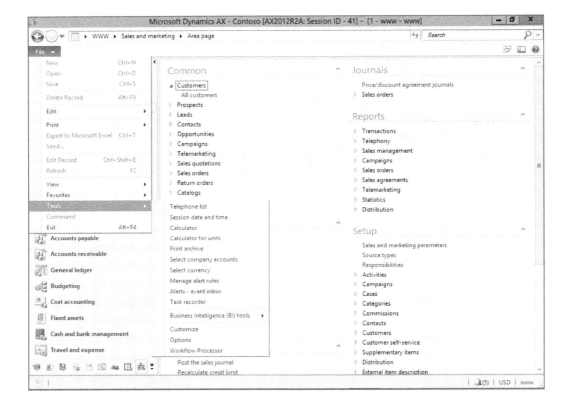

To change the language that your rich client uses, open up the Files menu select the Tools submenu, and then click on the Options menu item.

Change The Default Language Within The Rich Client

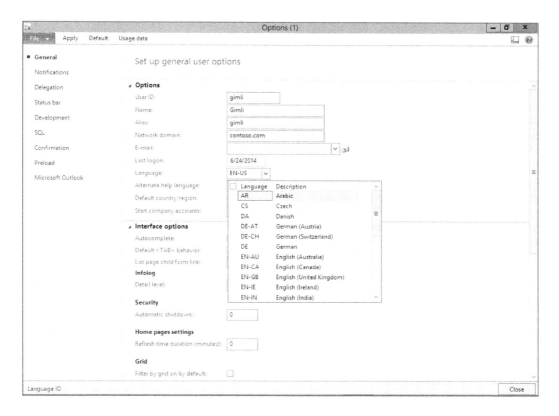

When the Options form is displayed, click on the Language dropdown field and you will be able to see all of the default languages that you can use for your client.

Change The Default Language Within The Rich Client

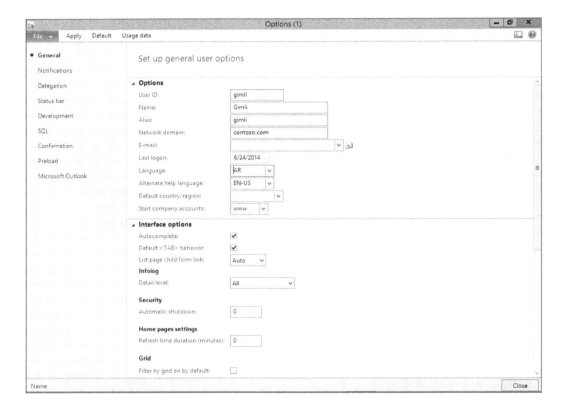

Select the language that you want to use and then close the Options form, and restart the client.

تغيير اللغة الافتراضية ضمن العميل الغنية

الآن يجب على العميل سوف تبدو مختلفة قليلاً.

تغيير اللغة الافتراضية ضمن العميل الغنية

لتغيير اللغة مرة أخرى، تفتح الملفات القائمة حدد القائمة الفرعية أدوات، ومن ثم انقر فوق عنصر القائمة "خيارات".

تغيير اللغة الافتراضية ضمن العميل الغنية

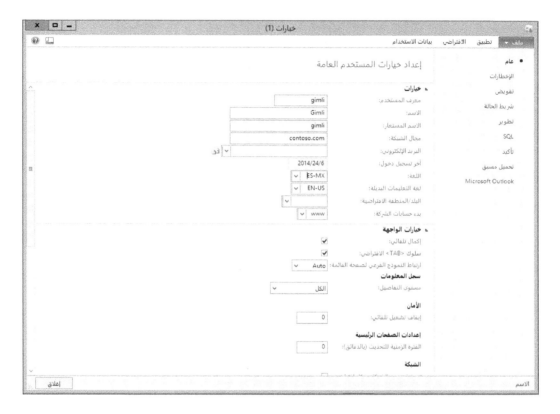

عندما يتم عرض النموذج خيارات، انقر فوق القائمة المنسدلة لحقل اللغة، وسوف تكون قادراً على مشاهدة
كافة اللغات الافتراضية التي يمكنك استخدامها للعميل الخاص بك.

Cambiar El Idioma Predeterminado Dentro Del Cliente Rico

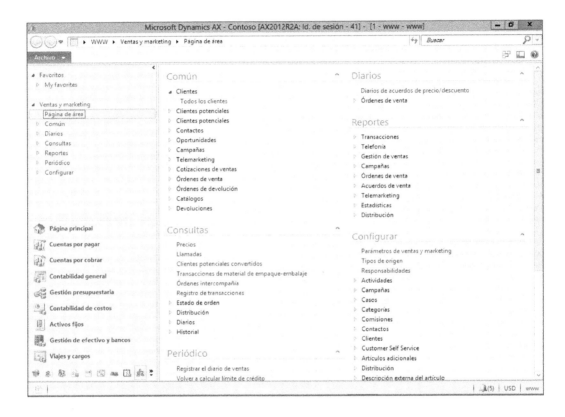

Ahora estarás en un idioma diferente.

Cambiar El Idioma Predeterminado Dentro Del Cl'ente Rico

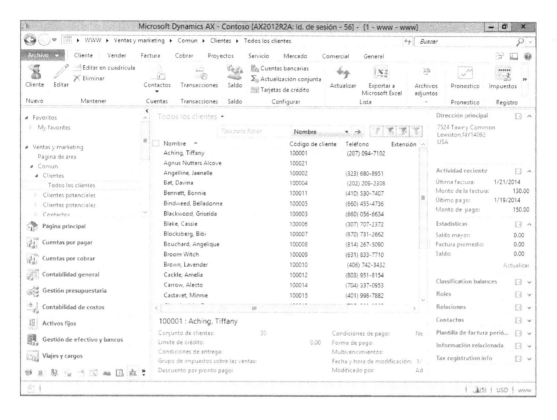

Observe que todas las cajas de hecho y las partidas son cambiadas, así cuando taladra en los formularios.

Cambiar El Idioma Predeterminado Dentro Del Cliente Rico

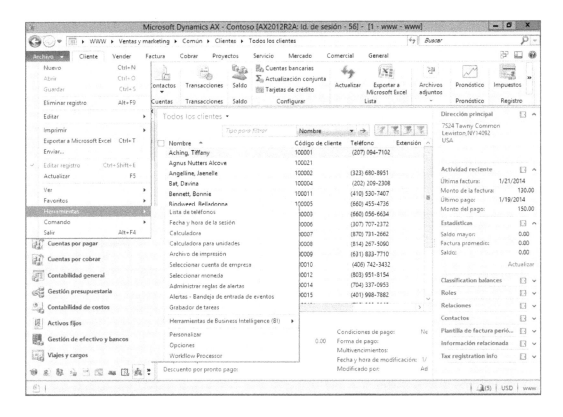

Para volver a los ingleses, abra los archivos de menú Seleccione el submenú herramientas y luego haga clic en el menú de opciones.

Cambiar El Idioma Predeterminado Dentro Del Cliente Rico

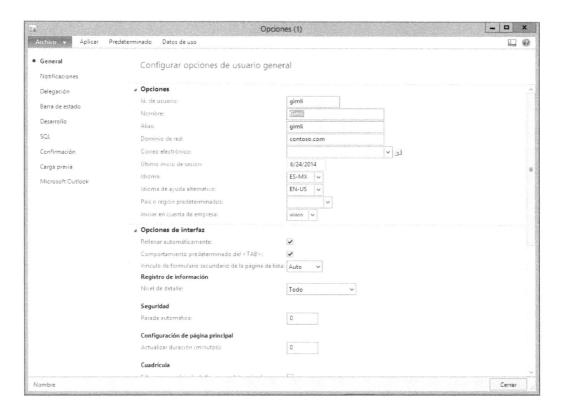

Cambiar el idioma a tu idioma original quiere usar y luego cerrar el formulario de opciones y reiniciar el cliente.

Cambiar El Idioma Predeterminado Dentro Del Cliente Rico

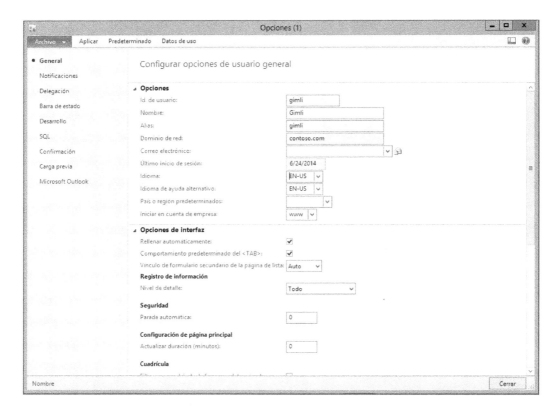

Cambiar el idioma a tu idioma original quiere usar y luego cerrar el formulario de opciones y reiniciar el cliente.

Change The Default Language Within The Rich Client

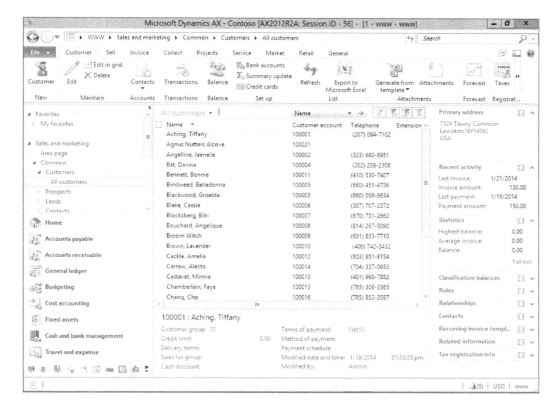

Now we're back to the base language.

How cool is that!

If You Don't Like The Way Your Data Looks The Rename It

If you are as OCD about tidy data as I am, then you probably hate data that does not quite match up with everything else in the database. Maybe it's because you made a mistake in adding some data, or maybe you just want the data to look a little cleaner, we don't judge. Luckily you don't have to live with odd data within Dynamics AX, you can rename the records at any time and all of the related records will be renamed as well.

If it's good enough for Gordon Matthew Thomas Sumner then it's good enough for your data.

If You Don't Like The Way Your Data Looks The Rename It

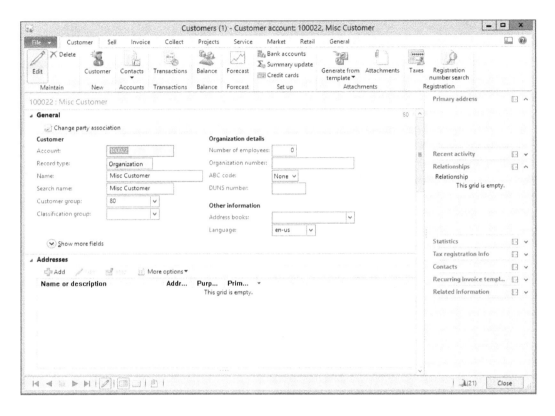

Start off by opening up the record that you want to rename.

If You Don't Like The Way Your Data Looks The Rename It

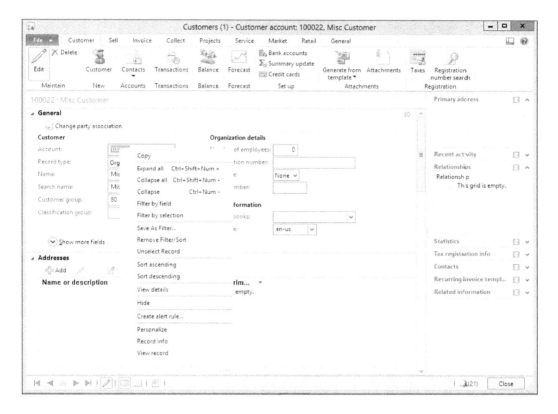

Then right-mouse-click on the form and select the Record Info menu item

If You Don't Like The Way Your Data Looks The Rename It

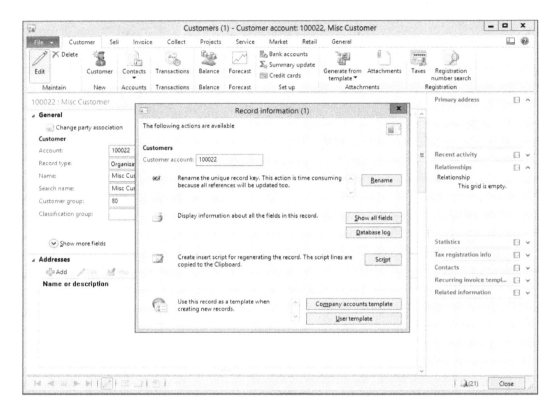

When the Record Information dialog box is displayed, click on the Rename button.

If You Don't Like The Way Your Data Looks The Rename It

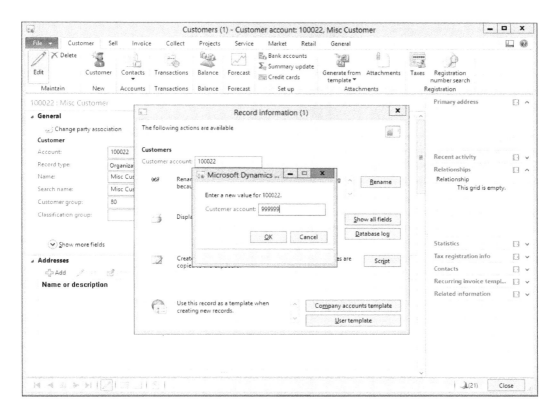

Then the Rename dialog box is displayed, just type in the new record key that you want to use and then click on the OK button.

If You Don't Like The Way Your Data Looks The Rename It

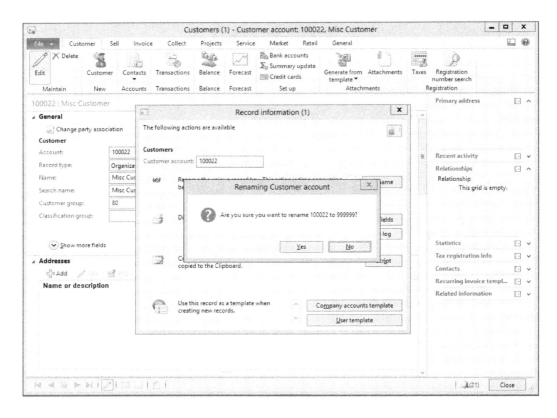

If you are sure that you want to rename the record then click Yes when the dialog box is displayed.

If You Don't Like The Way Your Data Looks The Rename It

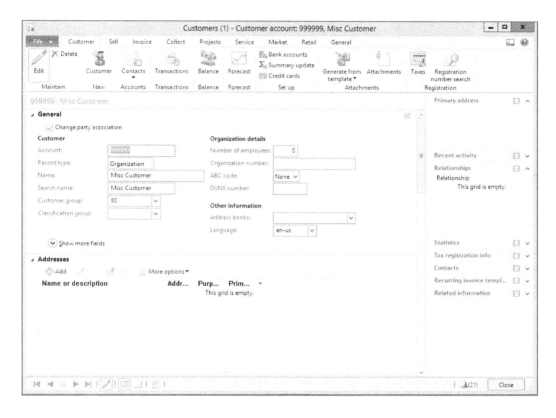

Now when you return to the record you will notice that the record index has been changed.

If You Don't Like The Way Your Data Looks The Rename It

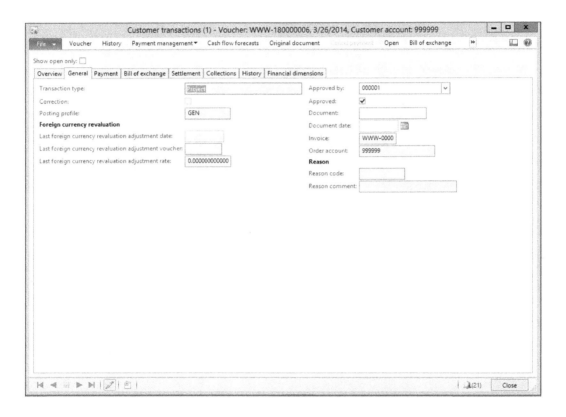

Also, all of the associated records have been changed as well.

How cool is that.

Convert Any Record Into A Template

You may be familiar with the template capabilities that are available within the Released Products, but that isn't the only place that you can create templates. You can turn any record within Dynamics AX into a public or personal template that you can use to pre-populate fields saving you setup time, and also ensuring that all of the miscellaneous fields are configures just how you like them.

It's like having your own cookie cutter creator.

Convert Any Record Into A Template

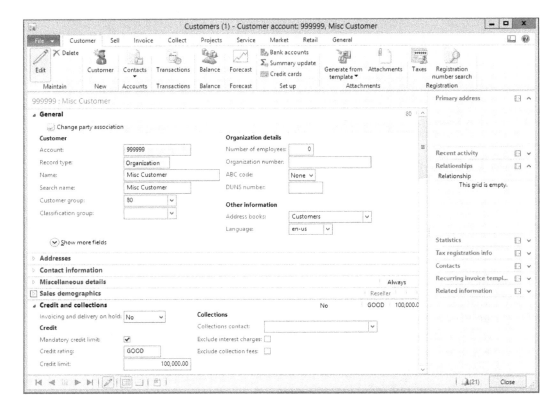

To do this, find the record that you want to use as a template.

Convert Any Record Into A Template

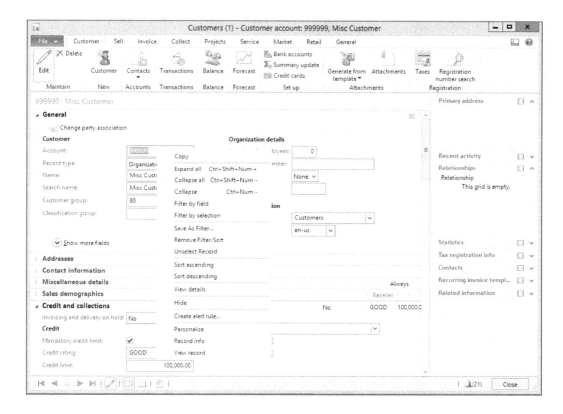

Then right-mouse-click on the form and select the Record Info menu item.

Convert Any Record Into A Template

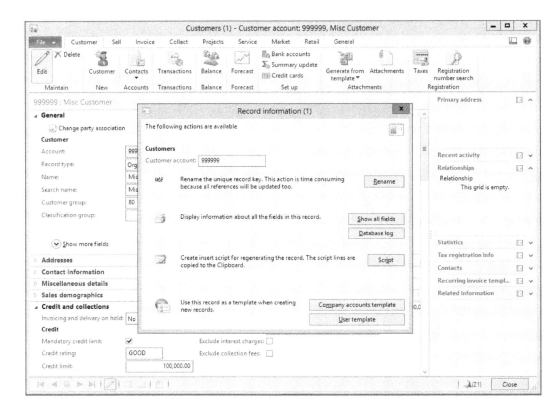

When the Record Information dialog box is displayed, click on either the Company Accounts Template button if you want to make this template available to everyone, or the User Template button if you just want to create a template for your own personal use.

Convert Any Record Into A Template

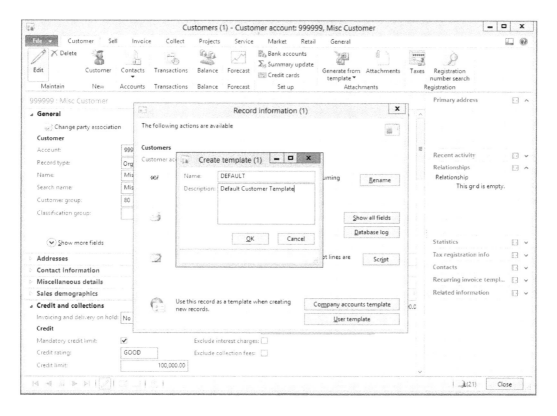

This will open up a Create Template dialog box where you just need to assign your template a Name and a Description and then click on the OK button.

Convert Any Record Into A Template

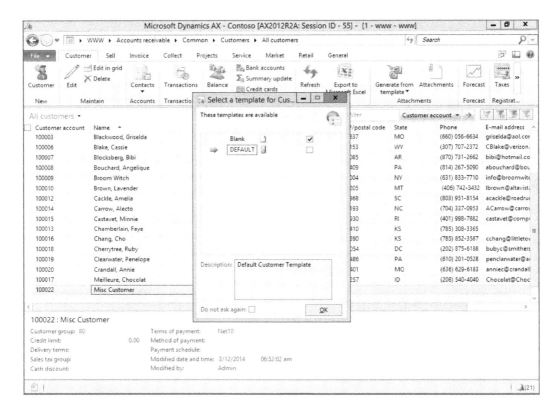

Now when you create a new record, a Select A Template dialog box will be displayed where you can select which template you want to use as the foundation. All you need to do is select one and then click the OK button.

Convert Any Record Into A Template

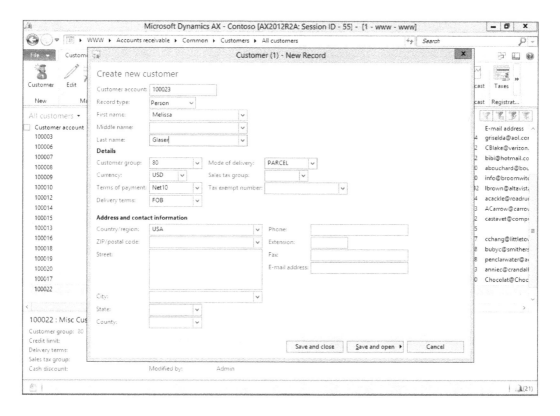

All of the information from the template will default in.

Convert Any Record Into A Template

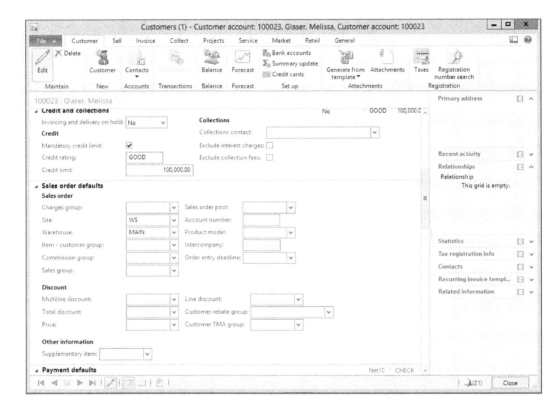

And all of those miscellaneous fields that takes the real setup time will be set up for you.

That should make life a lot easier.

FUNCTIONAL TRICKS

There is a lot that you can do functionally within Dynamics AX, but that should just be the starting point. There are a lot of features that are built into the application to support the core functions that allow you to take it to the next level. You just need to know what they are.

In this section we will show how you can use features like Workflow to streamline your approvals, Cases to manage incidents and issues, Print Management to automate document delivery, Portals for collaboration with partners, and also the Registration Forms to simplify production.

Clock Workers In And Out Using Job Registration

The Job Registration screens within the Production Management area gives you a great way to update your production jobs through touchscreens, but it can also be used for a lot of other functions as well including time clock checking in and out. Workers just need to swipe their badge and the clock starts ticking.

Clock Workers In And Out Using Job Registration

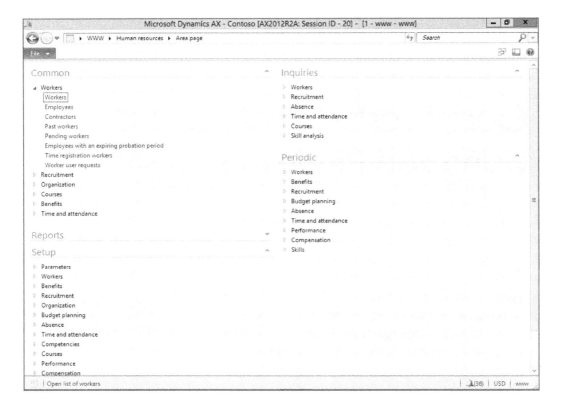

The first step is to configure the workers so that they are allowed to use the Registration screens, and enable the clocking in feature. To do this, click on the Workers menu item within the Workers folder of the Common group of the Human Resources area page.

Clock Workers In And Out Using Job Registration

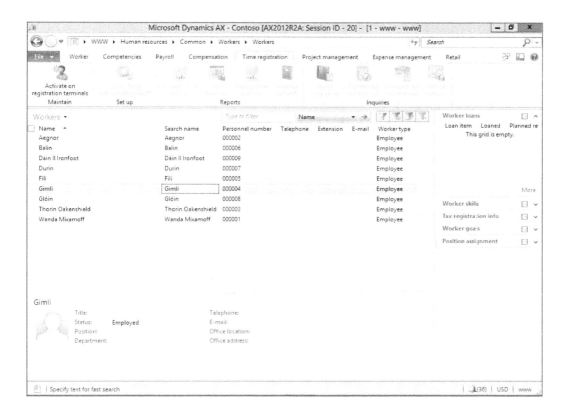

Select the worker (or workers) that you want to enable for clocking in and out, and then click on the Activate on Registration Terminals button within the Maintain group of the Time Registration ribbon bar.

Clock Workers In And Out Using Job Registration

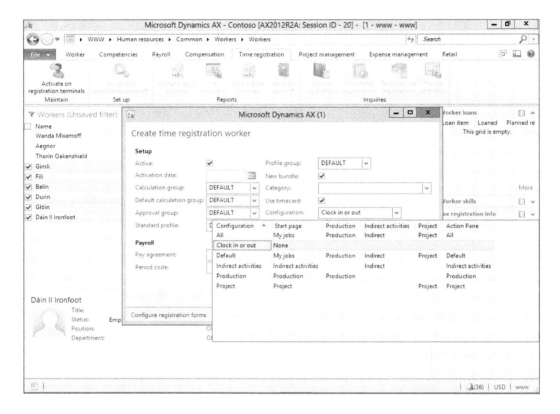

When the Create Time Registration Worker dialog box is displayed, configure all of the required groups and profile defaults and then select the Check In or Out Configuration profile.

Note: if you only want the user to check in and out, then check the Use Timecard option.

When you are done, just click the Close button to exit from the form.

Clock Workers In And Out Using Job Registration

One other configuration that you will need to perform is to assign a Password to the Worker. To do this, just open up the Worker record, select the Employment group, and you will find the Password field within the Time Registration tab group.

Clock Workers In And Out Using Job Registration

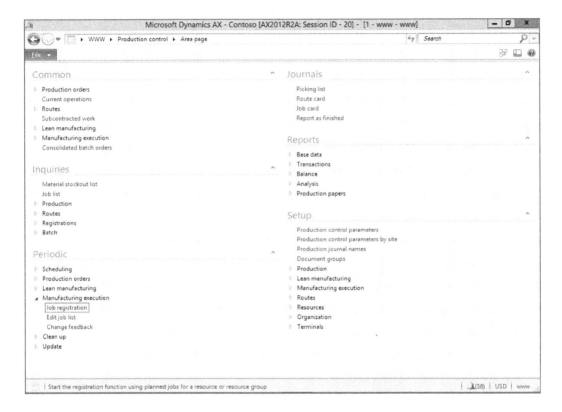

Now you can click on the Job Registration menu item within the Manufacturing Execution folder of the Periodic group within the Production Control area page.

Clock Workers In And Out Using Job Registration

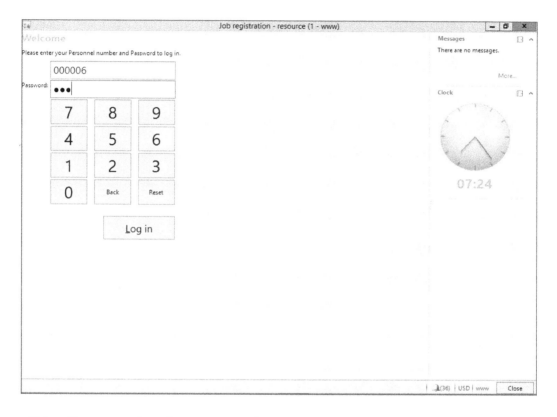

This will open up the Job Registration form where the user is able to type in their ID (or scan their badge) and then type in their password.

Clock Workers In And Out Using Job Registration

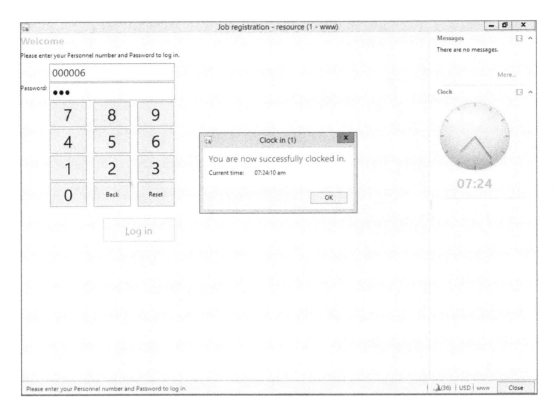

If they are a Time Registration enabled worker then it will check them in.

Clock Workers In And Out Using Job Registration

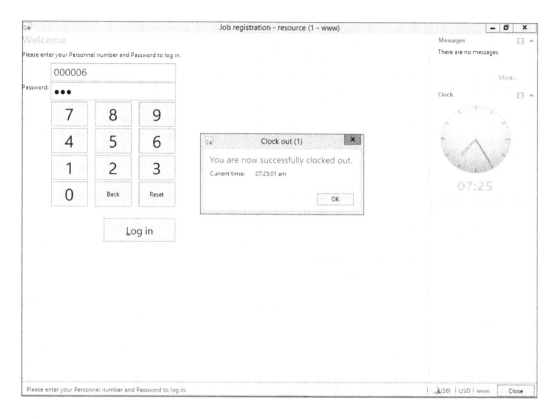

The next time that they log in, it will check them out.

Clock Workers In And Out Using Job Registration

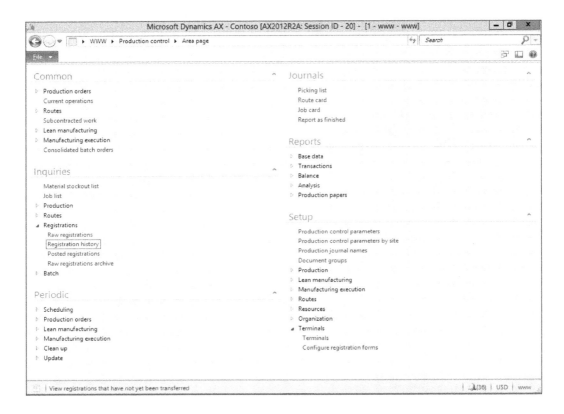

Also, to see all of the check ins and outs, all you need to do is click on the Registration History menu item within the Registration folder of the Inquiries group within the Production Control area page.

Clock Workers In And Out Using Job Registration

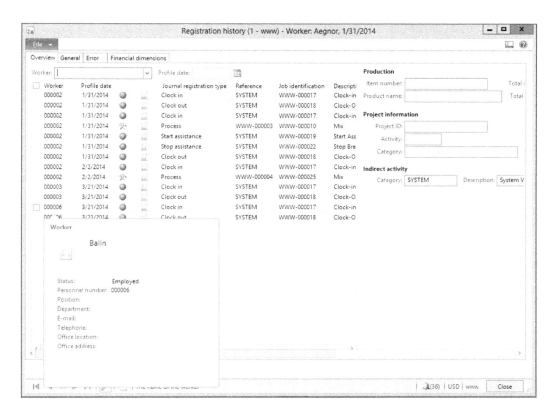

This will show you everyone's records, and all of the check in and out time stamps.

How cool is that.

Change The Default Party Types From Organizations To Person

When you create a new Party record like a Customer, Vendor, Prospect etc. The default Record Type that is used is Organization, which is OK if you are always working with companies. But if you are working with people as your main account, then every time you create the record, you need to change the Record Type to Person. This soon becomes a little annoying.

Rather than torture yourself, just change the default Record Type for those Parties to Person and life will be good again.

Change The Default Party Types From Organizations To Person

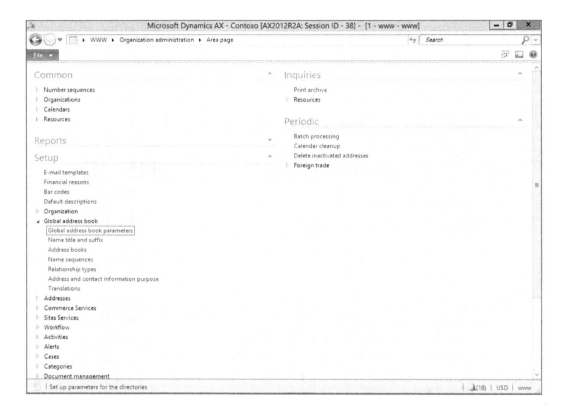

To do this, click on the Global Address Book Parameters menu item within the Global Address Book folder of the Setup group within the Organization Administration area page.

Change The Default Party Types From Organizations To Person

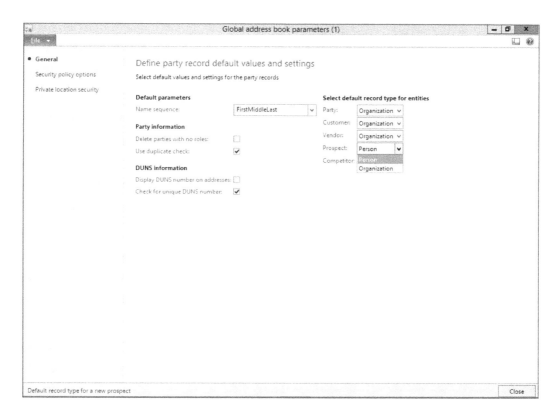

Within the General group you will see the field group titled Select default record types for entities, where you can change the default type from Organization to Person.

Change The Default Party Types From Organizations To Person

Just change the records that you don't want to be Organizations by default to Persons and then click the Close button.

Change The Default Party Types From Organizations To Person

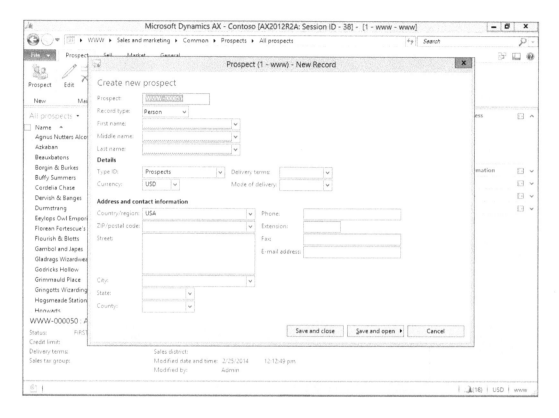

Now when you create a Party record that you changed the type for it will automatically default in as Person.

Add Additional Email Purposes To Route Emails To Different Groups In An Organization

The Print Management function within Dynamics AX is great, and got even better with the CU7 release of R2 when the ability to tokenize your e-mail destinations were added. But by default, there are only a handful of ways that you can segregate out your contact details, and if you have a customer that has multiple departments and you need to send out emails to different people depending on the purpose, it is still a little restrictive. Don't worry though, you can create your own new Business Purpose codes within Dynamics AX and then use them within the Print Management to route different documents to different addresses.

Rain or shine, that e-mail will now get to the right person.

Add Additional Email Purposes To Route Emails To Different Groups In An Organization

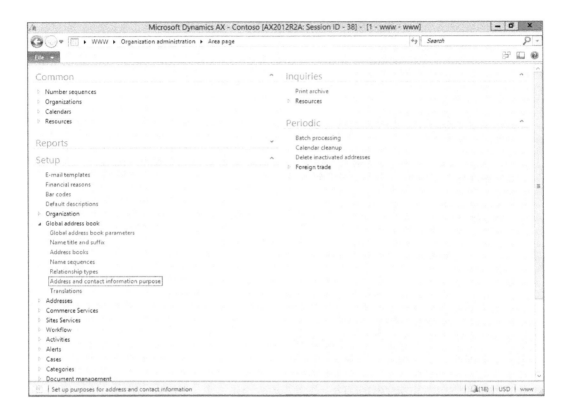

Click on the Address and Contact Information Purpose menu item within the Global Address Book folder of the Setup group within the Organization Administration area page.

Add Additional Email Purposes To Route Emails To Different Groups In An Organization

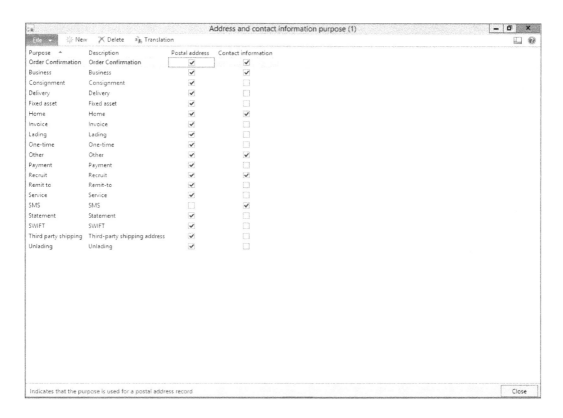

When the Address and Contact Information Purpose maintenance form is displayed, click on the New button within the menu bar to create a new record.

Assign your record a Purpose code, and a Description and then check the Postal Address checkbox if you want this to apply to the postal addresses, and check the Contact Information checkbox if you want this purpose to apply to emails and phone numbers.

Add Additional Email Purposes To Route Emails To Different Groups In An Organization

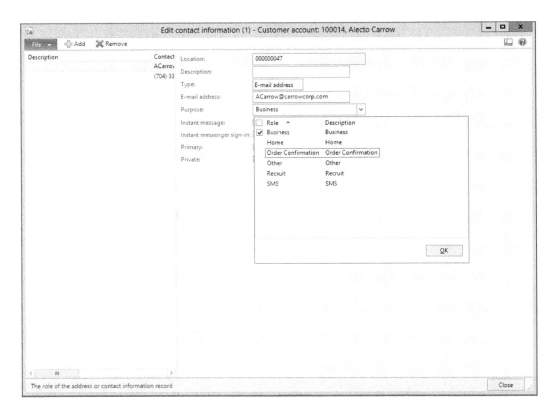

Now when you open up your contact details you will see your new Purpose shows up in the list, and you can mark your e-mails to be associated with it.

Add Additional Email Purposes To Route Emails To Different Groups In An Organization

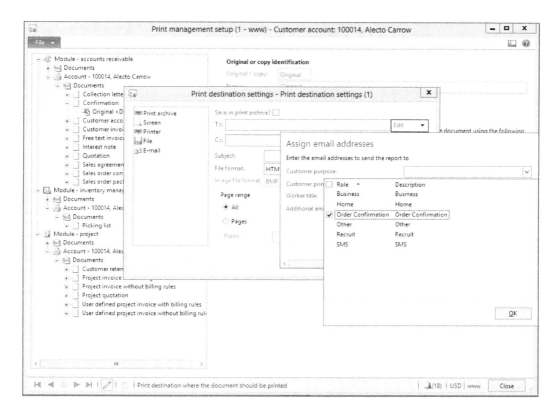

Now when you configure your Print Management you will be able to select your Purpose from the list when you assign the emails using a token.

Add Additional Email Purposes To Route Emails To Different Groups In An Organization

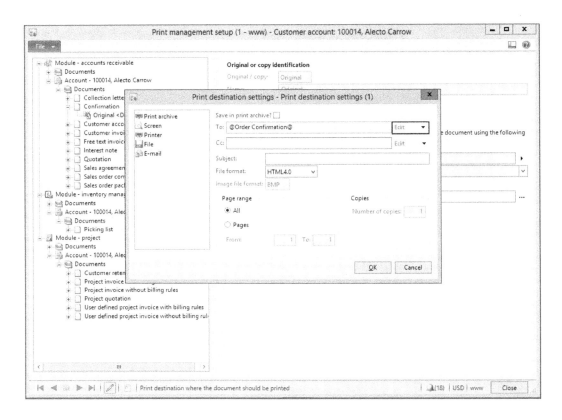

And from now on when you print out the report and have it automatically emailed, it will look for the contact details that match the purpose.

Invoices can go to one account, and confirmations can go to another.

Showing Contacts First Names Last and Last Names First

The order in which contacts names are displayed is a divisive debate that has been raging ever since there have been address books. Should the first name come first, or the last name? Microsoft Dynamics AX has made it's stand by showing the first name first, but if you are a firm believer that the last name is king, then dor't worry, with a quick parameter change you can change the way that all of the contact names are displayed.

Now everyone is able to live in peace and harmony with their contact lists ordered how they like.

Showing Contacts First Names Last and Last Names First

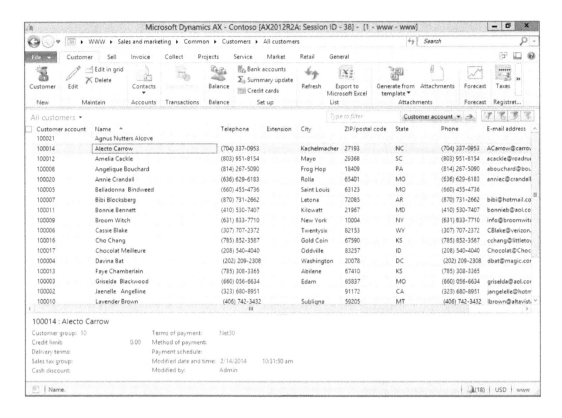

Initially all of your contacts within Dynamics AX show up with their names showing up as first and then last name.

Showing Contacts First Names Last and Last Names First

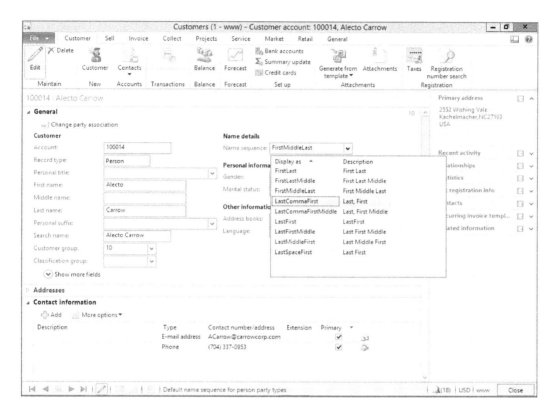

To manually change the way that the contacts name show up, open up the record and then change the Name Sequence to LastCommaFirst.

Note: These formats are completely user configurable, so if you look into the details, then just drill into the details and you will see all of the formats, and also be able to add your own Name Sequences.

Showing Contacts First Names Last and Last Names First

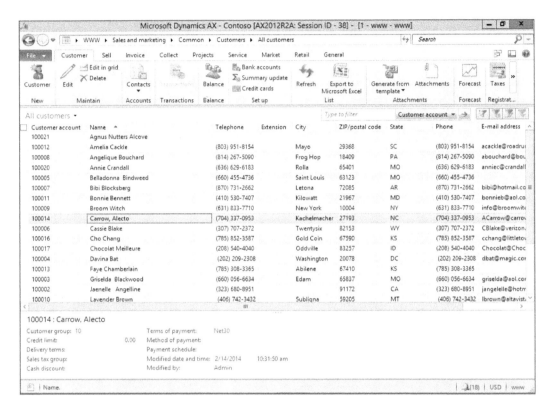

Now when you return to the list, the records name will be displayed with the last name first.

Showing Contacts First Names Last and Last Names First

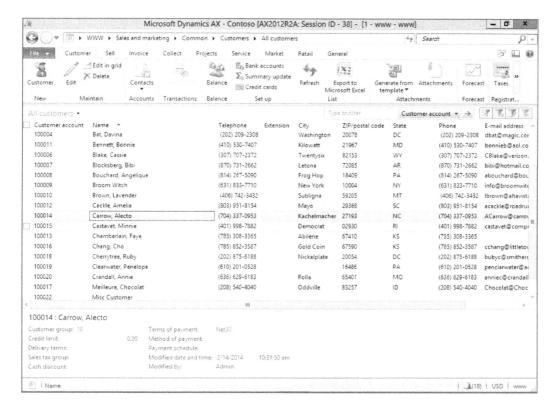

After a little maintenance, all of the contacts now show up the same way.

Showing Contacts First Names Last and Last Names First

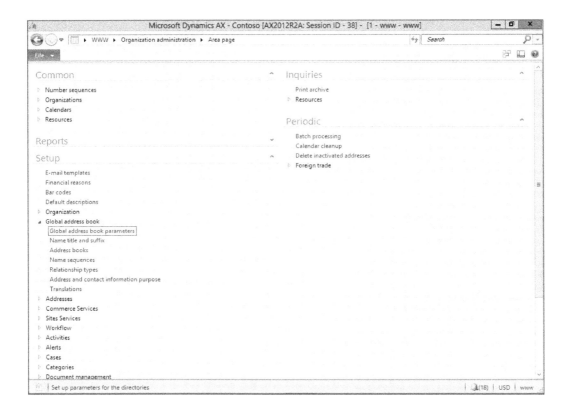

Rather than manually changing all of the records, you can set Dynamics AX up with a default Name Sequence so that all of your contacts show up wit their names the way that you like it. To do this, click on the Global Address Book Parameters menu item within the Global Address Book folder of the Setup group within the Organization Administration area page.

Showing Contacts First Names Last and Last Names First

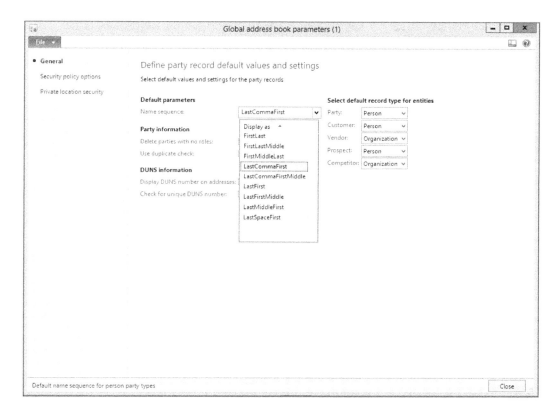

From within the General tab of the Global Address Book Parameters you can set the Name Sequence default.

Track Relationships Between Parties Through The Global Address Book

In addition to needing to track all of the common information within Dynamics AX like the Customers and Vendors, there is a lot of relationship information that you may want to record as well. You may want to track relationships between companies such as lenders, subsidiaries etc., between people such as recruiters, family members etc. or even between companies and people like board members, founders etc. The good news is that through the Global Address Book you can do just that.

Now we finally have a way to model the six degrees of Kevin Bacon.

Track Relationships Between Parties Through The Global Address Book

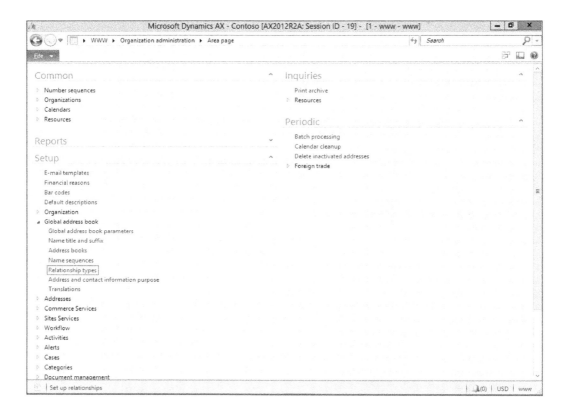

Click on the Relationship Types menu item within the Global Address Book folder of the Setup group within the Organization Administration area page.

Track Relationships Between Parties Through The Global Address Book

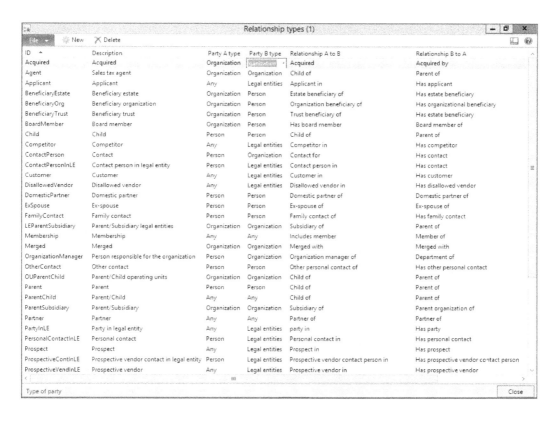

When the Relationship Types maintenance form is displayed you will see all of the different relationships that you can track by default within Dynamics AX.

Track Relationships Between Parties Through The Global Address Book

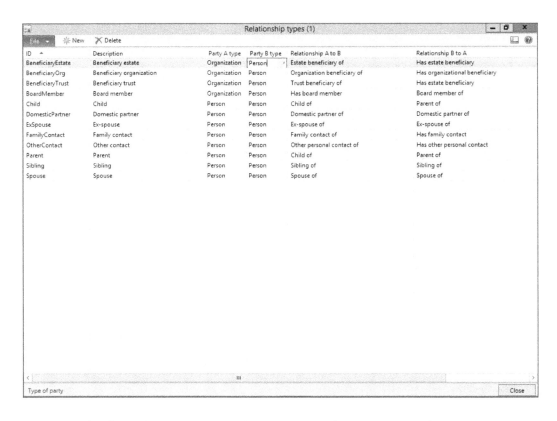

You can also filter the types just to the ones that relate to a particular Party Type.

Track Relationships Between Parties Through The Global Address Book

To create a relationship between the entities click on the Global Address Book menu within the Common group of the Home area page.

Track Relationships Between Parties Through The Global Address Book

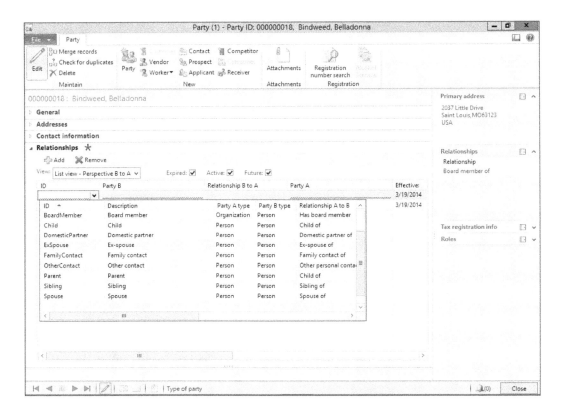

When the Global Address Book list page is displayed, open up the Party record that you want to create a relationship against and the jump to the Relationship tab.

To add a new Relationship click on the Add button within the tabs menu bar.

Then select the type of Relationship from the ID dropdown list.

Track Relationships Between Parties Through The Global Address Book

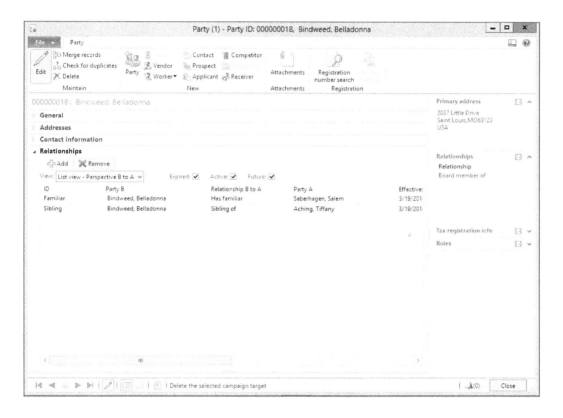

Then select the A and B parties that you want to relate with each other.

Repeat the process until you have defined all of the relationships and then click the Close button.

Track Social Media Information Against Contacts

The contact management feature within Dynamics AX allows you to track an unlimited number of phone numbers, email addresses, and websites against a contact. But these are just the direct contact types. We live in the age of Social Media, and there are so many other different sources of information that we want to track against our contacts. Don't' despair, with a small tweak to the configuration within Dynamics AX, you can add additional contact media types and start tracking all this information.

Now you will be able to get the full scoop on you customers and contacts.

Track Social Media Information Against Contacts

By default, Dynamics AX lets you track the common information against contacts like phone numbers, email addresses, web sites, and telex (who the heck even uses that).

Track Social Media Information Against Contacts

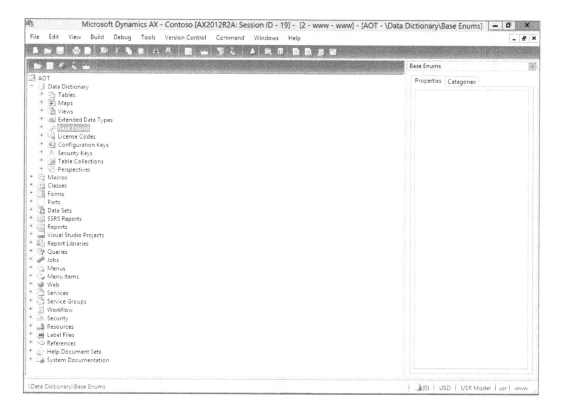

To add more types to Dynamics AX, open up AOT, expand the Data Dictionary group, and then expand the Base Enums group.

Track Social Media Information Against Contacts

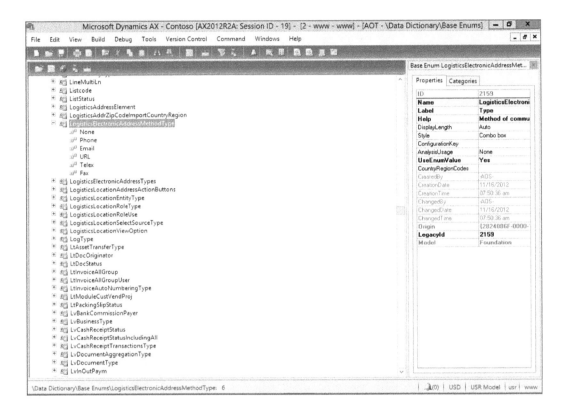

Within the Base Enums, find the LogisticsElectronicAddressMethodTypes enumeration and expand it.

You will see all of the standard types are listed there.

Track Social Media Information Against Contacts

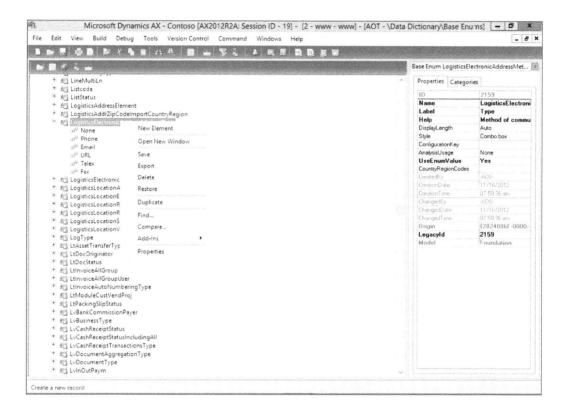

Now right-mouse-click on the LogisticsElectronicAddressMethodTypes
enumeration, and select the New Element menu item.

Track Social Media Information Against Contacts

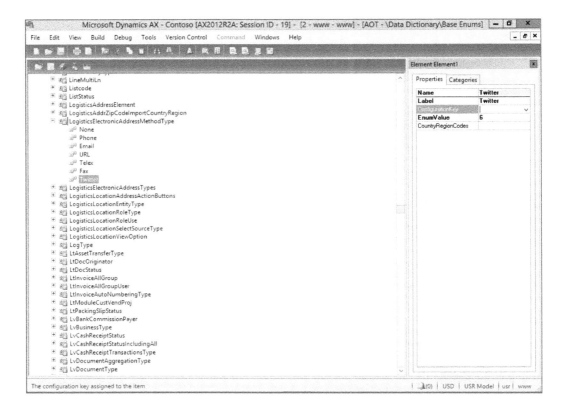

When the new element is created, change the Name and Label to be your new method type – in this case Twitter.

Track Social Media Information Against Contacts

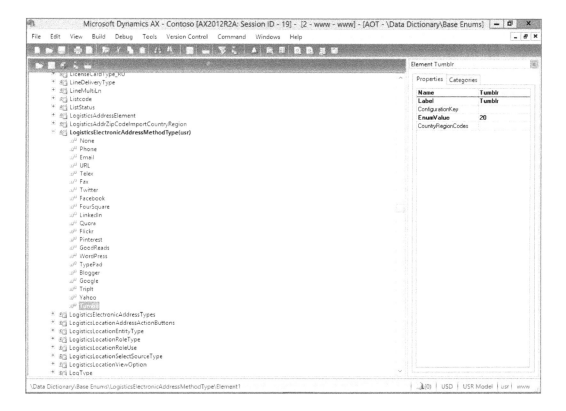

If you want to be an overachiever, then you can add a few more contact method types through AOT.

To test this, save your model and then restart Dynamics AX.

Track Social Media Information Against Contacts

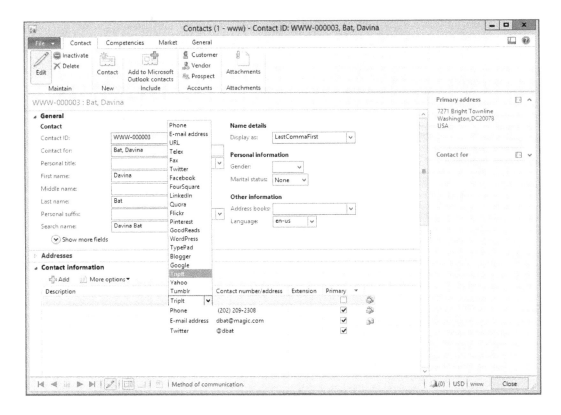

Now when you look at the types that are available for you within the Contact Information you will see that you have the option for all for the different social media types.

Track Social Media Information Against Contacts

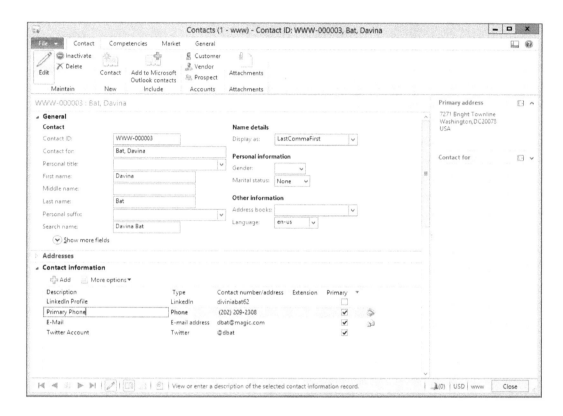

Now you can track everything properly.

How cool is that?

Schedule Multiple Discussions At Once Through The Mass Creation Option

Discussions are a polite term for being called into a meeting with HR, but the creation of them does not have to be a painful affair – at least for the HR department. There is a mass creation feature that allows you to create a block of discussion appointments for a group of employees that makes this process a breeze.

Being called into the principal's office has never been so automated.

Schedule Multiple Discussions At Once Through The Mass Creation Option

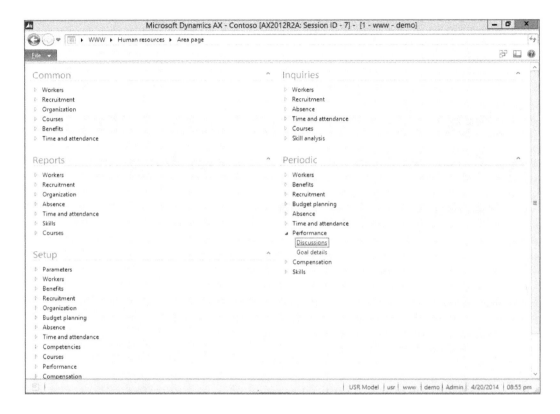

Click on the Discussions menu item within the Performance folder of the Periodic group within the Human Resources area page.

Schedule Multiple Discussions At Once Through The Mass Creation Option

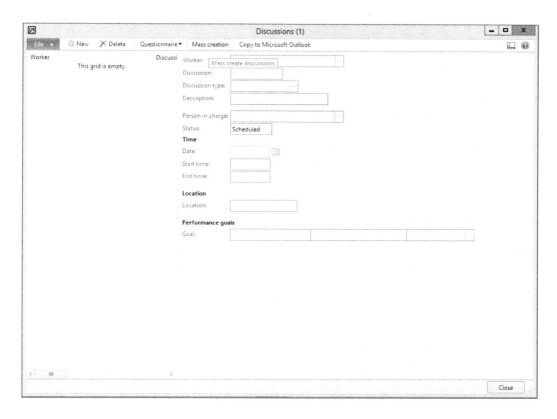

When the Discussions maintenance form is displayed, click on the Mass Creation button in the menu bar.

Schedule Multiple Discussions At Once Through The Mass Creation Option

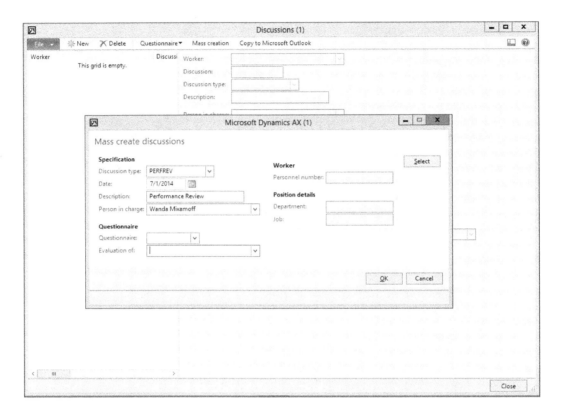

When the Mass Create Discussions dialog box is displayed, enter in all of the discussion information and the date of the planned discussion.

If you want to refine the workers that are included in the discussion group, then you can click on the Select button and refine the selection criteria.

When you have set up your discussion template, just click on the OK button.

Schedule Multiple Discussions At Once Through The Mass Creation Option

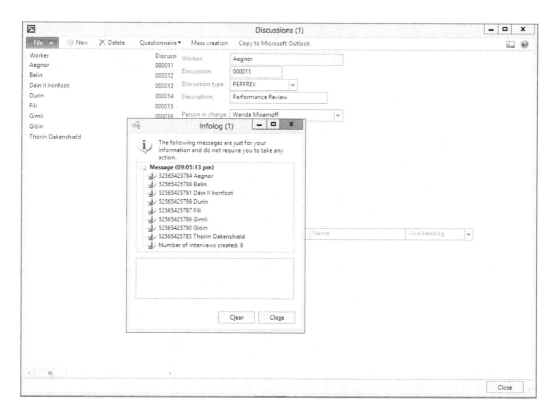

You will get an Infolog notification of all the discussions that have been created.

Schedule Multiple Discussions At Once Through The Mass Creation Option

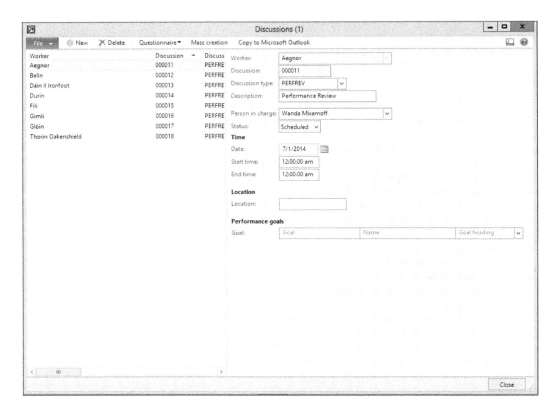

And when you return to the Discussions maintenance form you will see that everything has been scheduled for you.

Create Appointments In Outlook Directly From The Discussions

The only thing worse that having a "Discussion" with Human Resources is to miss a "Discussion", and have another "Discussion" created to discuss your poor time planning. To solve this, you may want to think about creating sending out meeting reminders when Discussions are created, which is just the click on the button within Dynamics AX.

Even if the discussion isn't pleasant, then at least the creation of one isn't.

Create Appointments In Outlook Directly From The Discussions

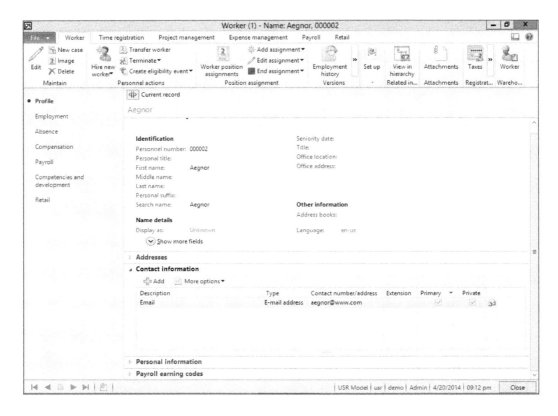

Before you start, make sure that you have an e-mail address associated with your employees...

Create Appointments In Outlook Directly From The Discussions

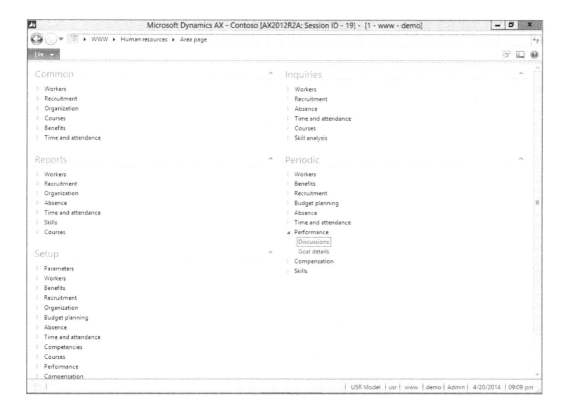

Click on the Discussions menu item within the Performance folder of the Periodic group within the Human Resources area page.

Create Appointments In Outlook Directly From The Discussions

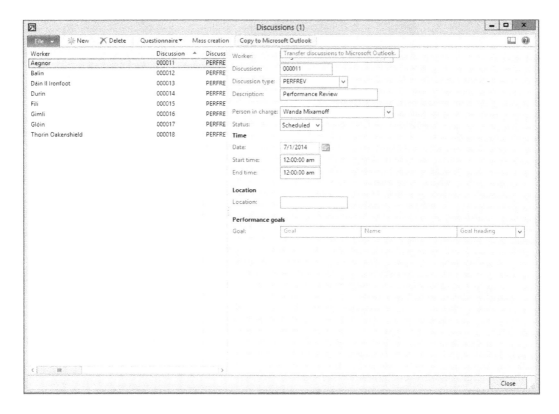

When the Discussions maintenance form is displayed, select the Discussion that you want to send out the appointment for and then click on the Copy To Microsoft Outlook button on the menu bar.

Create Appointments In Outlook Directly From The Discussions

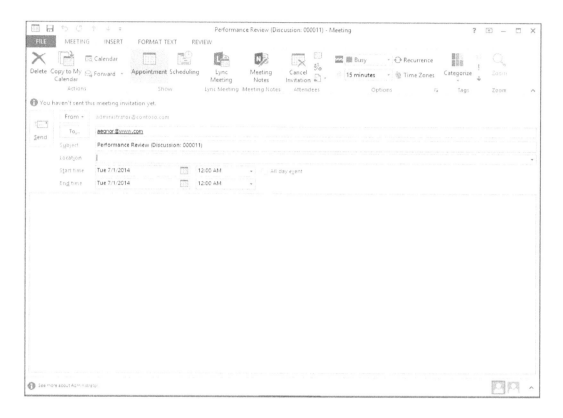

This will create an Outlook appointment for you with the date and time from the Discussion record, and also pre-populate it with the workers email address in the To box.

All you really need to do is click the Send button and the worker will have it on their calendar.

Create Appointments In Outlook Directly From The Discussions

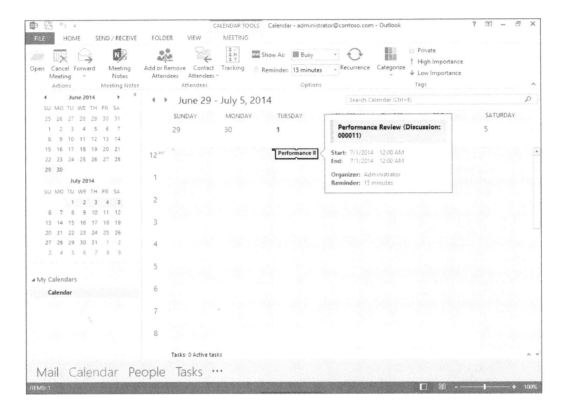

If you look at Outlook you will now see the appointment has been added to your calendar as well.

This is too organized.

Tally Packaging Quantities On Order Lines

If you are putting your products into boxes before you ship them out, or if you are worried about the cube space that the order lines will take up when being shipped then you might want to get Dynamics AX to calculate them on the fly as you enter in the order lines. The package calculation allows you to define how many items of a product goes into a standard package, and then it will tell you how many of those packages will be used on the order. For example, if you can fit 4 items in a box and the customer orders 6 then it will tell you that you need 2 boxes.

Now you can optimize you packing regardless of the product.

Tally Packaging Quantities On Order Lines

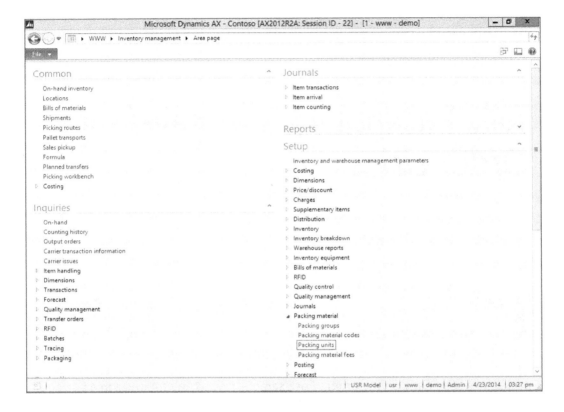

Click on the Packing Units menu item within the Packing Material folder of the Setup group within the Inventory Management area page.

Tally Packaging Quantities On Order Lines

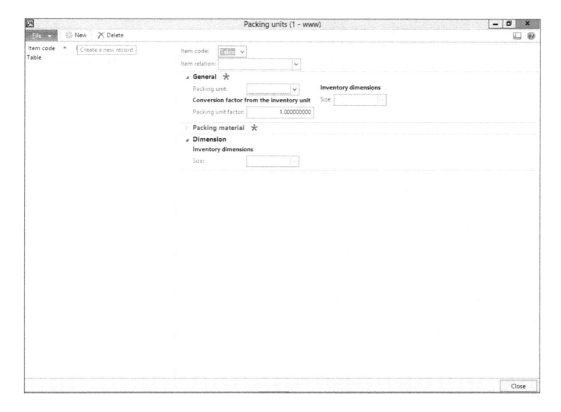

Then the Packaging Units maintenance form is displayed, click on the New button in the menu bar to add a new packaging record.

Tally Packaging Quantities On Order Lines

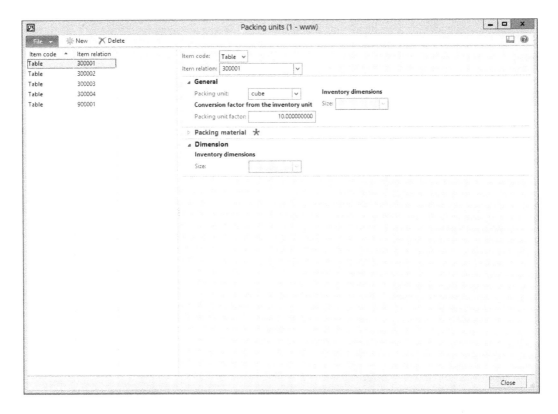

Now just add an Item Relation for the product that you want to track the packaging quantity for, and enter the Packaging Unit and Packaging Unit Factor within the General tab.

When you are done configuring the packaging quantities, click on the Close button to exit from the form.

Tally Packaging Quantities On Order Lines

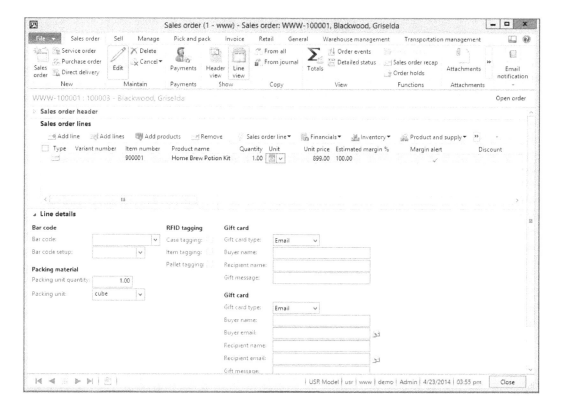

Now when you look at your Sales Order Lines, if you open up the Line Details tab, and then look within the Packing sub-tab, you will see that the Packing Material group shows the number of packages that you will need to the quantity.

Tally Packaging Quantities On Order Lines

To make this even better, right-mouse-click on the order line and select the Personalize option.

Tally Packaging Quantities On Order Lines

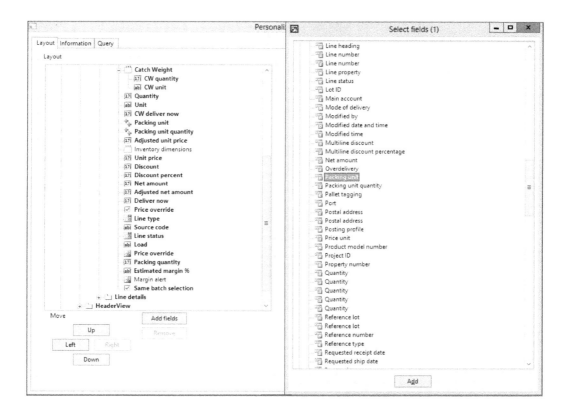

Then find the Packing Unit and Packing Unit Quantity fields and add them to the order lines table.

Tally Packaging Quantities On Order Lines

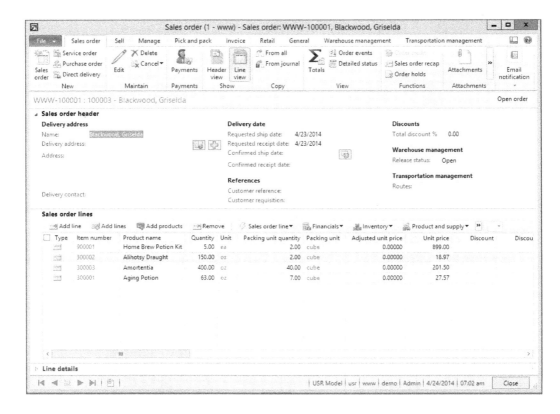

Now as you build up the order, the packing units will show up alongside the order quantities.

Isn't that so useful?

Generate Product Bar Code Labels Through Retail

The Retail area of Dynamics AX has a boat load of goodies embedded within it. One example of this is the capability to configure bar code labels for products that you can print at use for scanning and product identification. But just because it is configured through the Retail area it doesn't mean that you have to be a retail style company in order to take advantage of it. All you need to do is get over the stigma of the Retail label and set it up.

I know it feels naughty to use the Retail area, but it feels so good to do it...

Generate Product Bar Code Labels Through Retail

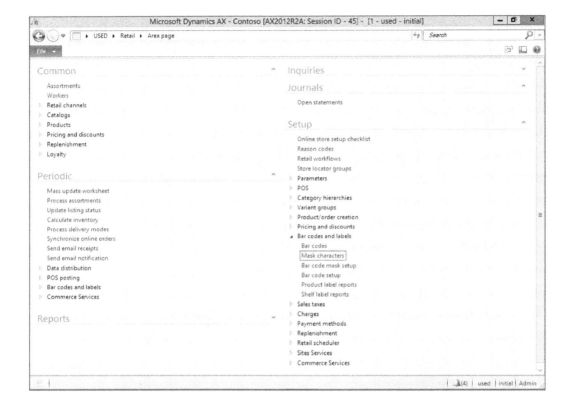

First we need to do a little bit of setup to configure the bar codes themselves. And the first step is to configure the bar code Mask Characters.

To do this, click on the Mask Characters menu item within the Bar Codes and Labels folder of the Setup group within the Retail area page.

Generate Product Bar Code Labels Through Retail

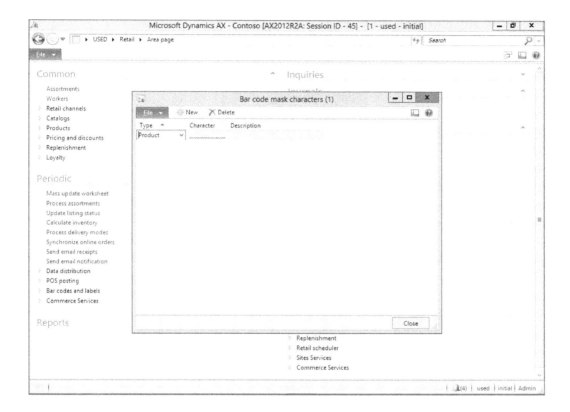

When the Bar Code Mask Characters maintenance form is displayed, click on the New button on the menu bar to add a new record.

Generate Product Bar Code Labels Through Retail

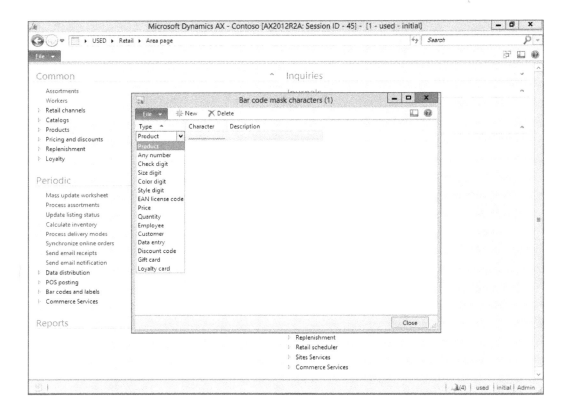

For each different type of field that we are including in the bar code, we need to create a mask. For this example, select the Product option from the Type dropdown list.

Generate Product Bar Code Labels Through Retail

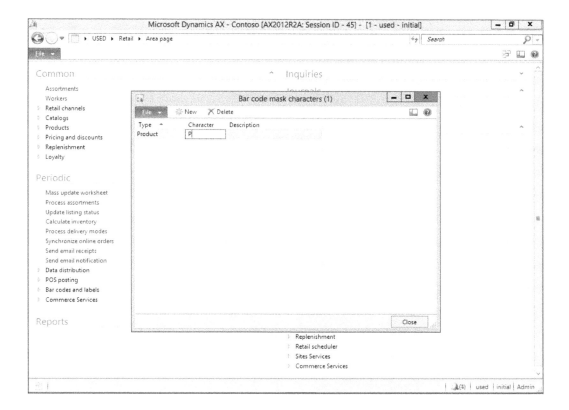

Then set the Character to P.

Generate Product Bar Code Labels Through Retail

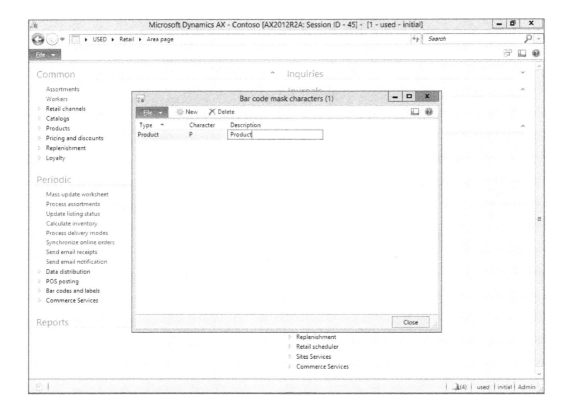

Finally, add a Description and then click on the Close button to exit from the form.

Generate Product Bar Code Labels Through Retail

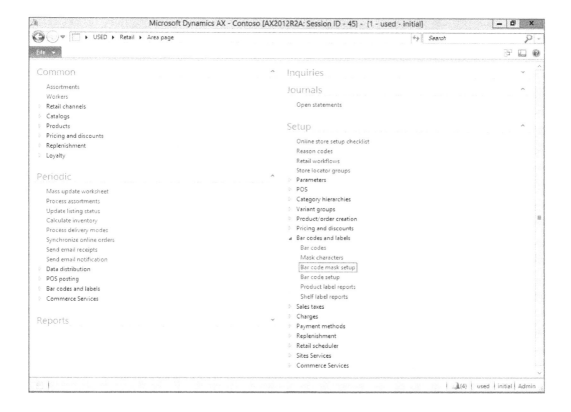

Now we need to configure a mask to use on the bar codes. To do this, click on the Bar Code Mask Setup menu item within the Bar Codes and Labels folder of the Setup group within the Retail area page.

Generate Product Bar Code Labels Through Retail

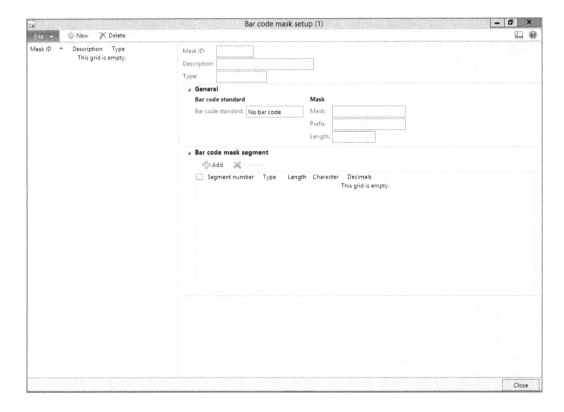

When the Bar Code Mask Setup maintenance form is displayed, click on the New button in the menu bar to create a new record.

Generate Product Bar Code Labels Through Retail

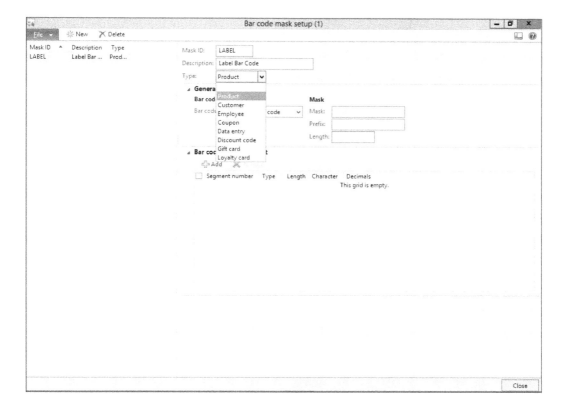

Set the Mask ID, and Description, and then select the Product option from the Type dropdown list.

Generate Product Bar Code Labels Through Retail

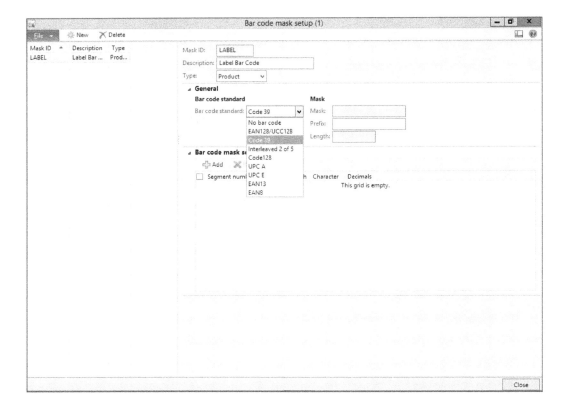

Then select the Bar Code Standard that you want to use to generate the bar code with.

Generate Product Bar Code Labels Through Retail

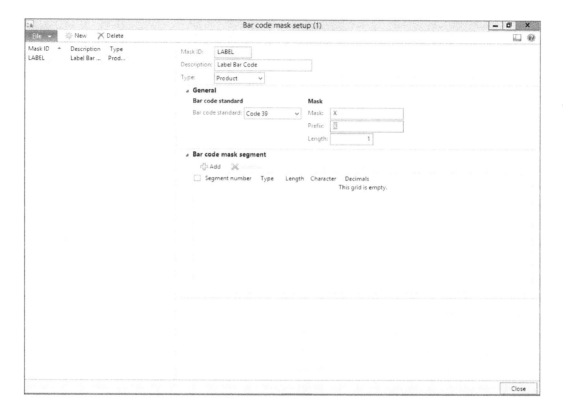

And add a Prefix to the bar code record – I just used X for mine.

Then click on the Add button within the menu bar for the Bar Code Mask Segment to create a new segment within the bar code.

Generate Product Bar Code Labels Through Retail

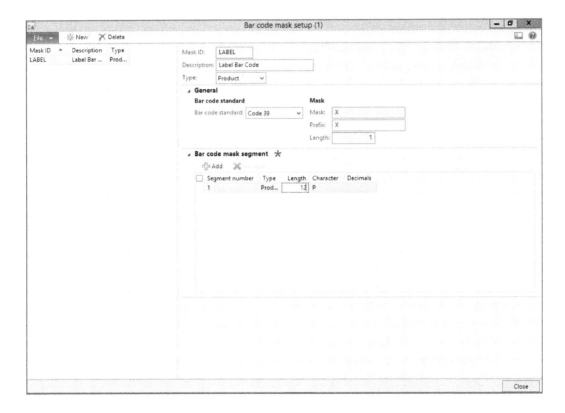

Set the Type to be Product and then set the Length of the bar code.

Generate Product Bar Code Labels Through Retail

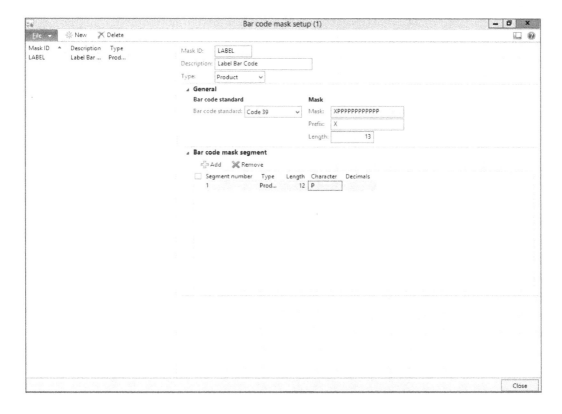

Now you will notice that the Mask field has been populated for you, and you can click on the Close button to exit from the form.

Generate Product Bar Code Labels Through Retail

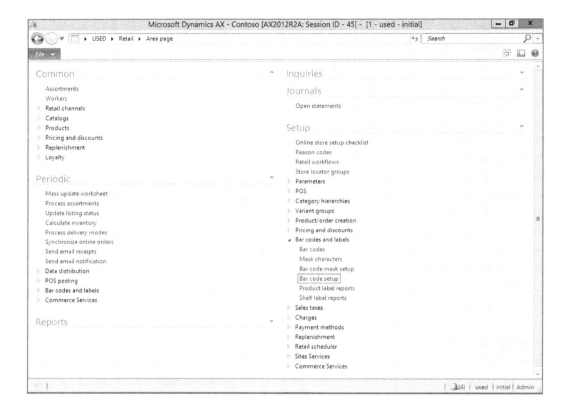

Now click on the Bar Code Setup menu item within the Bar Codes and Labels folder of the Setup group within the Retail area page.

Generate Product Bar Code Labels Through Retail

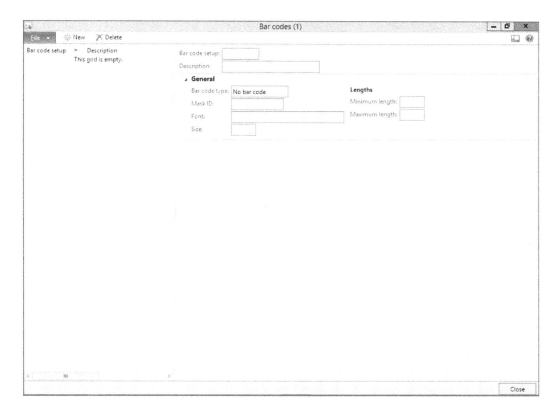

When the Bar Codes maintenance form is displayed, click on the New button in the menu bar to create a new record.

Generate Product Bar Code Labels Through Retail

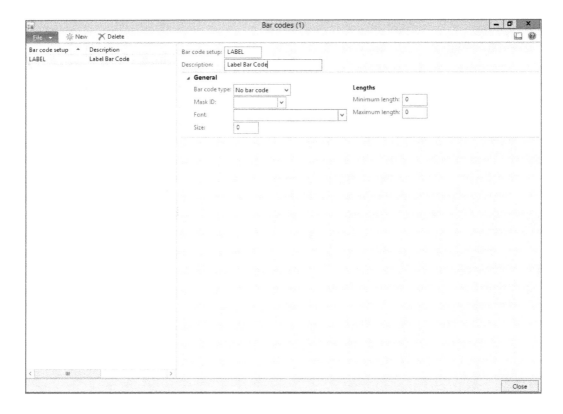

Assign your new record a Bar Code Setup code, and also a Description.

Generate Product Bar Code Labels Through Retail

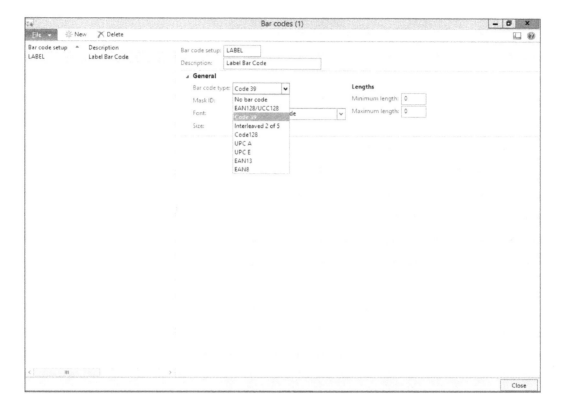

Then select the same Bar Code Type as you configured in the previous step.

Generate Product Bar Code Labels Through Retail

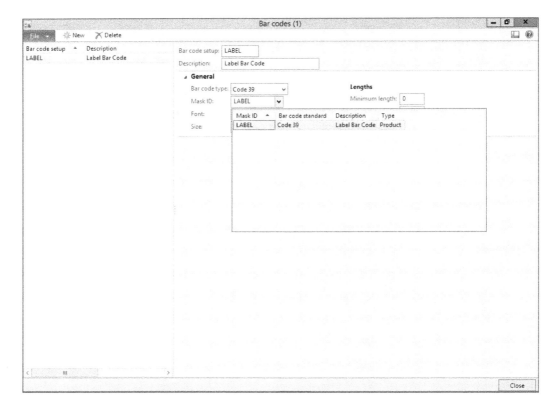

From the Mask ID dropdown, select the Mask that you just configured as well.

Generate Product Bar Code Labels Through Retail

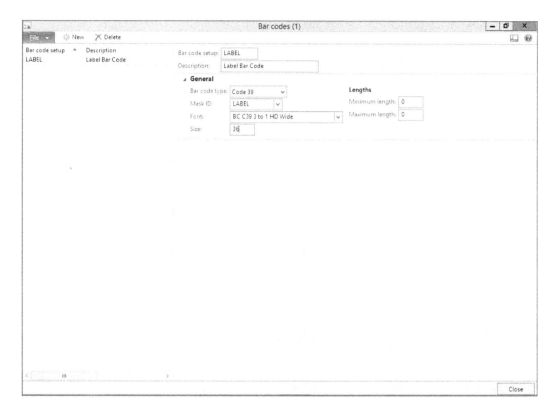

Set the Size field to be the font size that you want to use for the bar code.

Generate Product Bar Code Labels Through Retail

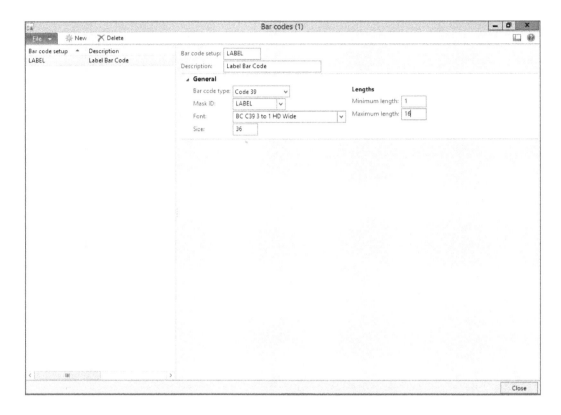

And then set the Minimum and Maximum Length for the bar code.

When you have done that, just click on the Close button to exit from the form.

Generate Product Bar Code Labels Through Retail

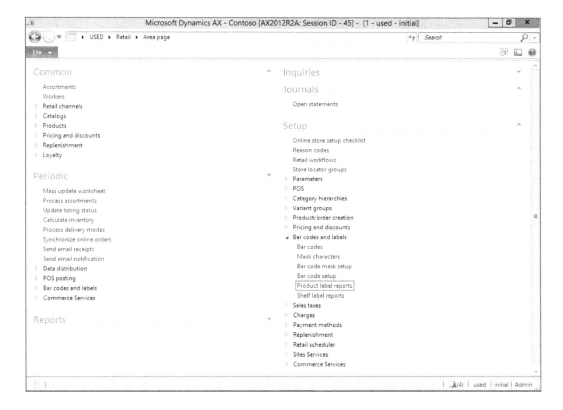

Nearly done with the setup. We just have to configure the label report. Do this by clicking on the Product Label Reports menu item within the Bar Codes and Labels folder of the Setup group within the Retail area page.

Generate Product Bar Code Labels Through Retail

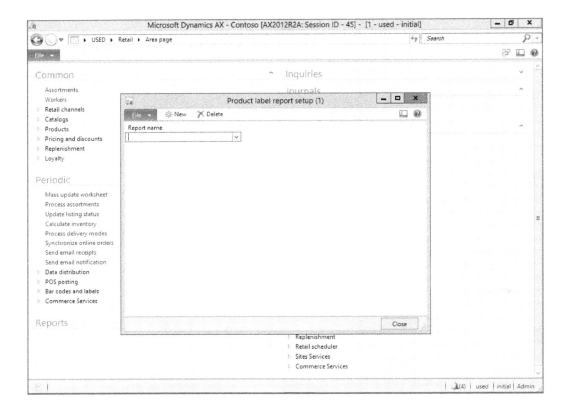

When the Product Label Report Setup maintenance form is displayed, click on the New button in the menu bar to create a new record.

Generate Product Bar Code Labels Through Retail

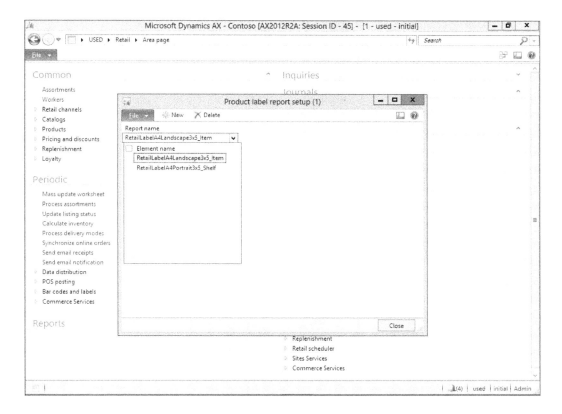

Then select the label form that is delivered with Dynamics AX for the Item.

Generate Product Bar Code Labels Through Retail

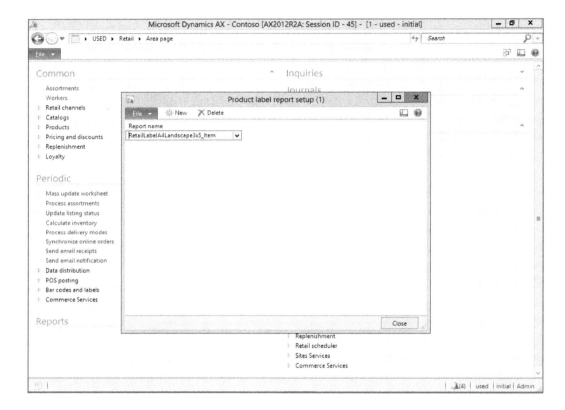

When you have done that, click on the Close button to exit from the form.

Generate Product Bar Code Labels Through Retail

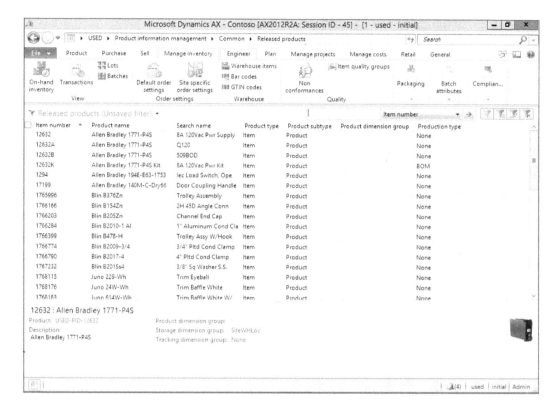

Now we can configure the bar codes for the products. To do this, open up the Released Products maintenance form, and click on the Bar Codes menu item within the Maintenance group of the Manage Inventory ribbon bar.

Generate Product Bar Code Labels Through Retail

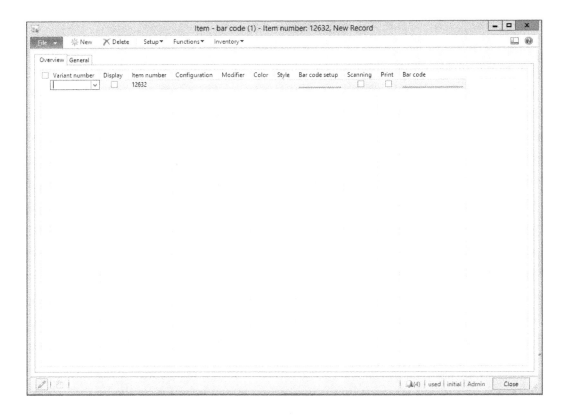

When the Item Bar Codes maintenance form is displayed it will automatically have a line shown in edit mode. You can create the Bar Code record by hand if you like, although a better way is to get Dynamics AX to do it. So click on the Delete button in the menu bar to remove the automatically created line.

Generate Product Bar Code Labels Through Retail

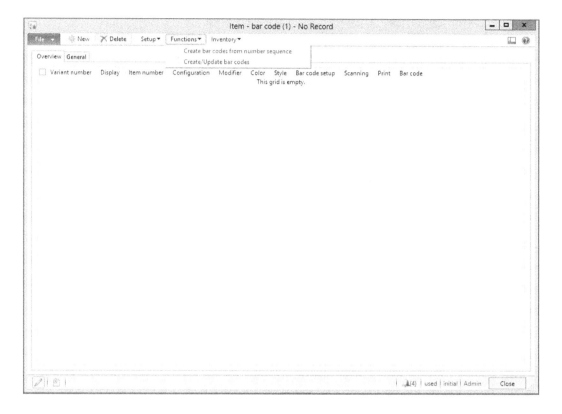

Then click on the Create/Update Bar Codes menu item within the Functions dropdown menu.

Generate Product Bar Code Labels Through Retail

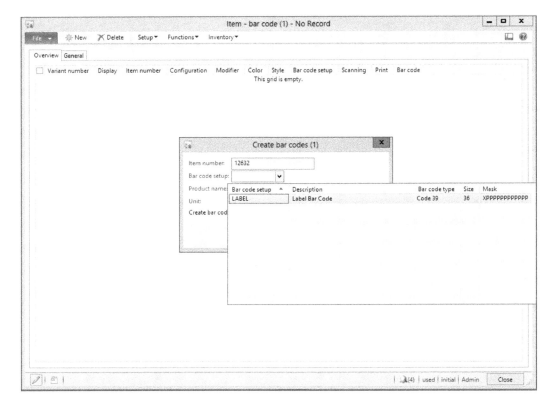

When the Create Bar Codes dialog box is displayed, select the Bar Code Setup that you just configured from the dropdown list.

Generate Product Bar Code Labels Through Retail

Then click on the OK button.

Generate Product Bar Code Labels Through Retail

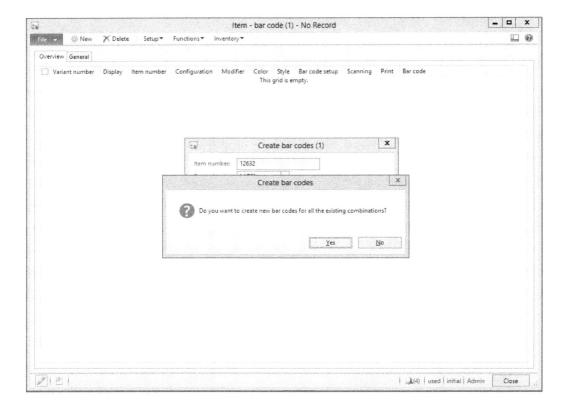

When the Create Bar Codes confirmation dialog box is displayed, click on the Yes button.

Generate Product Bar Code Labels Through Retail

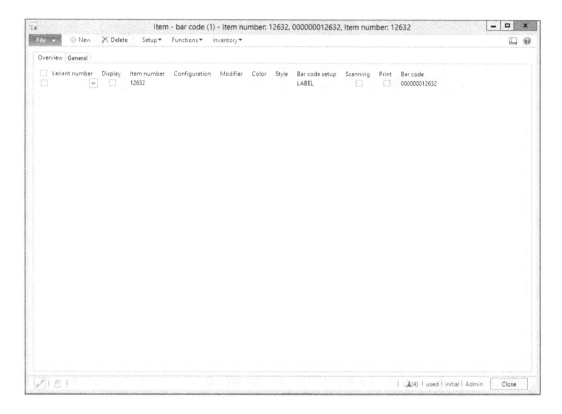

When you return to the Item Bar Codes maintenance form you will now have a bar code record.

Generate Product Bar Code Labels Through Retail

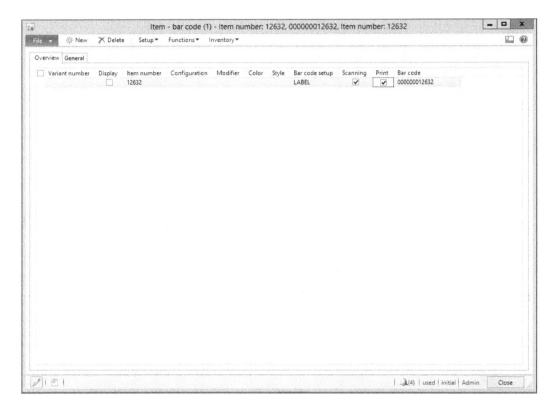

Check the Scanning and Print check boxes, and then click the Close button to exit from the form.

Generate Product Bar Code Labels Through Retail

Nearly there. All that is left now is to click on the Product Label button within the Setup group of the Retail ribbon bar.

Generate Product Bar Code Labels Through Retail

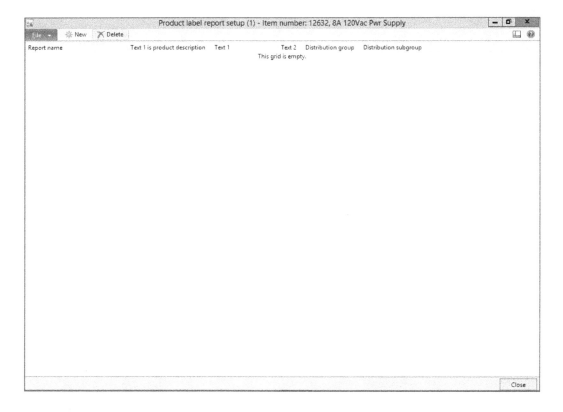

When the Product Label Report Setup maintenance form is displayed, click on the New button within the menu bar to create a new record.

Generate Product Bar Code Labels Through Retail

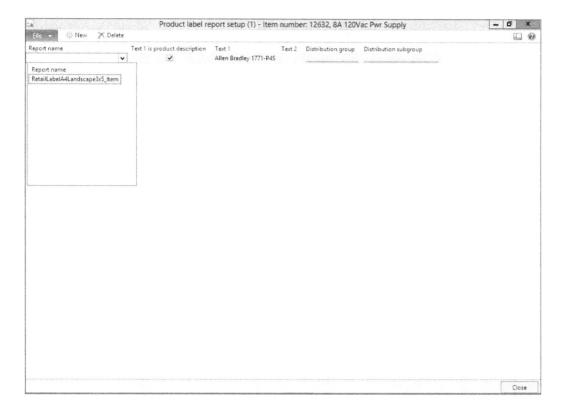

Select the Report Name from the dropdown list for the product label.

Generate Product Bar Code Labels Through Retail

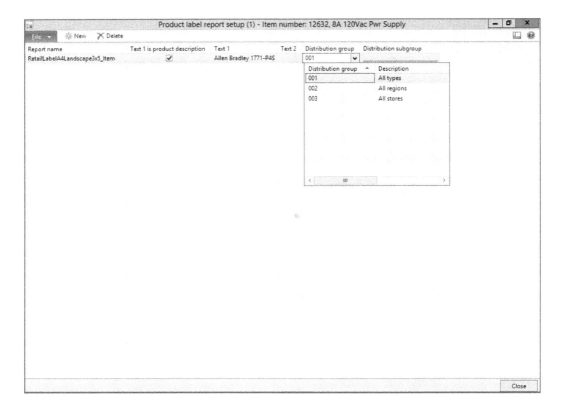

Then select a Distribution Group.

Generate Product Bar Code Labels Through Retail

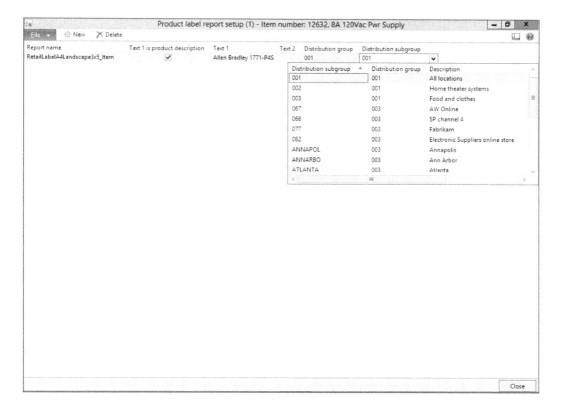

And finally select a Distribution Subgroup.

Generate Product Bar Code Labels Through Retail

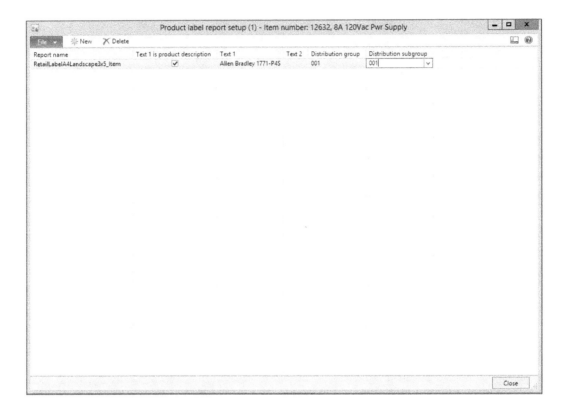

Now that you have the label configured, click on the Close button to exit from the form.

Generate Product Bar Code Labels Through Retail

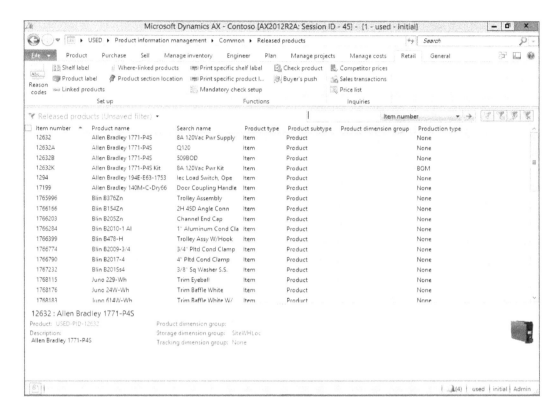

Now we can print our labels. To do that, click on the Print Specific Product Label button within the Functions group of the Retail ribbon bar.

Generate Product Bar Code Labels Through Retail

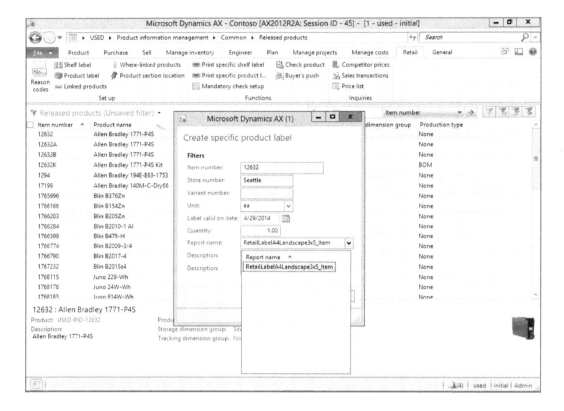

When the Create Specific Product Label select the Report Name from the dropdown list, and then click on the OK button.

Generate Product Bar Code Labels Through Retail

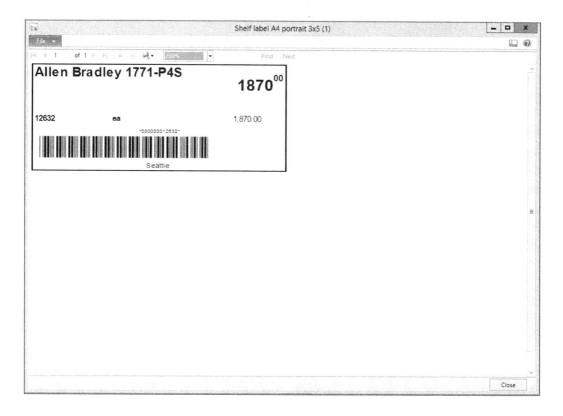

Now that's a pretty label.

Quickly Update Prices For Released Products

Updating prices through the standard Pricing Journals maintenance form can sometimes get a little unwieldy, especially when you just need to update one or two products. Fortunately if you want, you can update your prices directly from within the Released Products maintenance form, and with just a matter of clicks you will have a new and updated price list.

Now you can wheel and deal like a space cargo trader.

Quickly Update Prices For Released Products

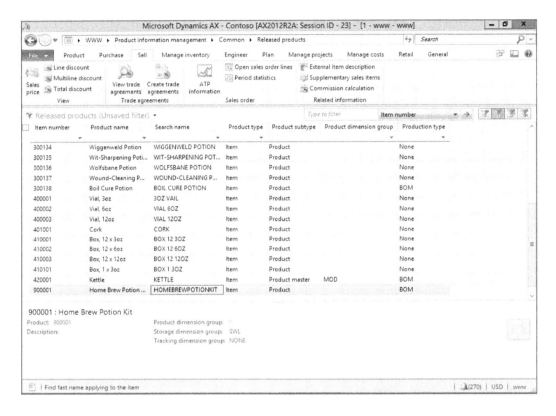

Open up the Released Products list page, select the product that you want to change the price for and then click on the View Trade Agreements button within the Trade Agreements group of the Sell ribbon bar.

Quickly Update Prices For Released Products

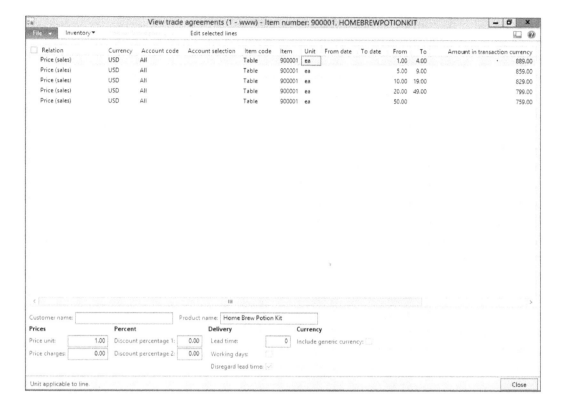

When the View Trade Agreements inquiry is displayed you will see all of the current pricing for the product.

Quickly Update Prices For Released Products

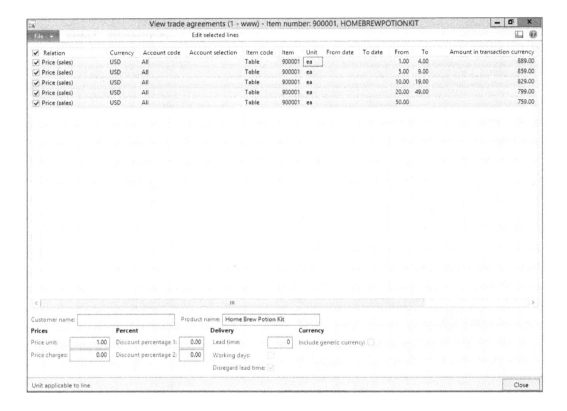

Select all of the lines that you want to update, and then click on the Edit Selected Lines button in the menu bar.

Quickly Update Prices For Released Products

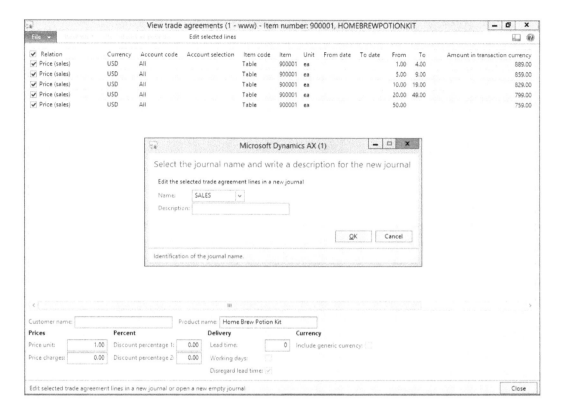

When the Select The Journal Name dialog box is displayed the Journal Name should already be populated, and all you need to do is click on the OK button.

Quickly Update Prices For Released Products

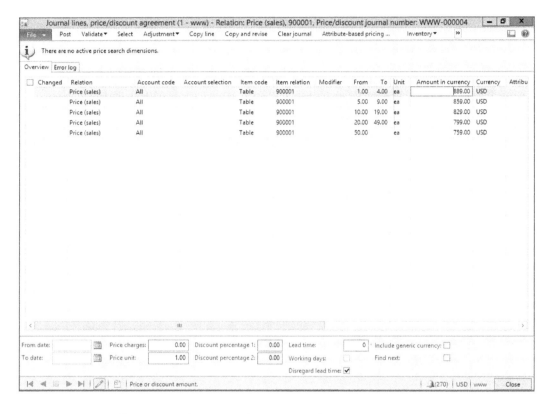

Dynamics AX will open up the Journal Lines Price/Discount Agreement maintenance form with all of the old prices copied over into the journal.

Quickly Update Prices For Released Products

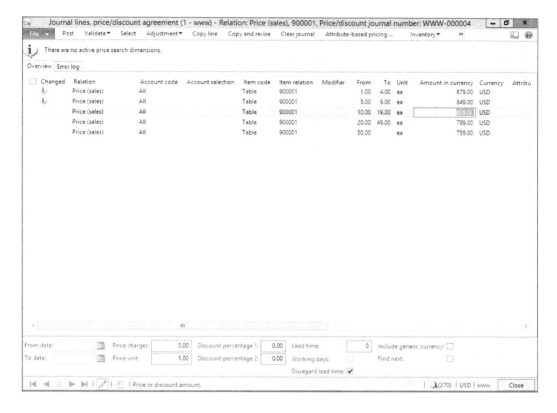

Now you can just update the prices that you want to adjust, and when you are done, just click on the Post button in the menu bar.

Quickly Update Prices For Released Products

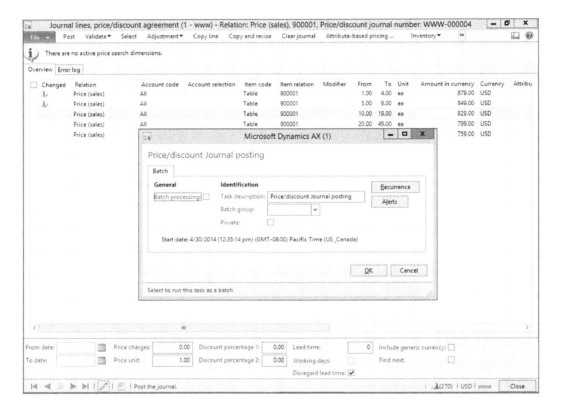

When the Price/Discount Journal Posting dialog box is displayed, just click on the OK button.

Quickly Update Prices For Released Products

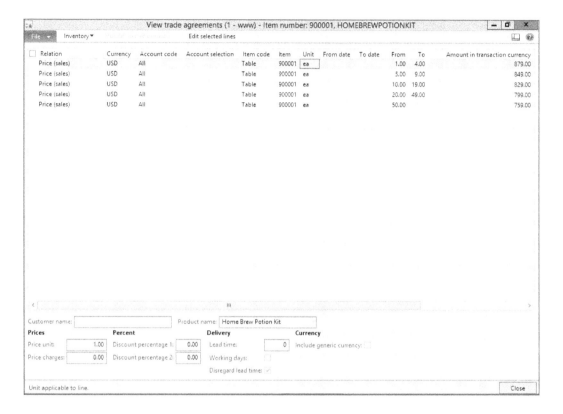

When you return to the View Trade Agreements inquiry is displayed, you will see that the prices have now been updated based on your price journal.

How easy is that!

Mark Deleted Sales Orders As Voided To Track Lost Sales

Every sales order is special, even the deleted ones because they allow you to track you lost sales. If you don't want all of the deleted orders to disappear from Dynamics AX, then you can turn on the Voided Order Tracking and it will save all of the deleted order details for you for posterity.

Now your deleted sales orders will be gone, but not forgotten.

Mark Deleted Sales Orders As Voided To Track Lost Sales

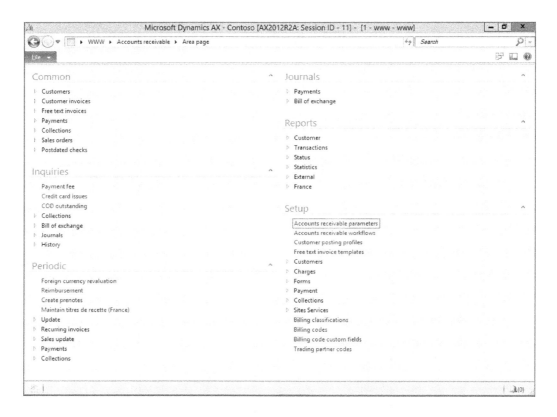

To turn on the voided order tracking click on the Accounts Receivable Parameters menu item within the Setup group of the Accounts Receivable area page.

Mark Deleted Sales Orders As Voided To Track Lost Sales

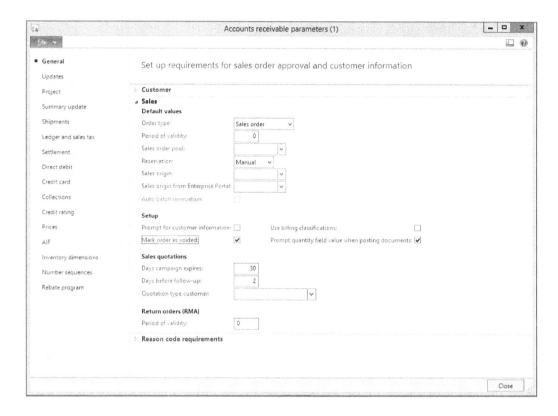

Then check the Mark Order As Voided checkbox within the Setup group of the Sales tab in the General section.

Mark Deleted Sales Orders As Voided To Track Lost Sales

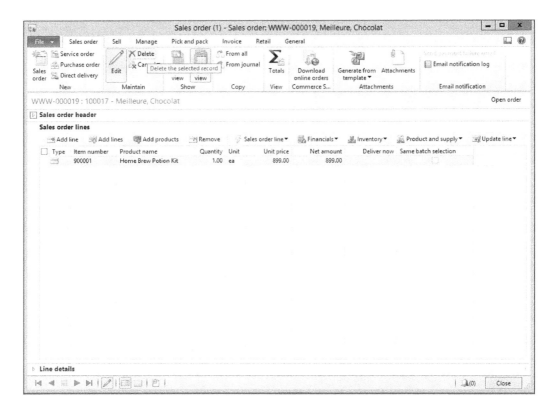

Now go to any order that you don't need and click the Delete button within the Maintain group of the Sales Order ribbon bar.

Mark Deleted Sales Orders As Voided To Track Lost Sales

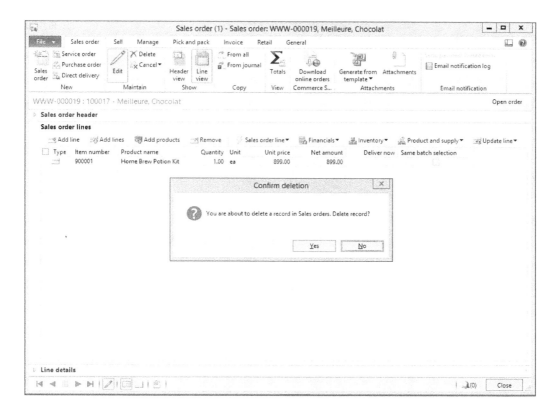

And click the Yes button on the Confirm Deletion dialog box.

Mark Deleted Sales Orders As Voided To Track Lost Sales

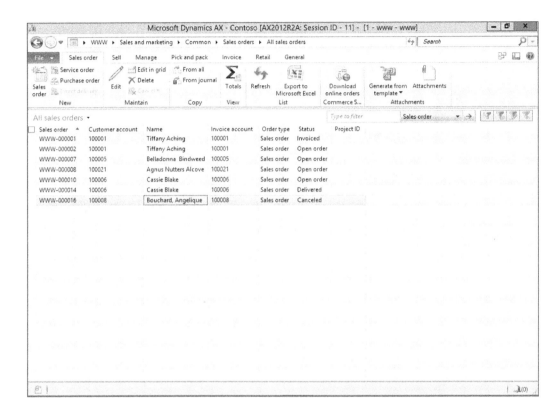

Now there is no trace of the order... or is there?

Mark Deleted Sales Orders As Voided To Track Lost Sales

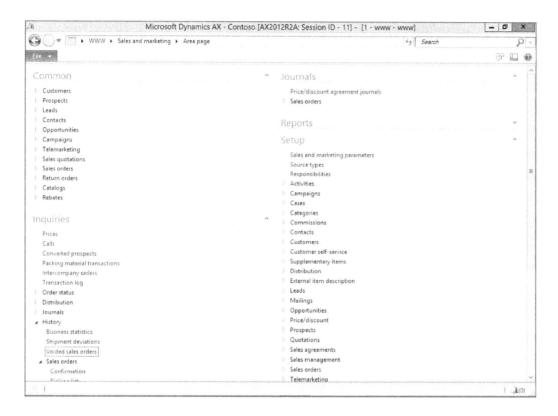

To see your deleted orders and lines, click on the Voided Sales Orders menu item within the History folder of the Inquiries group of the Sales And Marketing area page.

Mark Deleted Sales Orders As Voided To Track Lost Sales

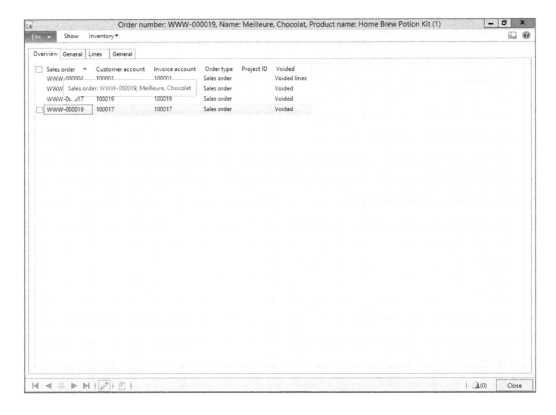

You will see the order that you just deleted is tracked here.

Mark Deleted Sales Orders As Voided To Track Lost Sales

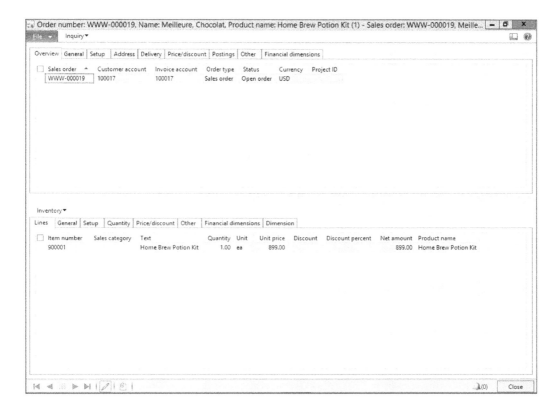

If you click on the Show button in the menu bar then you will see all of the history of the sales order that you voided as well.

Maybe you should bring some flowers next time...

Block Users From Using Particular Journal Names By Making Them Private

If the General Ledger is the heart and soul of Dynamics AX, and then the Journals are the DNA that builds up all of the information about the company. So it makes sense that you would want to make sure that people aren't just making postings willy nilly within the system. Some of the postings are automatic, some will be controlled through approval processes, but for the special journals that the finance department use, you may want to secure them down by making them private so that only certain people are able to see them.

The finance group is not a secret group, but that doesn't mean that it's not a group with secrets.

Block Users From Using Particular Journal Names By Making Them Private

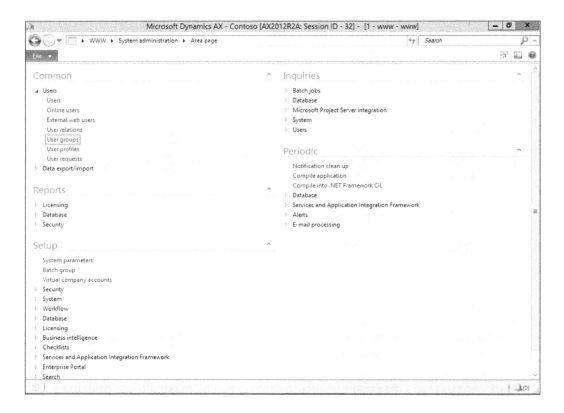

First you need to set up a user group that contains all of the users that you want to allow to use the journal. To do that, click on the User Groups menu item within the Users folder of the Common group of the System Administration area page.

Block Users From Using Particular Journal Names By Making Them Private

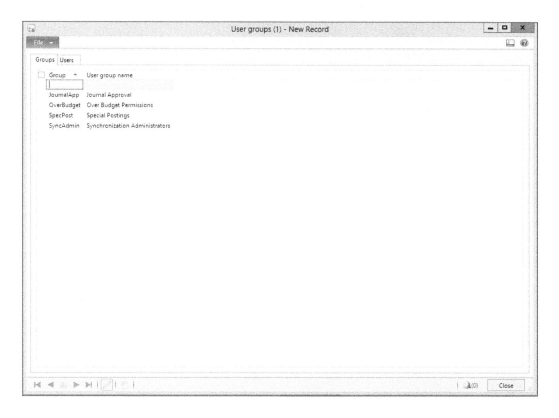

When the User Group maintenance form is displayed, create a new record by pressing CTRL+N - there is no New button in the menu bar of this form, so you have to do this a little old school.

Block Users From Using Particular Journal Names By Making Them Private

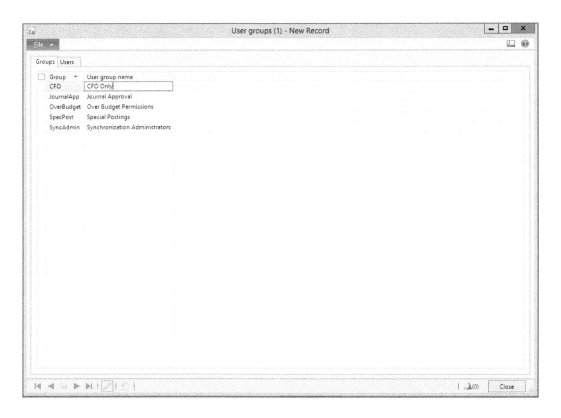

Then assign your User Group a Group name, and a description.

Block Users From Using Particular Journal Names By Making Them Private

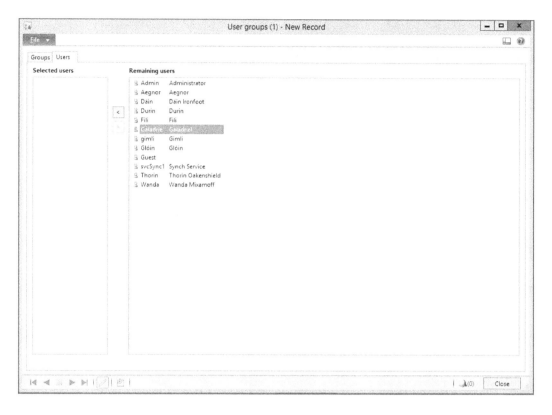

Then click on the Users tab, select the users that you want to include in the group, and then click on the < button.

Block Users From Using Particular Journal Names By Making Them Private

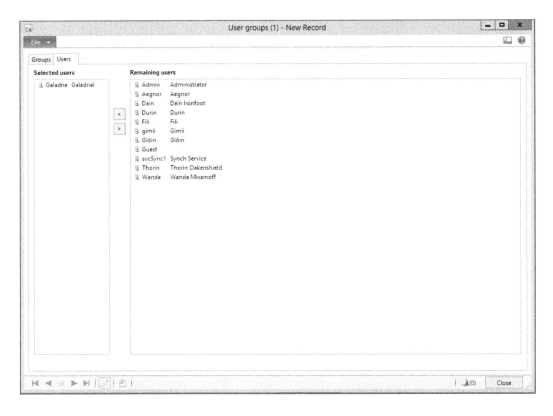

After you have selected all of the users then you can click on the Close button to exit from the form.

Block Users From Using Particular Journal Names By Making Them Private

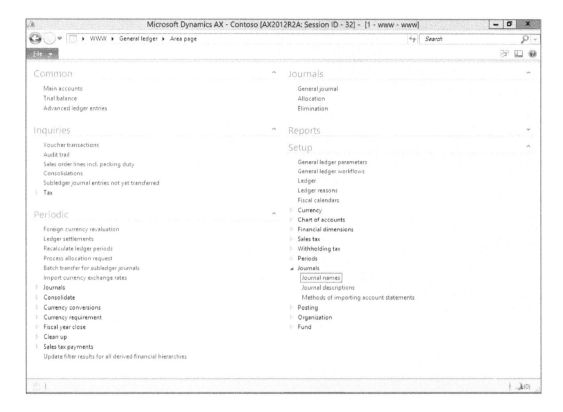

Now we need to lock down the Journal by associating the User Group to it. To do this, click on the Journal Names menu item within the Journals folder of the Setup group within the General Ledger area page.

Block Users From Using Particular Journal Names By Making Them Private

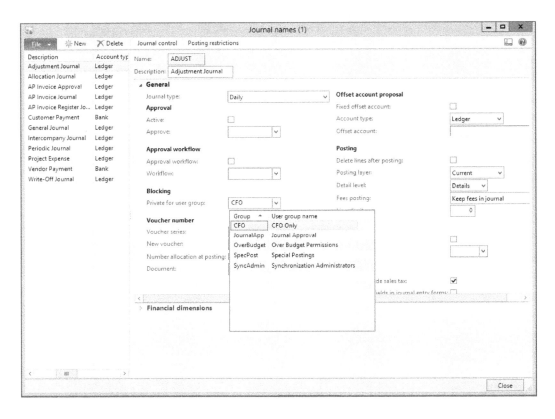

When the Journal Names maintenance form is displayed, select the Journal that you want to make private, and select the User Group that you just configured from the list within the Private For User Group drop down list within the Blocking section of the General tab.

Block Users From Using Particular Journal Names By Making Them Private

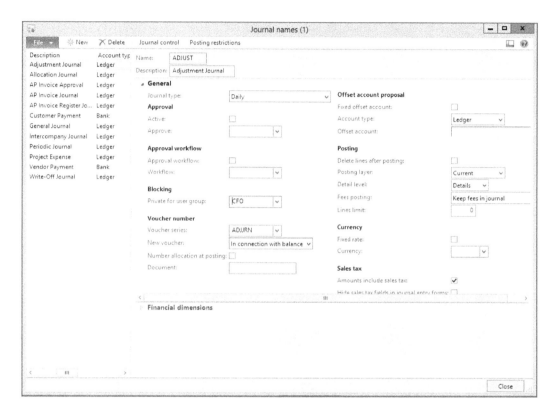

After you have done that you are set, and you can click on the Close button to exit from the form.

Block Users From Using Particular Journal Names By Making Them Private

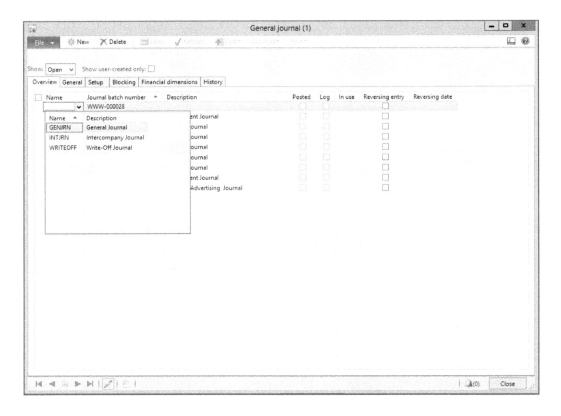

Now, if you are not part of the cool kids that have access to the Journal you will not see it.

Block Users From Using Particular Journal Names By Making Them Private

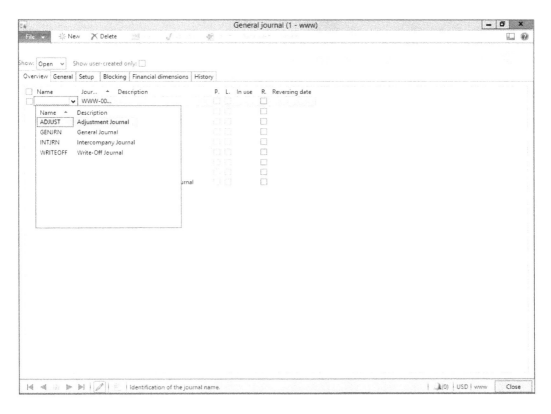

But for the lucky ones, it will show up on their list of available Journal Names.

Use Workflows To Process AP Invoices Through Unattached Documents

The Document Attachment feature within Dynamics AX is great, because you can attach files to any record in the system. But sometimes you have document attachments that do not have records that they can be attached to yet, and may have to create records and then attach them after the fact. In these cases you can take advantage of the unattached document feature and even add workflow processes around the document to make sure that it gets processed by the right people.

It's like matchmaking, except for files.

Use Workflows To Process AP Invoices Through Unattached Documents

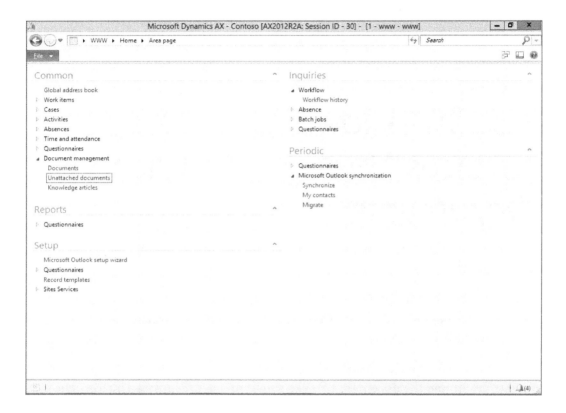

Start off by clicking on the Unattached Documents link within the Document Management folder of the Common group of the Home area page.

Use Workflows To Process AP Invoices Through Unattached Documents

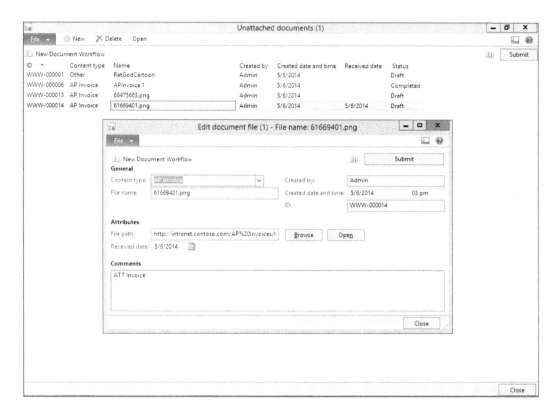

Select the document that you want to process and submit it to the Document Management workflow process.

Use Workflows To Process AP Invoices Through Unattached Documents

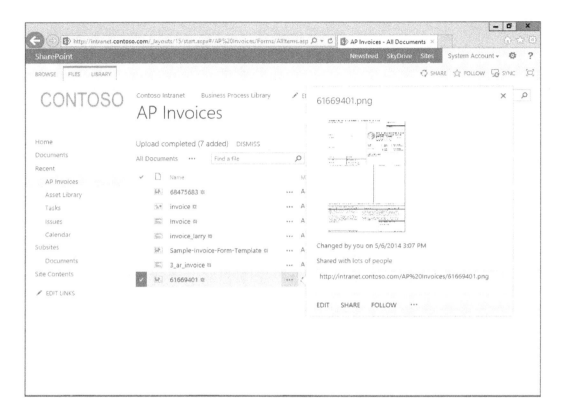

Note: In this case we are linking the Unattached Document record to a scanned image that we have loaded into SharePoint.

Use Workflows To Process AP Invoices Through Unattached Documents

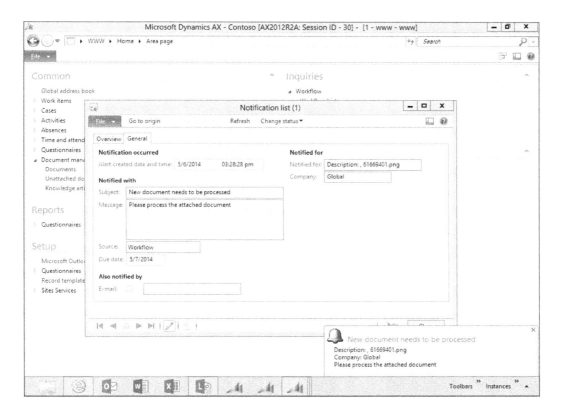

Through the workflow process the AP clerk will be notified that they have a document that they need to process.

Use Workflows To Process AP Invoices Through Unattached Documents

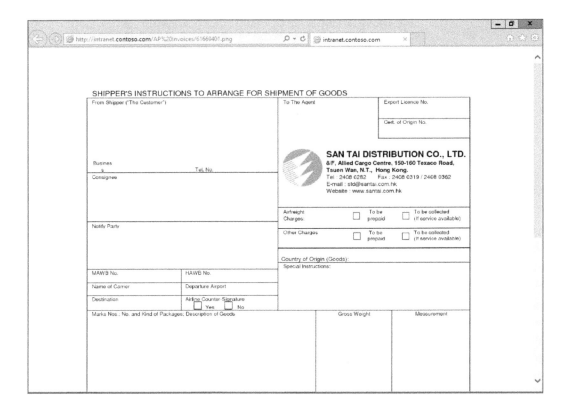

By following the Unattached Document link they are able to view the scanned image directly from within SharePoint.

Use Workflows To Process AP Invoices Through Unattached Documents

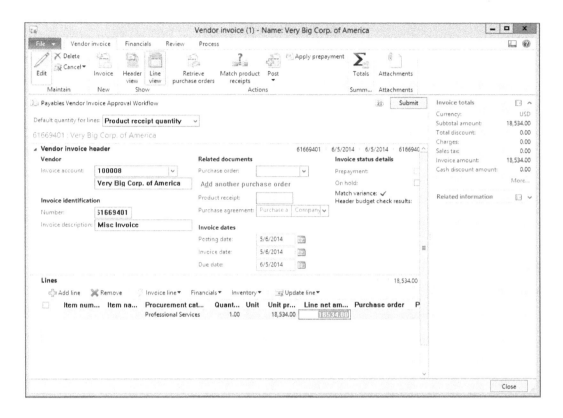

The next step is to create the AP Invoice record based off the scanned image.

Use Workflows To Process AP Invoices Through Unattached Documents

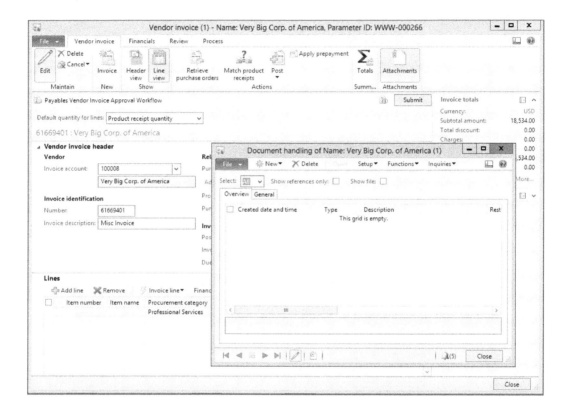

To attach the Unattached Document to the invoice for reference, click on the Attachments button within the Attachments group of the Vendor Invoices ribbon bar.

Use Workflows To Process AP Invoices Through Unattached Documents

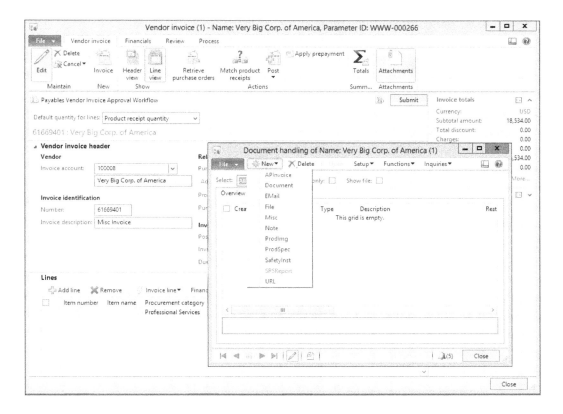

Then click on the New button in the menu bar and select the type of document that you want to associate the scanned invoice to.

Use Workflows To Process AP Invoices Through Unattached Documents

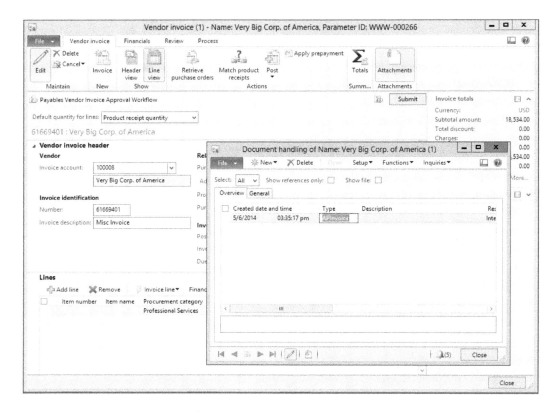

In our case we will use the AP Invoice document type.

Use Workflows To Process AP Invoices Through Unattached Documents

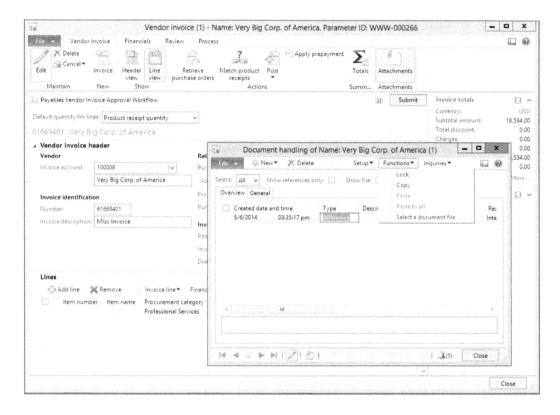

To search for the Unattached Document and link it to the attachment record, click on the Functions menu and click on the Select A Document File menu item.

Use Workflows To Process AP Invoices Through Unattached Documents

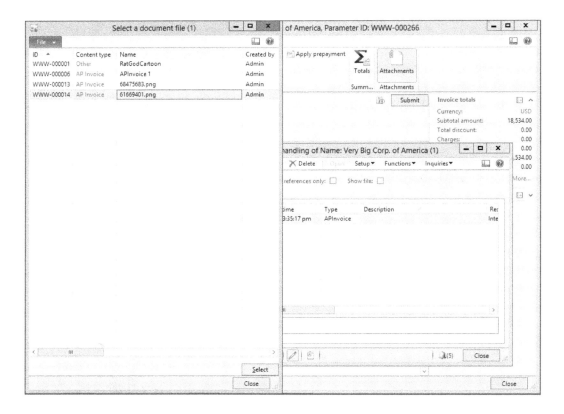

This will give you a list of all the Unattached Documents. Just select the record for the scanned invoice, click on the Select button, and then click the Close button.

Use Workflows To Process AP Invoices Through Unattached Documents

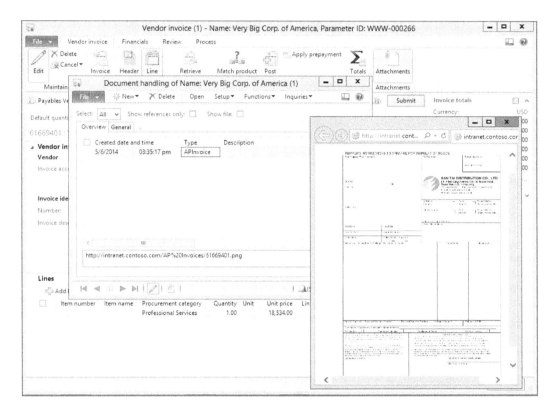

This will add a link to the document within SharePoint and you can even click on the Open button in the menu bar to view the record within SharePoint.

Use Workflows To Process AP Invoices Through Unattached Documents

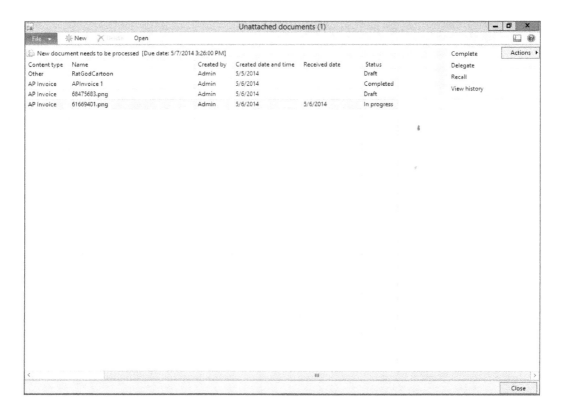

All that is left to do now is to return back to the work item list and complete the document management workflow.

Enable Change Management On Purchase Orders To Track Changes

If you want to track your Purchase Orders a little more closely, then you may want to turn on the Change Management feature within the Procurement & Sourcing module of Dynamics AX. This gives you the added ability to have workflow approvals on your Purchase Orders, but will also give you the ability to view the old versions of the Purchase Orders and see the differences between the versions.

Now you won't have to play "Spot The Difference" when trying to work out what was updated on the Purchase Order.

Enable Change Management On Purchase Orders To Track Changes

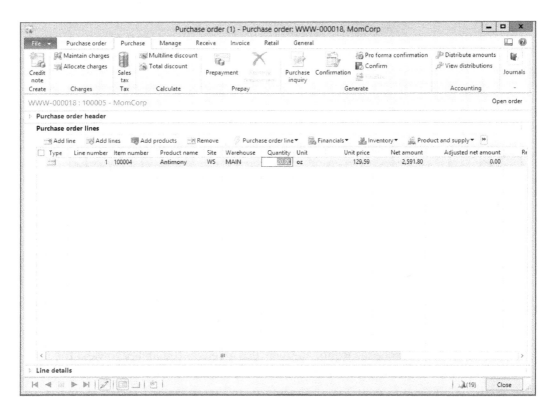

Normally if you create a Purchase Order within Dynamics AX you can immediately print out the Confirmation and then it is available for receiving.

Enable Change Management On Purchase Orders To Track Changes

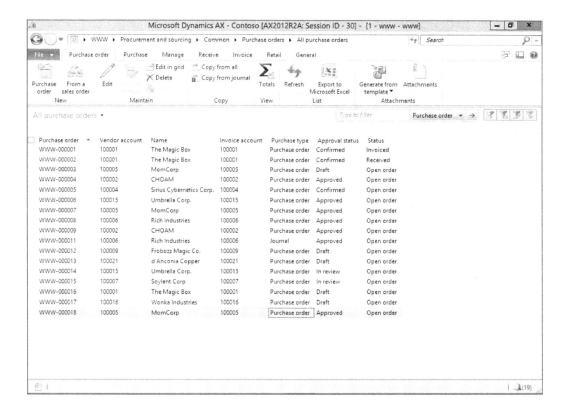

If you look at the Approval Status on the record created, then they will normally have the Approved status as soon as they have been entered into the system.

Enable Change Management On Purchase Orders To Track Changes

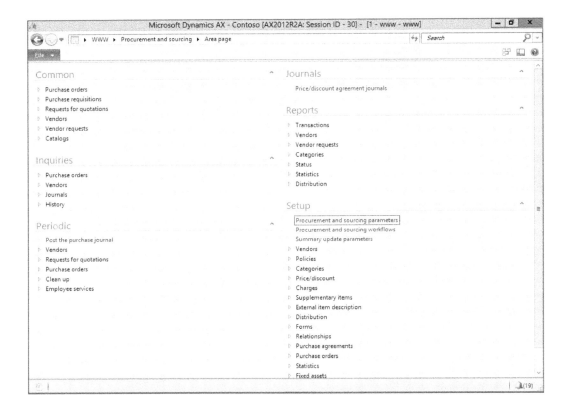

To add more control to the Purchase Order generation process you can turn on the Change Control feature. To do this click on the Procurement and Sourcing Parameters menu item within the Setup group of the Procurement and Sourcing area page.

Enable Change Management On Purchase Orders To Track Changes

When the Procurement and Sourcing Parameters maintenance form is displayed, check the Activate Change Management flag within the Change Management For Purchase Orders group in the General page.

Enable Change Management On Purchase Orders To Track Changes

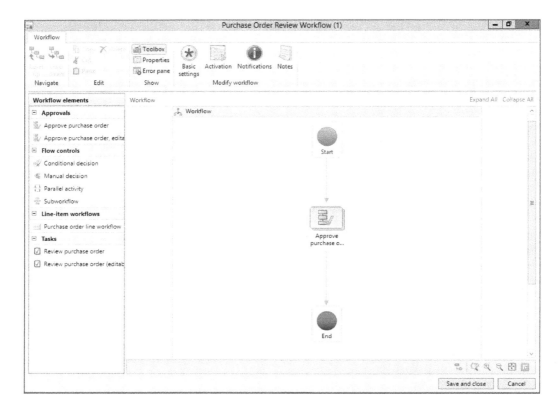

Purchase Orders that are tracked through Change Management are approved through the workflow engine within Dynamics AX. So there is one last step in the process and that is to create a new workflow that will allow you to approve the Purchase Orders when they are submitted.

Enable Change Management On Purchase Orders To Track Changes

Now create a new Purchase Order.

Enable Change Management On Purchase Orders To Track Changes

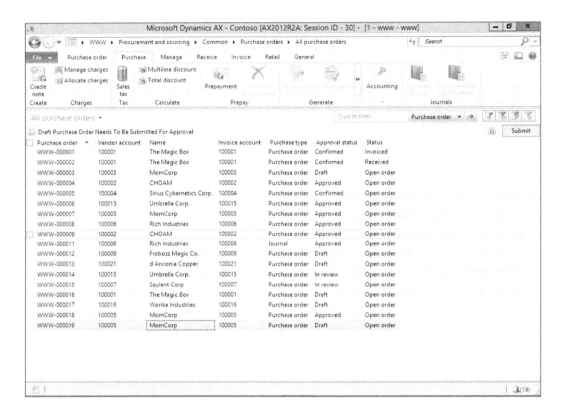

You will now notice that the Purchase Order has been set to a Draft approval status, and there is a submission option to send it to workflow for approval.

Also there is no option available to allow the user to confirm the Purchase Order. When you want to send the Purchase Order through the approval process, click on the Submit button.

Enable Change Management On Purchase Orders To Track Changes

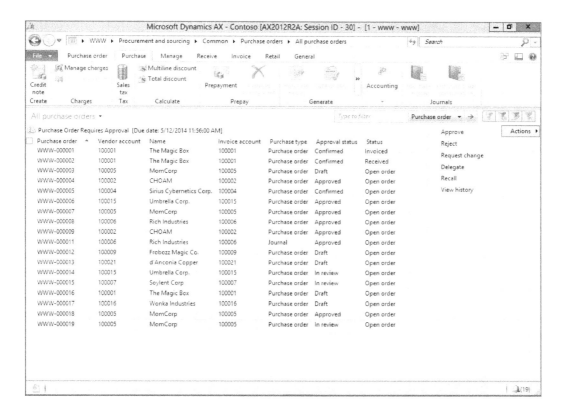

This will change the status of the purchase order to In Review and then allow you to approve the PO.

Enable Change Management On Purchase Orders To Track Changes

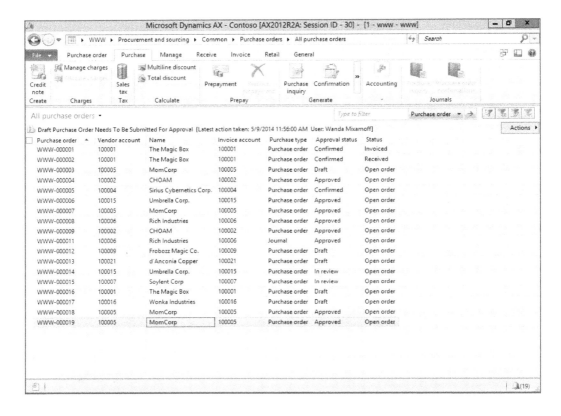

Once the Purchase Order is approved you will be able to send out the Purchase Order confirmation.

Enable Change Management On Purchase Orders To Track Changes

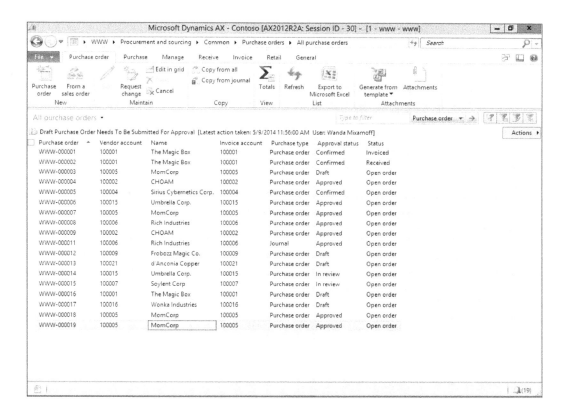

Also, if you look at the Purchase Order ribbon bar, you will notice that the Edit option within the Maintain group is disabled, but the Request Change option is now enabled. To make an update to the Purchase Order, click on the Request Change button.

Enable Change Management On Purchase Orders To Track Changes

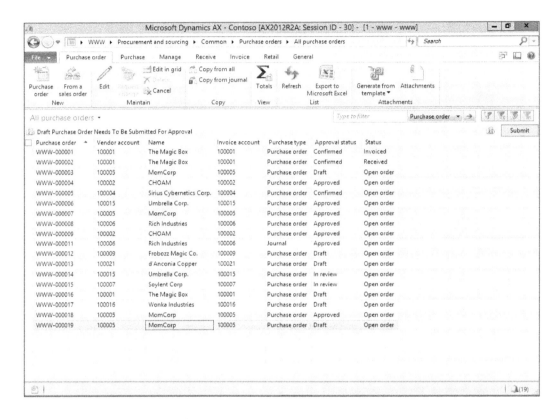

This will revert the Purchase Order back to a Draft approval status and the approval process needs to be completed before it is available to be sent out to the vendor again as a confirmation.

Enable Change Management On Purchase Orders To Track Changes

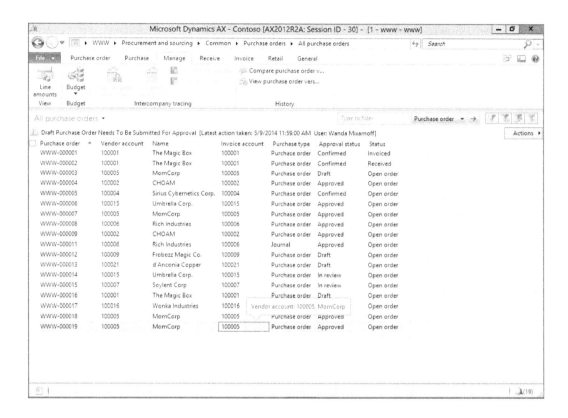

As a bonus, if you switch to the Manage ribbon bar, then the buttons within the History group of the ribbon bar will be enabled. If you want to see what the changes were over time, then click on the View Purchase Order History button.

Enable Change Management On Purchase Orders To Track Changes

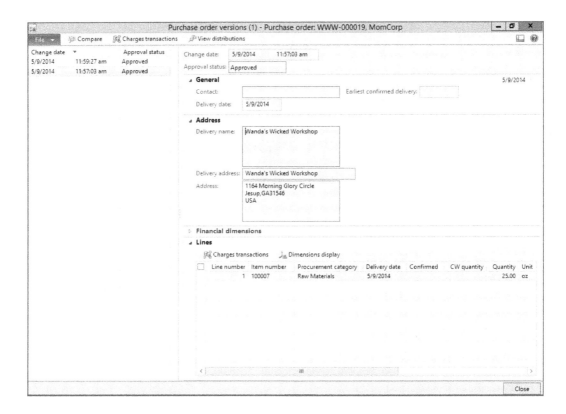

When the Purchase Order Versions inquiry form is displayed, then you will see all of the different version of the Purchase Order.

To see the changes made, click on the Compare button within the menu bar.

Enable Change Management On Purchase Orders To Track Changes

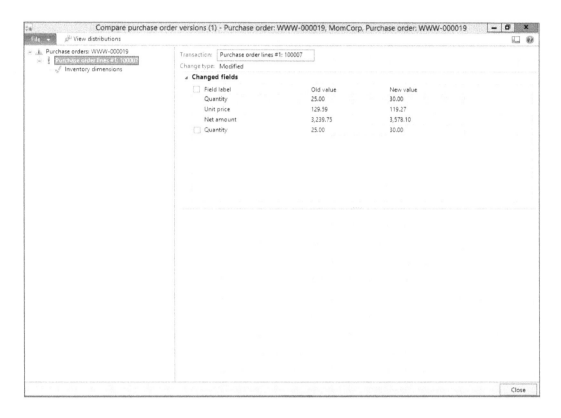

This will show you all of the changes between the two Purchase Orders.

How cool is that!

Use Auto-Numbering Unless You Don't Feel Like It

If you have implemented some sort if intelligence within your numbering or naming schemes within Dynamics AX, then having it automatically assign a sequential number through auto-numbering completely messes up all of your hard work, but having your numbering as just a manual process also has it's disadvantages because you need to find the right slot to fit your number into as well. Dynamics AX has an option to allow you to override the automatic numbering that gets assigned though allowing you to accept the number it suggests, or change it up or down based on your preferences. This gives you the best of both worlds when it comes to numbering.

Who said you can't have your cake and eat it too.

Use Auto-Numbering Unless You Don't Feel Like It

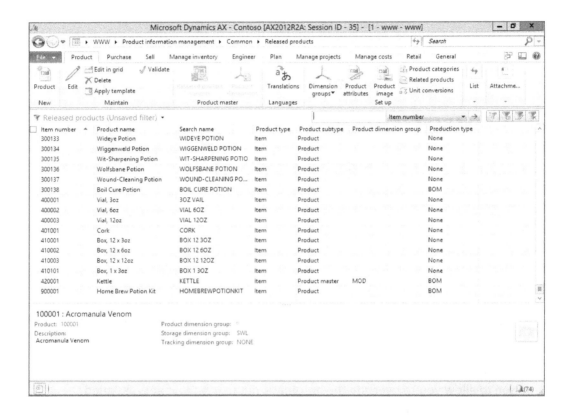

In my system I have a simple scheme for numbering my products i.e. 1XXXXX for Raw Ingredients, 3XXXXX for Finished Goods, 4XXXXX for Packaging Supplies and 9XXXXX for Configured Products. Most of the time I will be adding new finished goods, so I want my numbering sequence to default in within the 3XXXXX series.

Use Auto-Numbering Unless You Don't Feel Like It

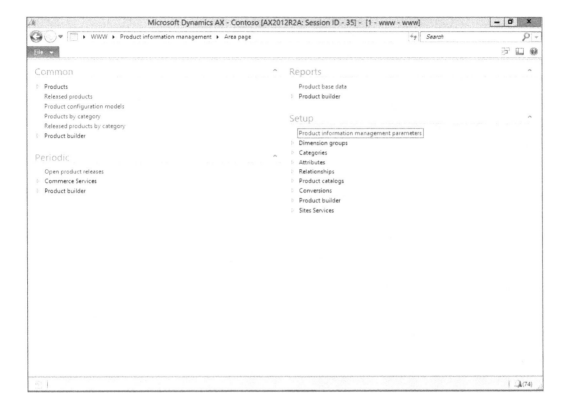

To do this, click on the Product Information Management Parameters menu item within the Setup group of the Product Information Management area page.

Use Auto-Numbering Unless You Don't Feel Like It

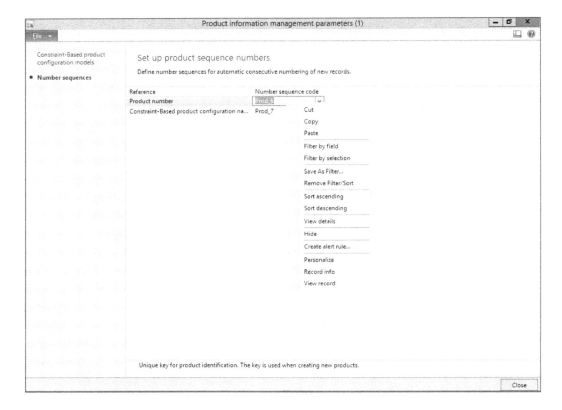

When the Product Information Management Parameters form is displayed, select the Number Sequence page, and then right-mouse-click on the Product Number number sequence and select View Details from the pop-up menu.

Use Auto-Numbering Unless You Don't Feel Like It

When the Number Sequence maintenance form is displayed, click on the Edit button within the Maintain group of the Number Sequence ribbon bar.

For this number sequence I have it set to manual so that I can enter in any number. To make this a semi-automated numbering sequence, uncheck the Manual flag within the General tab group.

Use Auto-Numbering Unless You Don't Feel Like It

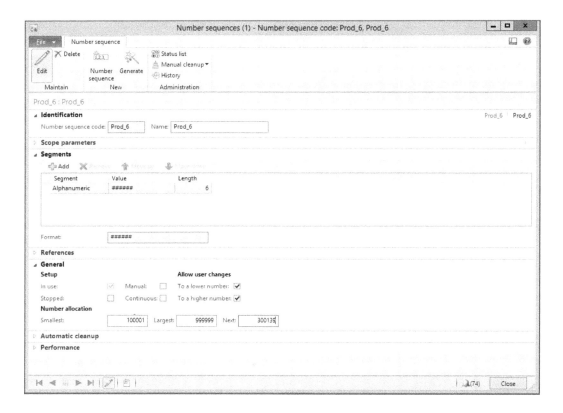

Then set the Next number to the next number in the sequence that you want to use.

Also, check the To A Lower Number and To A Higher Number flags within the Allow User Changes group of the General tab group. This will allow the users to change the number even when it is auto-assigned.

Once you are done, you can click the Close button and exit out of the form.

Use Auto-Numbering Unless You Don't Feel Like It

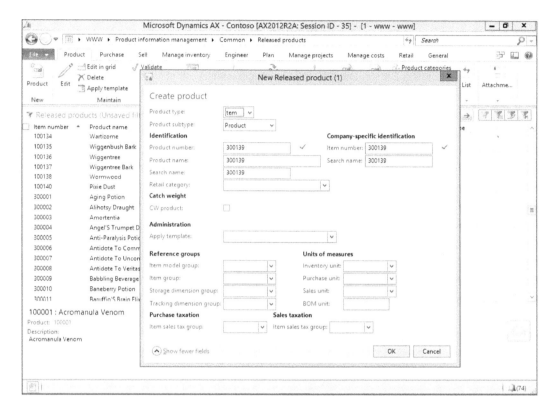

Now when I create a new record, Dynamics AX will suggest the next product number in the sequence that I normally add products within.

Use Auto-Numbering Unless You Don't Feel Like It

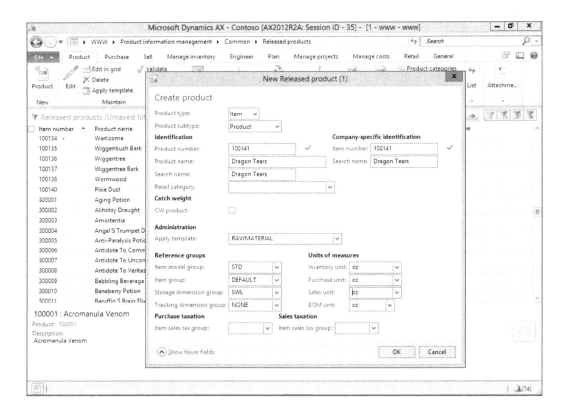

But, if I want to change it then there is nothing stopping me from adding a higher or lower number.

Split Your Number Sequences To Make Them Look Intelligent

The Number Sequences within Dynamics AX are great because they allow you to add a lot of intelligence to your document and transaction numbering. You can add constants to them so that you can quickly see where they came from and sort though them. But it doesn't stop there. If you have incorporated some logic into how you are actually numbering the records, then you can split the number up itself so that even though it's still continuous, there may be segment separators that highlight that certain numbers are significant.

Now you just need to train the users on what the numbers mean...

Split Your Number Sequences To Make Them Look Intelligent

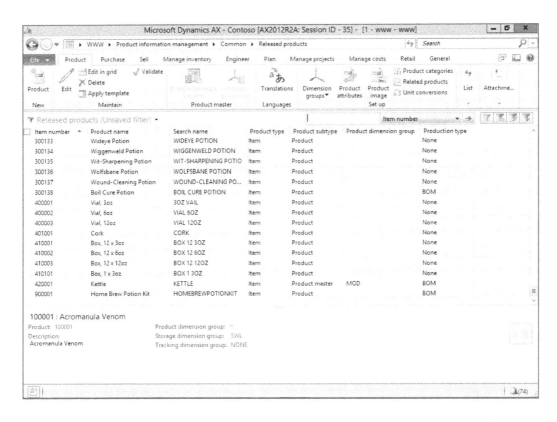

In my system I have a simple scheme for numbering my products i.e. 1XXXXX for Raw Ingredients, 3XXXXX for Finished Goods, 4XXXXX for Packaging Supplies and 9XXXXX for Configured Products. So I would really like to highlight this by separating out the first number when I create the products so that it has the format X-XXXXX.

Split Your Number Sequences To Make Them Look Intelligent

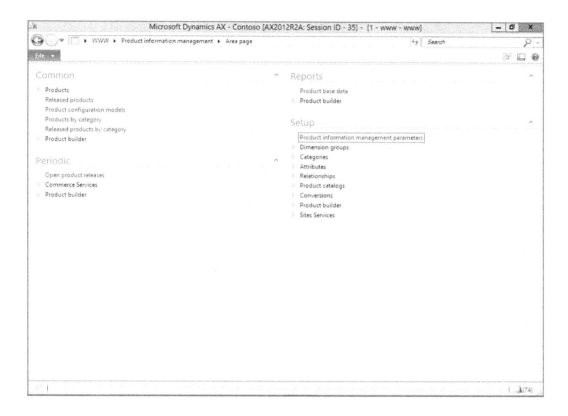

To do this, click on the Product Information Management Parameters menu item within the Setup group of the Product Information Management area page.

Split Your Number Sequences To Make Them Look Intelligent

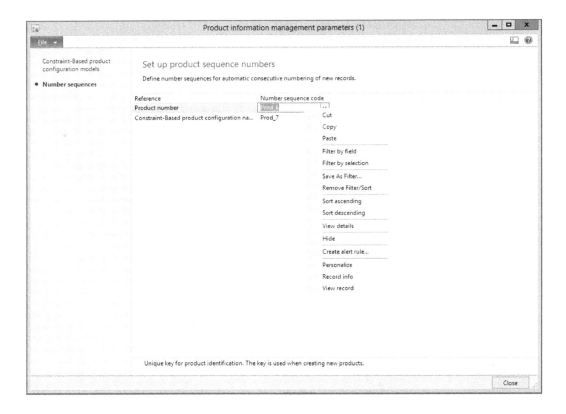

When the Product Information Management Parameters form is displayed, select the Number Sequence page, and then right-mouse-click on the Product Number number sequence and select View Details from the pop-up menu.

Split Your Number Sequences To Make Them Look Intelligent

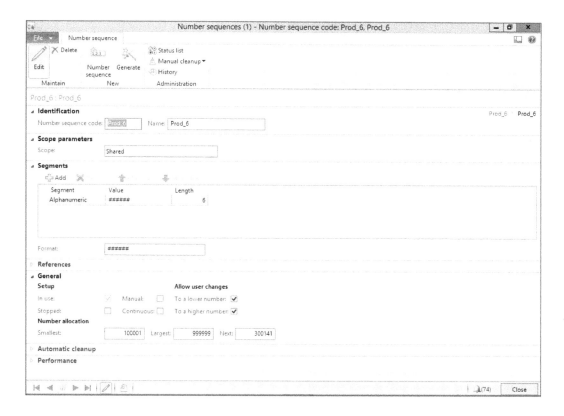

When the Number Sequence maintenance form is displayed, click on the Edit button within the Maintain group of the Number Sequence ribbon bar.

Our original Number Sequence in this example is 6 digits long, and is one continuous number string. Click on the Add button within the menu bar of the Segments tab group.

Split Your Number Sequences To Make Them Look Intelligent

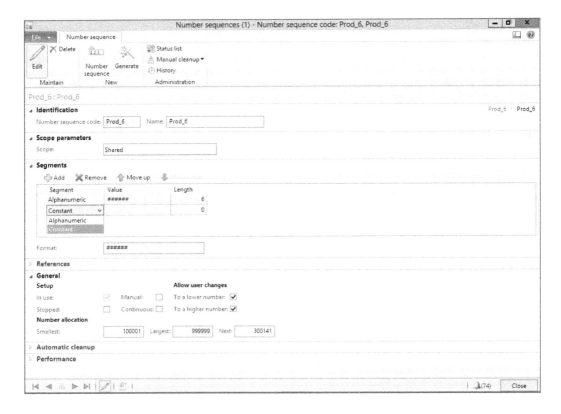

When the new segment record is created, change the Segment to Constant.

Split Your Number Sequences To Make Them Look Intelligent

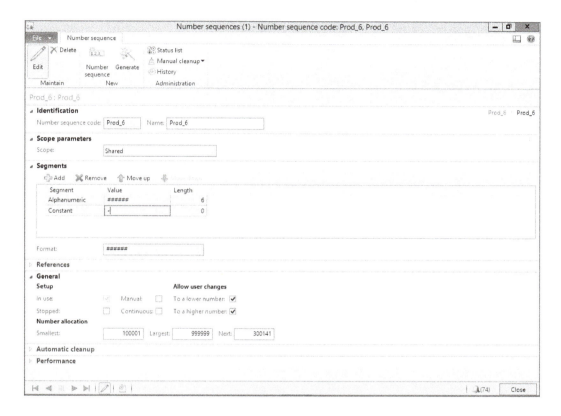

Then set the Value to -.

Split Your Number Sequences To Make Them Look Intelligent

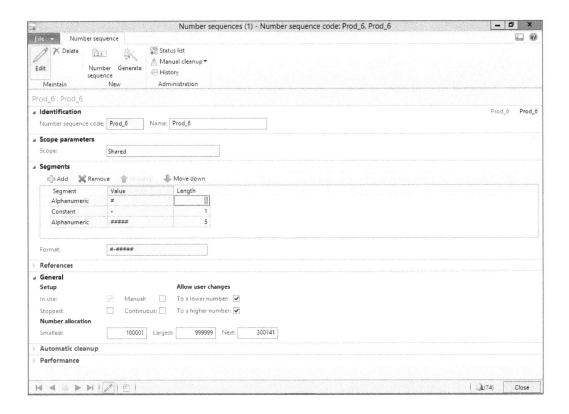

Repeat the process and add another Alphanumeric Segment and set the Value to #####.

So that there are still only 6 places in the total number of Alphanumeric placeholders, set the first Alphanumeric segment mask to #.

Note: Since the mask has 6 # placeholders then the numbers that are allocated to the sequence will remain the same even though there are 7 characters in the full product number record.

Split Your Number Sequences To Make Them Look Intelligent

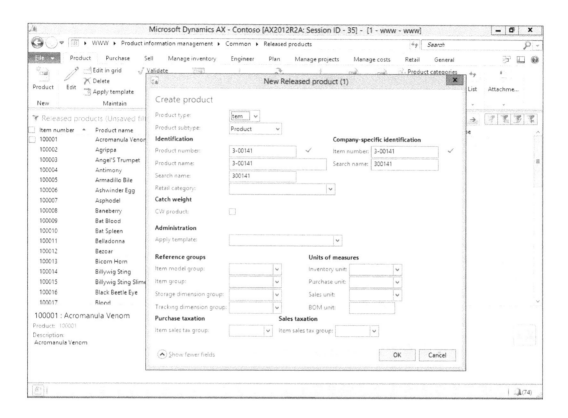

Now when I go out and create a new Product In Dynamics AX, it will format the number with my intelligent number separator after the first character.

Now if only I had done this from the start, then all of the products would have looked intelligent.

Use Pricing Models Within Configured Products To Calculate Prices Without A BOM

The Product Configurator within Dynamics AX is very cool and is a great way to capture options during the sales and quoting process. You don't have to go whole hog with it though and have it build BOM's and Routes in order to have it help you during the sales cycle in quoting prices though. The Product Configurator has a built in Price Modeler feature that allows you to design a price build up based on your configuration attributes, and then calculate prices dynamically as you are placing your orders.

You will now be able to rest easy that all of the costs have been taken into account when you price out jobs.

Use Pricing Models Within Configured Products To Calculate Prices Without A BOM

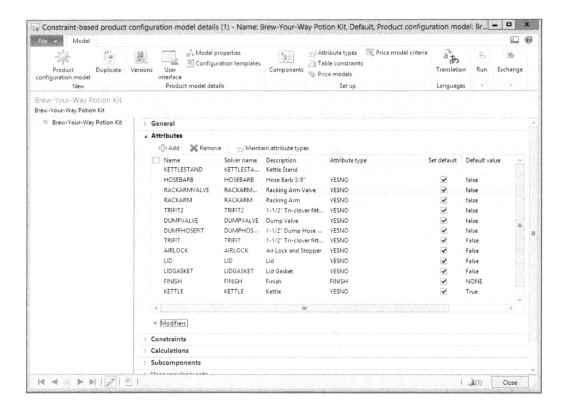

Start off by designing your configured product with all the options that you want to capture and then click on the Price Models button within the Setup group of the Model ribbon bar.

Use Pricing Models Within Configured Products To Calculate Prices Without A BOM

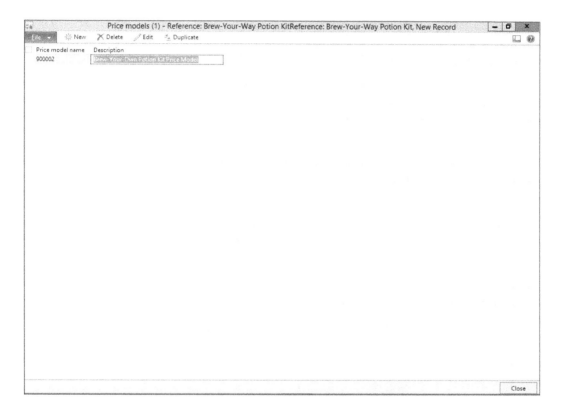

When the Price Models maintenance form is displayed, add a new record, and then click on the Edit button in the menu bar.

Use Pricing Models Within Configured Products To Calculate Prices Without A BOM

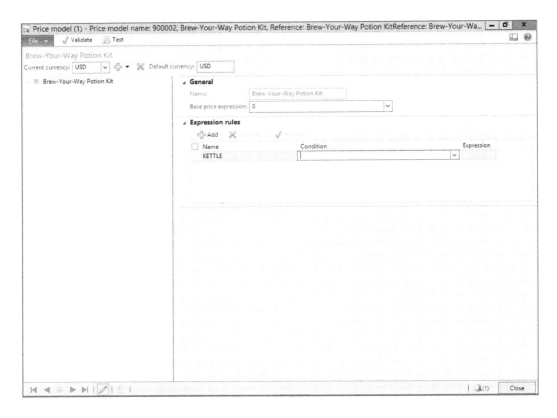

This will open up the Price Model designer. Click on the Add button within the Expression Rules tab to add a new price component.

Give your Expression a Name, and then click on the down-arrow on the Condition field to open up the condition editor.

Use Pricing Models Within Configured Products To Calculate Prices Without A BOM

When the Expression Editor is displayed, you can build your expression rule just by pointing and clicking through the columns. When you are done, just click on the OK button.

Use Pricing Models Within Configured Products To Calculate Prices Without A BOM

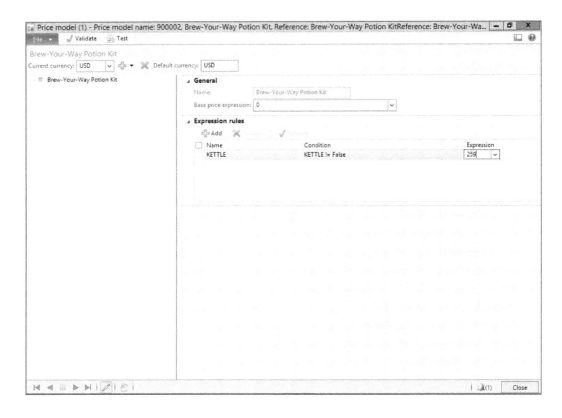

Then add a component price to the Expression field.

Note: You can also build an expression here as well like you did with the Condition field and use a formula to calculate the price.

Use Pricing Models Within Configured Products To Calculate Prices Without A BOM

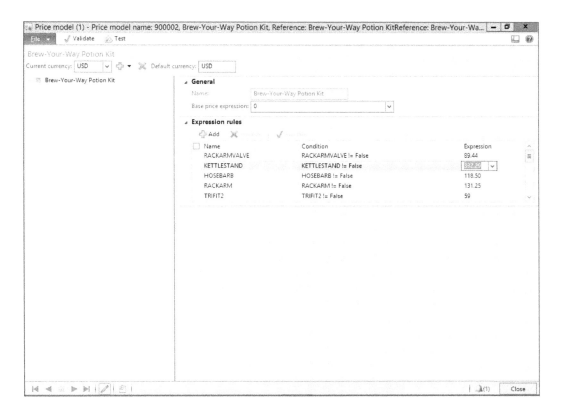

Continue adding additional Expression Rules to the pricing model for all the components that affect the price.

When you are done, just click on the Test button to see it in action.

Use Pricing Models Within Configured Products To Calculate Prices Without A BOM

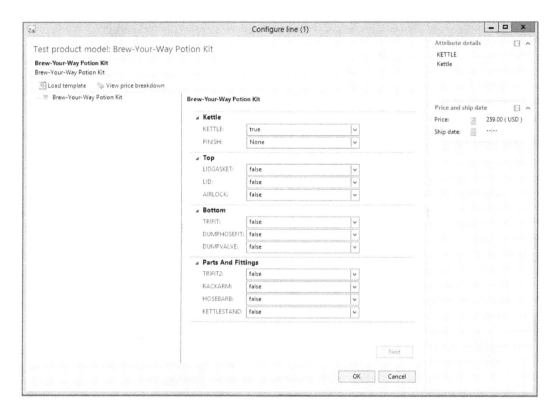

When the Test form is displayed, you will notice that there is a Price being calculated on the right in the fact boxes.

Use Pricing Models Within Configured Products To Calculate Prices Without A BOM

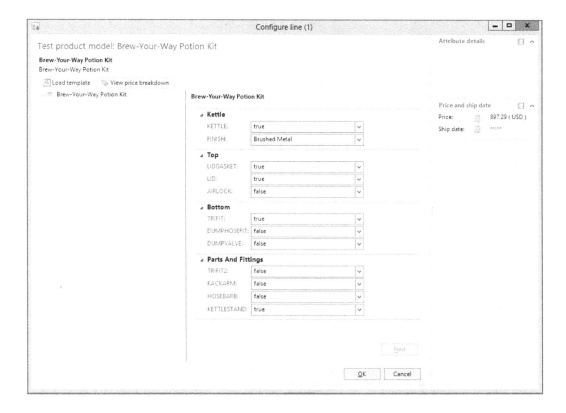

If you change the options within the product configuration, then the price changes as well.

If you want to see a breakdown of the prices in Excel, then click on the View Price Breakdown button.

Use Pricing Models Within Configured Products To Calculate Prices Without A BOM

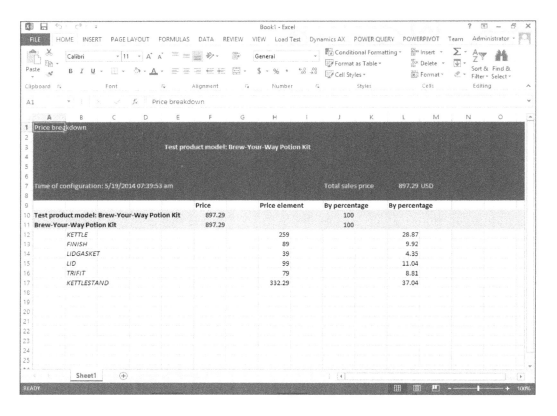

Dynamics AX will build you an Excel workbook with a summary of the prices.

How cool is that!

Use Pricing Models Within Configured Products To Calculate Prices Without A BOM

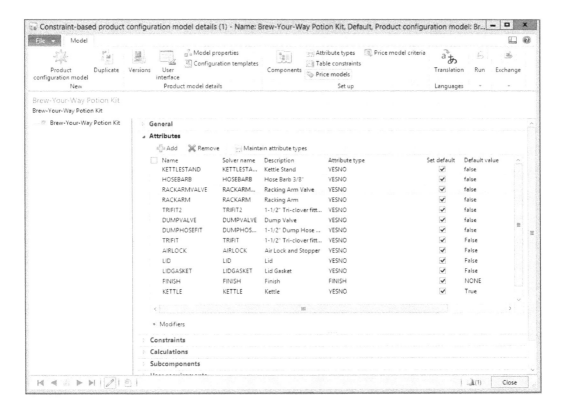

To use this within your Sales Orders, there is a little bit more setup required. Start off by clicking on the Price Model Criteria button within the Set Up group of the Model ribbon bar.

Use Pricing Models Within Configured Products To Calculate Prices Without A BOM

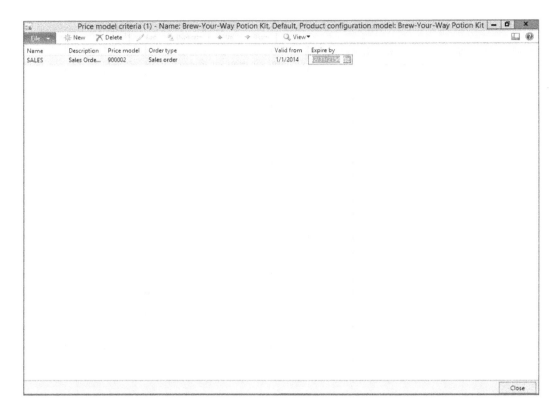

When the Price Model Criteria maintenance form is displayed, add a record, link it to the Price Model that you just created and also select the Sales Order type from the Order Type field.

When you are done then click on the Close button.

Use Pricing Models Within Configured Products To Calculate Prices Without A BOM

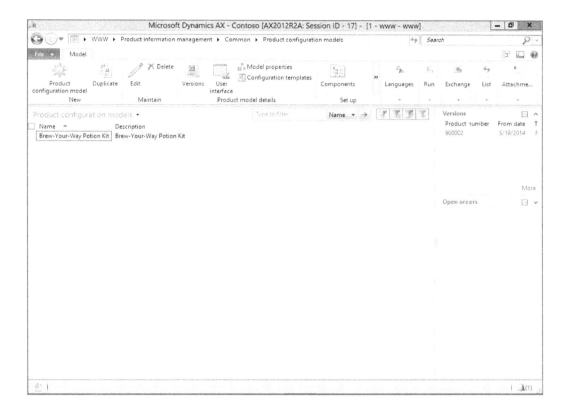

Also, you need to make sure that your product configuration is configured to use the pricing model. To do this, click on the Versions button within the Product Model Definition group of the Model area page.

Use Pricing Models Within Configured Products To Calculate Prices Without A BOM

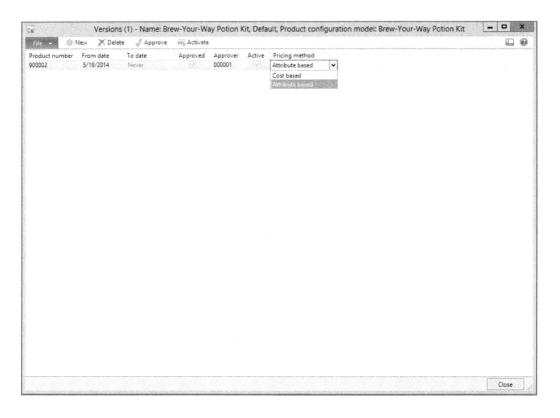

When the Versions maintenance form is displayed, make sure that the Pricing Method for the record is Attribute Based.

Use Pricing Models Within Configured Products To Calculate Prices Without A BOM

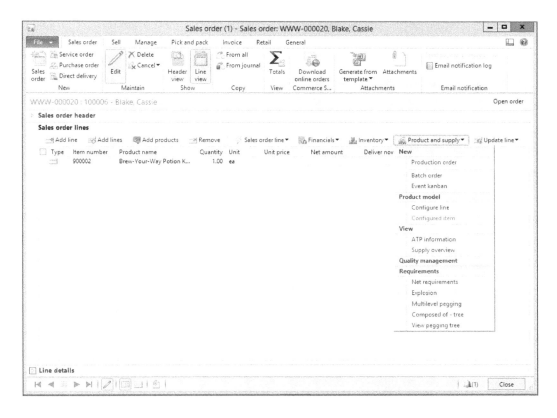

To see this in action, add a new Sales Order add a line for your configured product, and then configure it by clicking on the Configure Line option within the Product And Supply line menu item.

Use Pricing Models Within Configured Products To Calculate Prices Without A BOM

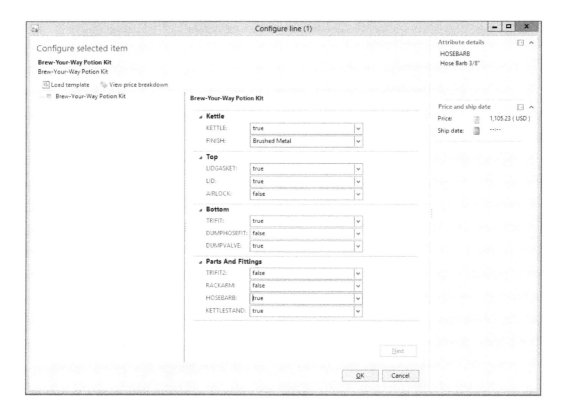

As you configure the line on the sales order, you will see the price is being updated based on the choices.

Use Pricing Models Within Configured Products To Calculate Prices Without A BOM

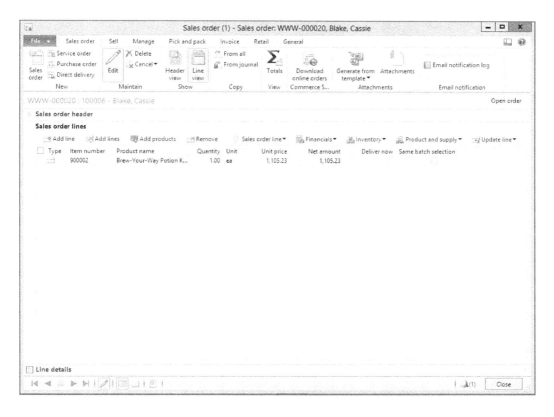

Also, when you return to the Sales Order the price that was calculated through the configuration is updated and applied to the order line.

Now that is super cool.

Control Price Adjustments On Sales Orders

You probably spend a lot of time trying to set up your pricing within Dynamics AX so that it is just right, and then the salespeople come along and just change it willey nilley as they are taking the sales orders. If a price change feels like a needle piercing your heart then don't worry, you can turn off the ability for the users to be able to update the price that you have set up, or at the very least, turn on reason codes so that when a price is changed, the user has to say why they made the change.

At least now when the users break your heart and ignore the suggested pricing, you will know why and receive a little closure.

Control Price Adjustments On Sales Orders

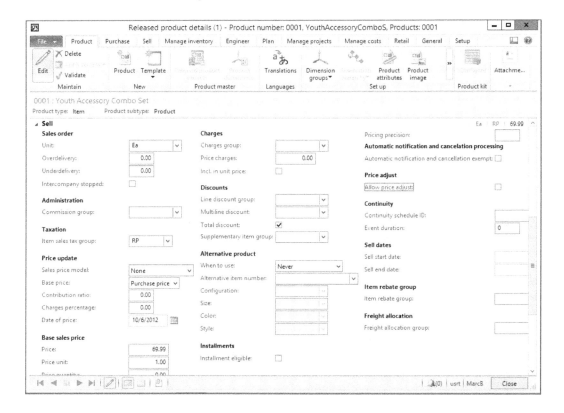

Open up your Released Product that you want to control the price updates on and within the Price Adjust field group of the Sell fast tab, notice that there is a new field called Allow Price Adjust.

To lock the price then uncheck this box.

Control Price Adjustments On Sales Orders

When you place an order for that product, there will be no way that the user is able to change the default price.

Control Price Adjustments On Sales Orders

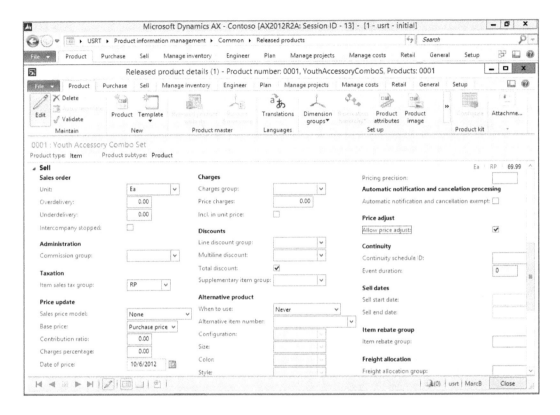

If you want to allow the users to change the price, then check the Allow Price Adjust flag.

Control Price Adjustments On Sales Orders

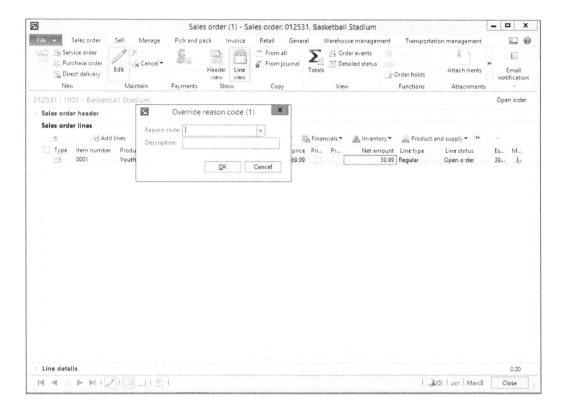

Now when you change the price on the order a Change Reason dialog box will be displayed.

Control Price Adjustments On Sales Orders

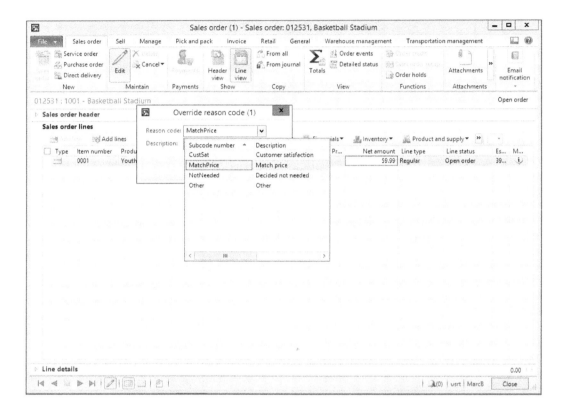

You will be required to select a reason from the reason codes that have been assigned to price changes.

Control Price Adjustments On Sales Orders

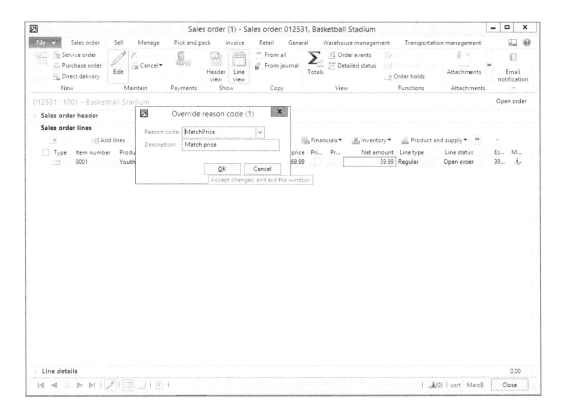

After selecting the reason code, just click the OK button.

Control Price Adjustments On Sales Orders

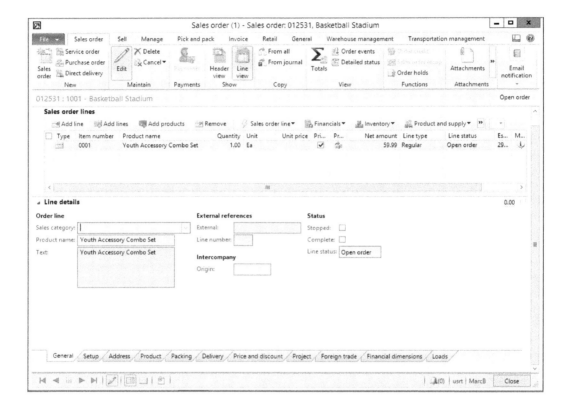

Now the price has been updated, and also an icon will show up on the order line that indicates that the price has been adjusted.

Also, the line details will be highlighted to give a visual cue that the price has been adjusted.

Control Price Adjustments On Sales Orders

Tip: If you want to change the default color for the price change highlighter, then click on the Call Center Parameters within the Setup group of the Call Center area page.

Control Price Adjustments On Sales Orders

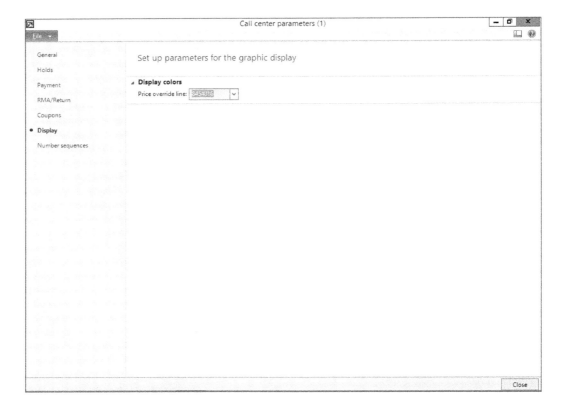

Within the Display page of the Properties you will find a color field called Price Override Line that you can change to any other color you like for the line highlighting.

Create Filtered Alerts To Sniff Out The Data You Really Want

Alerts are a great feature within Dynamics AX because they allow you to watch any information that you are interested in and then get alerts when the information is changed or updated. This is great for when you need status updates but are too busy (or lazy) to go into the list pages and look for yourself. But alerts are a double edged sword. If you are not careful you can end up spamming yourself. Having too much information being sent to you is just as bad as none at all. Luckily you can fine tune your alerts and notifications down from the shotgun approach to just the information that you are interested in.

It's like having your very own truffle sniffing pig, except it's not a pig and it sniffs out data, so really nothing like a truffle sniffing pig...

Create Filtered Alerts To Sniff Out The Data You Really Want

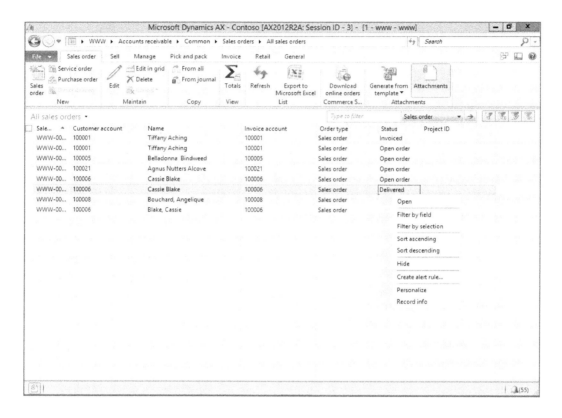

Start off by finding the data that you want to get alerted on. In this case we want to watch the status of our Sales Orders so we will watch the Status field. Then right-mouse-click on the field and select the Create Alert Rule menu item.

Create Filtered Alerts To Sniff Out The Data You Really Want

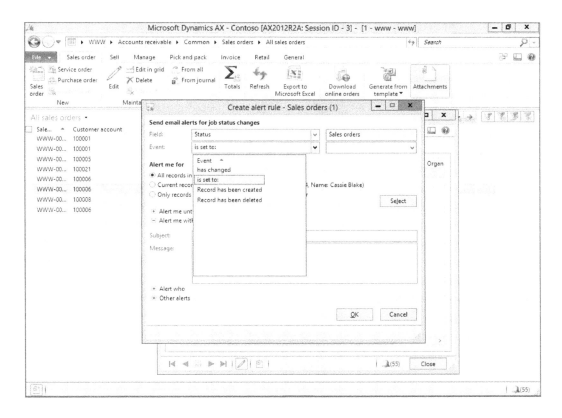

When the Create Alert Rule dialog box is displayed, change the Event to Is Set To so that we can track when the orders are placed in a certain status.

Create Filtered Alerts To Sniff Out The Data You Really Want

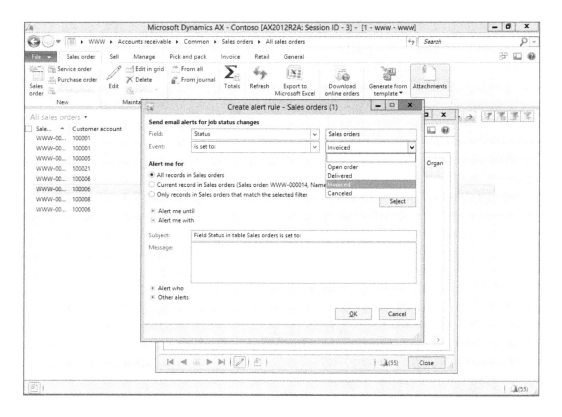

Then select the Status that you want to be notified on from the second dropdown list. In this case we only want to know when the orders are invoiced.

Create Filtered Alerts To Sniff Out The Data You Really Want

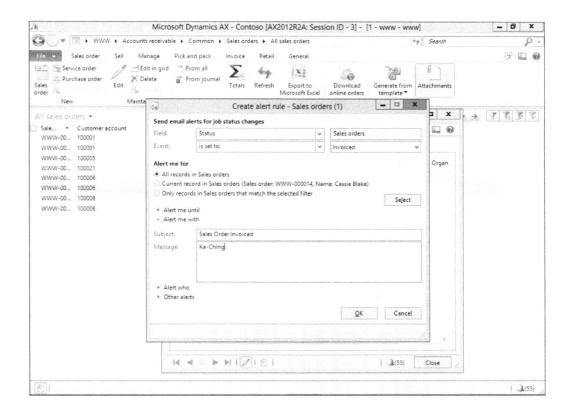

Then change the Subject and Message so that the alert is a little more informational.

Create Filtered Alerts To Sniff Out The Data You Really Want

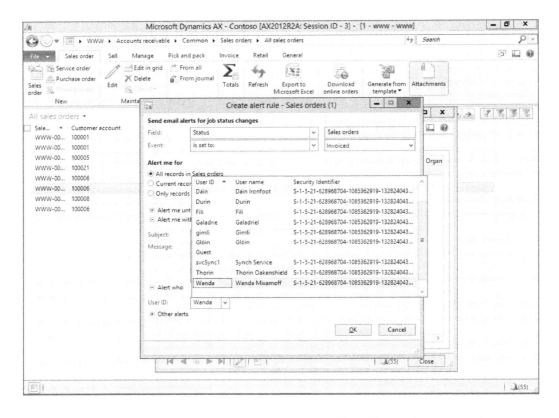

If you expand out the Alert Who group then you will be able to choose who is notified.

Create Filtered Alerts To Sniff Out The Data You Really Want

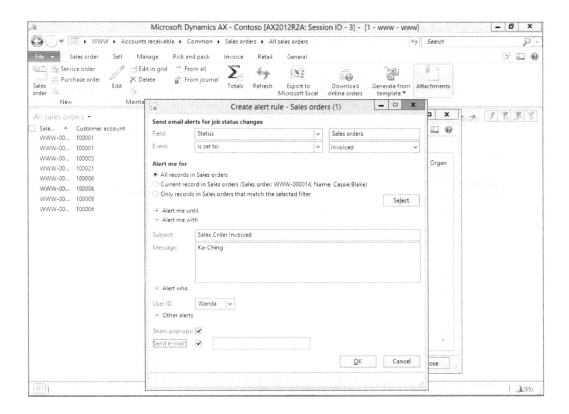

Also if you expand out the Other Alerts group then you can choose if you want to receive a Pop-Up, and/or an Email.

To make this even more useful we can restrict the records further to just the ones that we are interested in. In order to do this, click on the Select button within the Alert Me For group.

Create Filtered Alerts To Sniff Out The Data You Really Want

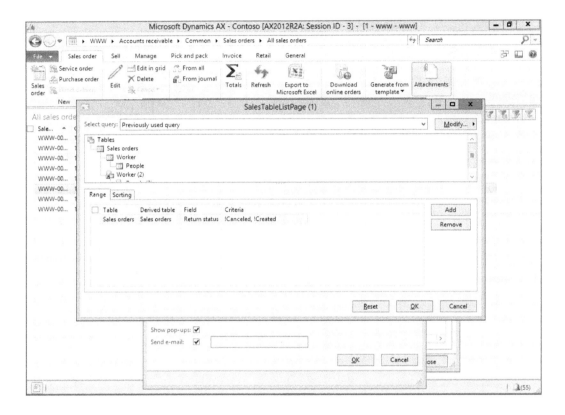

This will open up the default selection for this alert. To add another condition to this selection, click on the Add button.

Create Filtered Alerts To Sniff Out The Data You Really Want

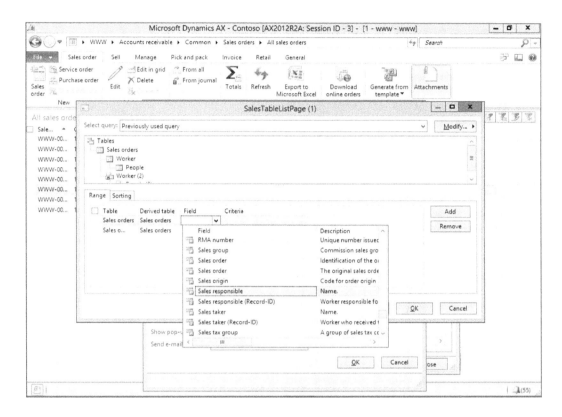

This will create a new line within the Range tab. You can then select the Field that you want to filter this alert on. In this case we will filter further on the Sales Responsible field so that we only get alerted on the orders that we are connected with.

Create Filtered Alerts To Sniff Out The Data You Really Want

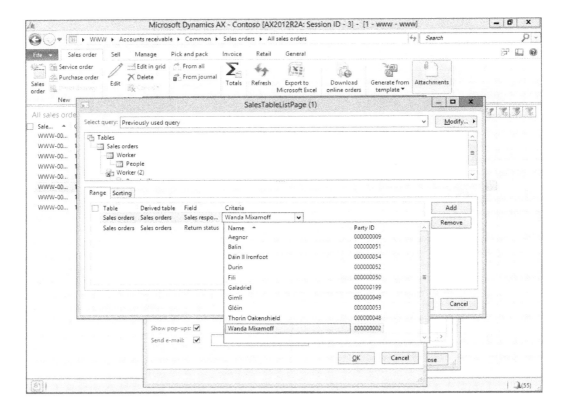

Then from the Criteria field we can select the user that we want to filter the selection on.

Create Filtered Alerts To Sniff Out The Data You Really Want

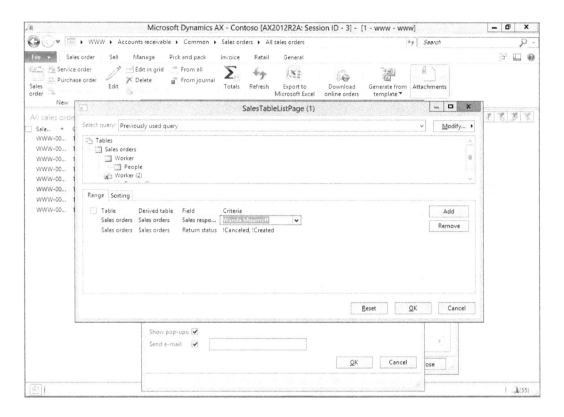

You can continue refining the search, and when you are done, click on the OK button to save the selection.

Create Filtered Alerts To Sniff Out The Data You Really Want

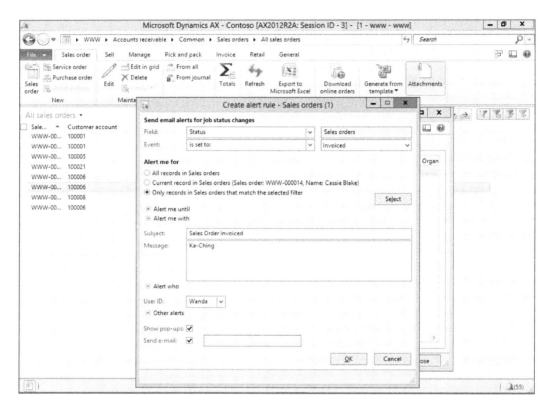

Now that you have created the alert, just click on the OK button to exit form.

Create Filtered Alerts To Sniff Out The Data You Really Want

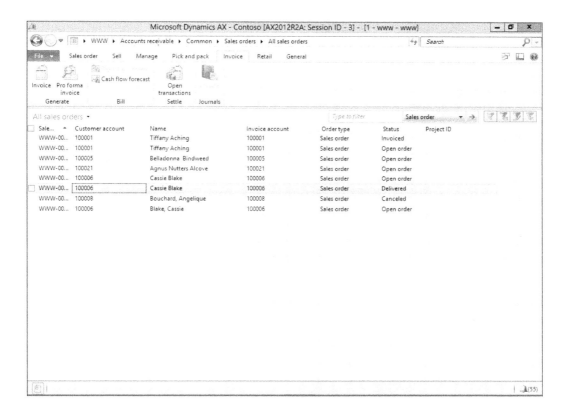

To see this in action, we will start off with our records that we want to watch.

Create Filtered Alerts To Sniff Out The Data You Really Want

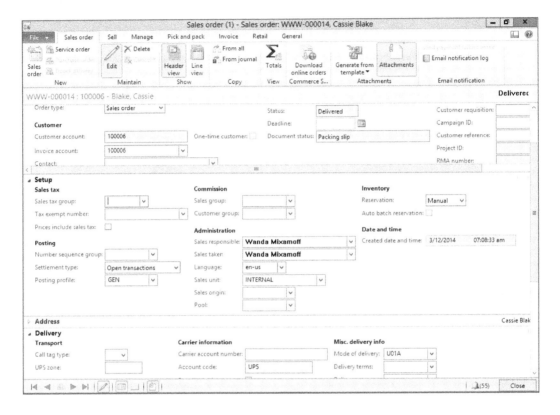

Just to be sure with this example we will make sure that the user is associated with the order before we continue on.

Create Filtered Alerts To Sniff Out The Data You Really Want

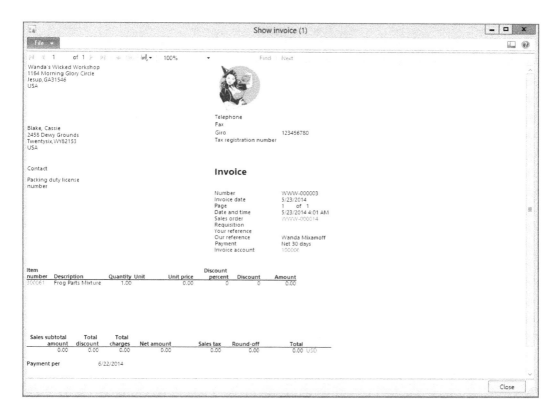

All that we need to do is invoice the sales order.

Create Filtered Alerts To Sniff Out The Data You Really Want

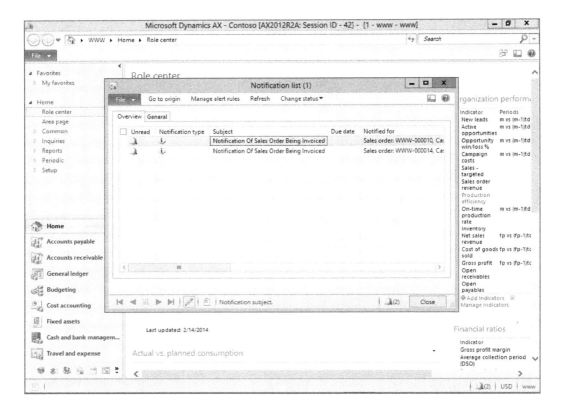

Behind the scenes Dynamics AX will send the user a notification that the order has been invoiced.

Create Filtered Alerts To Sniff Out The Data You Really Want

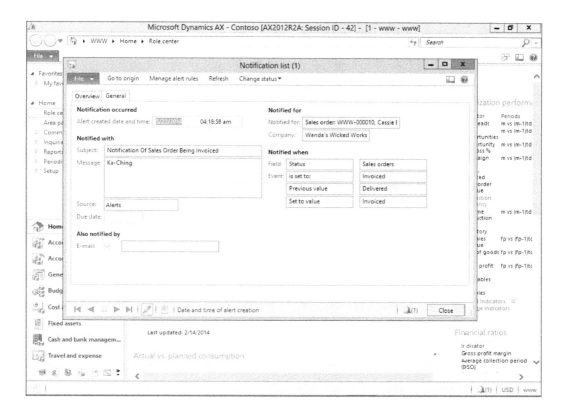

If you drill into the notification details then the subject and message will be copied from the alert to the notification as well.

How cool is that.

Declutter Customer Lists By Securing Them Through Address Books

Sometimes giving everyone access to every contact within the global address book is not necessary. Maybe you want to show people only contacts within their region, or legal entity, maybe you want to hide away inactive contacts from the default lists, or maybe you are just paranoid and don't want to give people access to all the contacts in the system. Regardless of the reason, you can do this easily with a click of the switch within Dynamics AX through the Address Book Security feature.

Now you can keep your special client list away from prying eyes.

Declutter Customer Lists By Securing Them Through Address Books

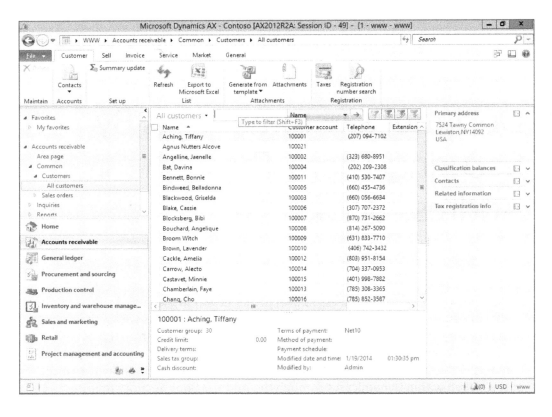

Just to show that there is nothing up my sleeves, this is the user before making this change. They have access to all of the contacts by default.

Declutter Customer Lists By Securing Them Through Address Books

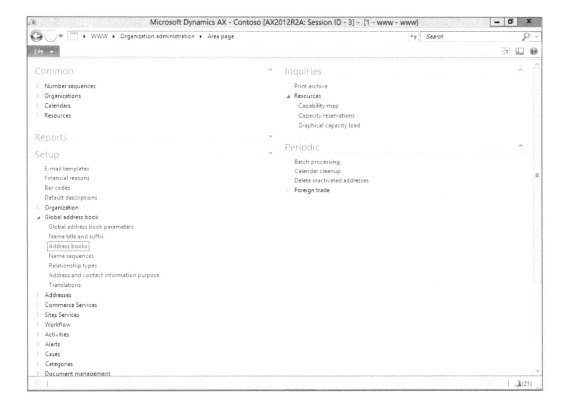

The first step to lock down the contact information is to set up some address books that we can use to classify them. To do this click on the Address Books menu item within the Global Address Book folder of the Setup group within the Organization Administration area page.

Declutter Customer Lists By Securing Them Through Address Books

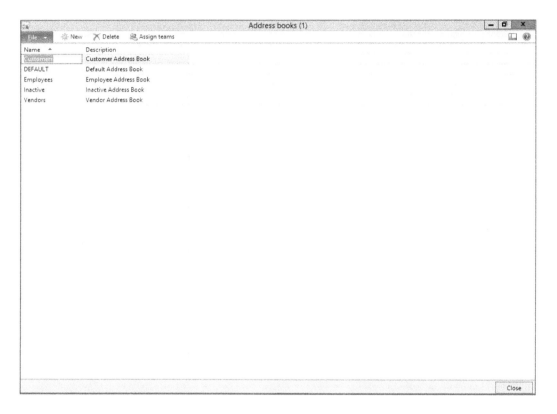

If when the Address Books maintenance form is displayed you don't have any records, just click on the New button in the ribbon bar to create new record.

Declutter Customer Lists By Securing Them Through Address Books

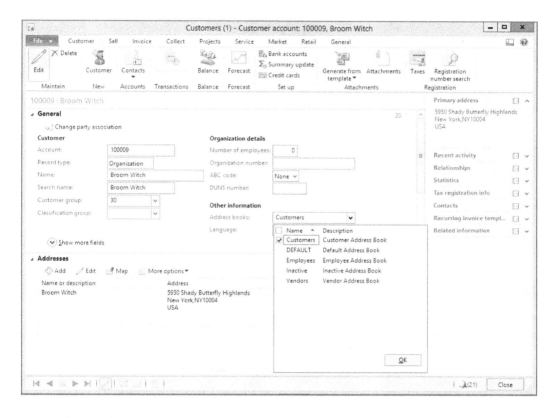

Now that we have address books configured we can start assigning them to the Customer records. To do this, open up your Customers detail page, and within the General fast tab, click on the Address Books field and select all of the address books that you want to assign to the customer record.

Repeat this for all the customers and then close out of the form.

Note: Any record that does not have an address book record will be treated as globally available.

Declutter Customer Lists By Securing Them Through Address Books

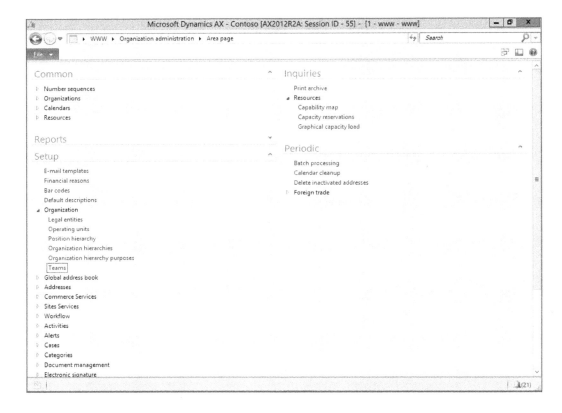

Dynamics AX restricts access to the Address Books by Teams to make the administration easier. So we need to make sure that we have some Teams defined. To do this, click on the Teams menu item within the Organization folder of the Setup group within the Organization Administration area page.

Declutter Customer Lists By Securing Them Through Address Books

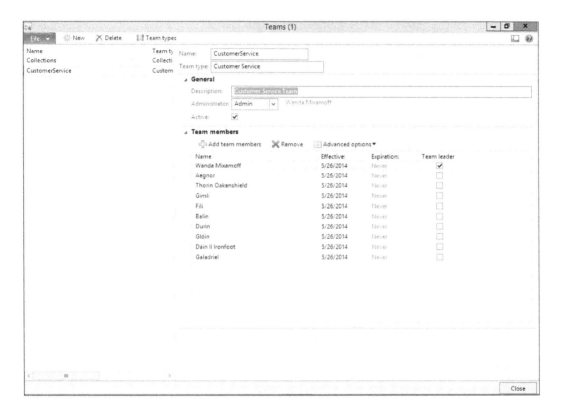

When the Teams maintenance form is displayed, make sure that all of your employees are configured within a Team and then close out of the form.

Declutter Customer Lists By Securing Them Through Address Books

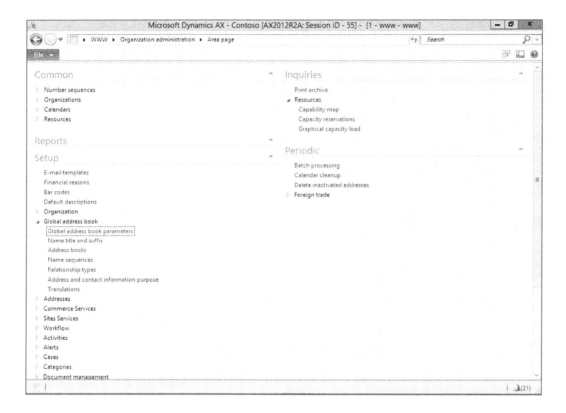

Now we will enable the security around the contacts. To do this, click on the Global Address Book Parameters menu item within the Global Address Book folder of the Setup group within the Organization Administration area page.

Declutter Customer Lists By Securing Them Through Address Books

When the Global Address Book Parameters maintenance form is displayed, select the Security Policy Options page.

Declutter Customer Lists By Securing Them Through Address Books

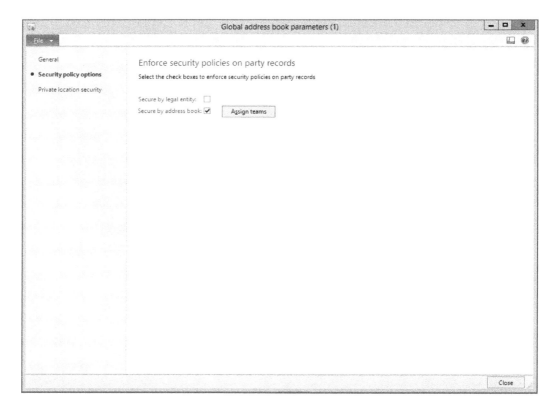

To secure the address books, just click on the Secure By Address Book check box.

Declutter Customer Lists By Securing Them Through Address Books

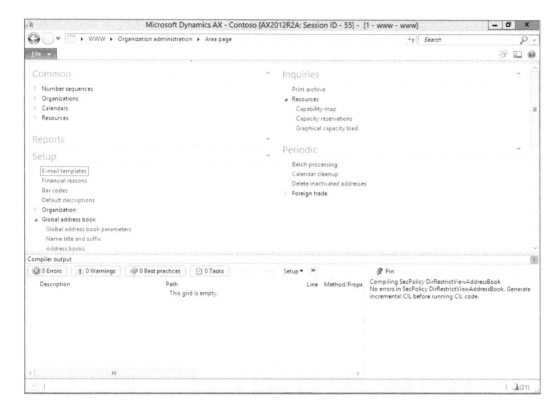

Note: When you save the change (CTRL+S) then Dynamics AX actually updates the database security so you may notice the log file trace pops up. After this is done, you can close the info panel.

Declutter Customer Lists By Securing Them Through Address Books

Now that the security has been enabled, we need to specify who has access to the Address Books. To do this, click on the Assign Teams button.

Declutter Customer Lists By Securing Them Through Address Books

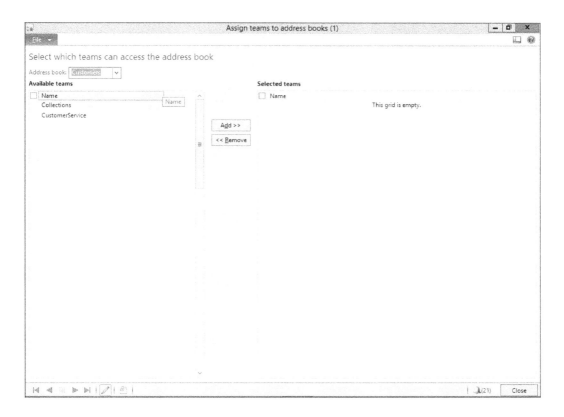

When the Assign Teams To Address Books maintenance form is displayed, select the Address Book that you want to secure.

Declutter Customer Lists By Securing Them Through Address Books

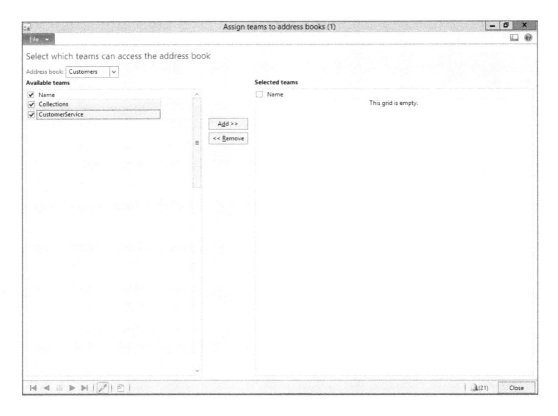

Then select all of the Teams that you want to give access to this address book from the Available Teams list and click the Add>> button.

Declutter Customer Lists By Securing Them Through Address Books

This will add them to the Selected Teams panel.

Declutter Customer Lists By Securing Them Through Address Books

Repeat the process for all of the other Address Books and when you are done, click on the Close button to exit from the form.

Declutter Customer Lists By Securing Them Through Address Books

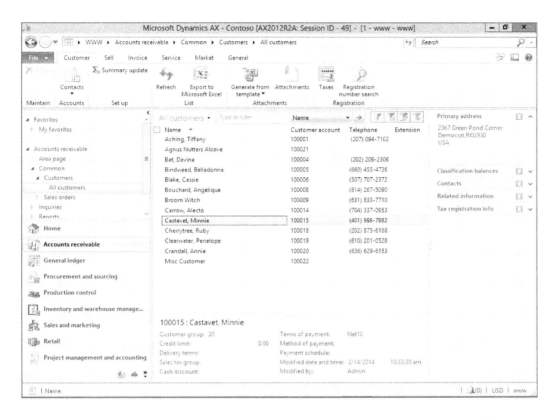

Now when our users look at the Customers, they only see the ones that they have been assigned.

Who said security is hard.

Set Default Parameter Values Into Posting Forms

There are usually a lot of different configuration choices that you can make choose from when you are performing updates and selections within the Dynamics AX forms. But you probably only use one option on a daily basis. Rather than going in and changing the selection parameters every time you open up the form, Dynamics AX allows you to set the default values and from then on you will always have the right parameters in your form.

This is definitely a case of set it and forget it.

Set Default Parameter Values Into Posting Forms

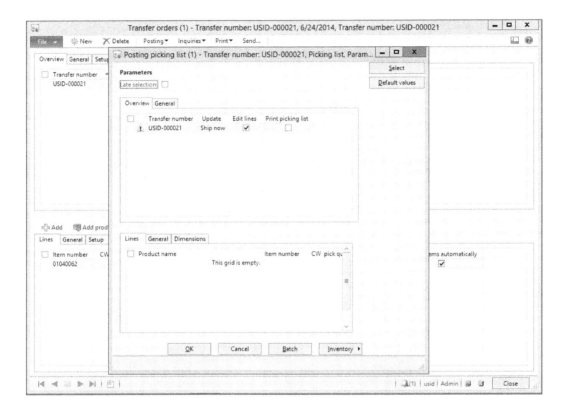

On some of the posting forms, you will notice that there is a Default button to the right of the form. If you want to change the default parameters that are used in the form, just click on it.

Set Default Parameter Values Into Posting Forms

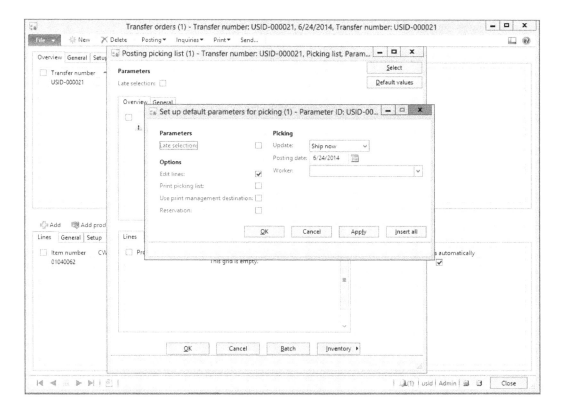

When the Set Up Default Parameters dialog box is displayed you will see all of the default values that are used for the form.

Set Default Parameter Values Into Posting Forms

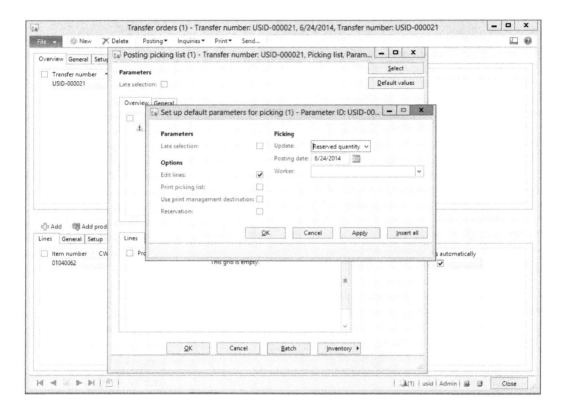

All you need to do is change them to what you want to use from now on and then click the Close button.

Set Default Parameter Values Into Posting Forms

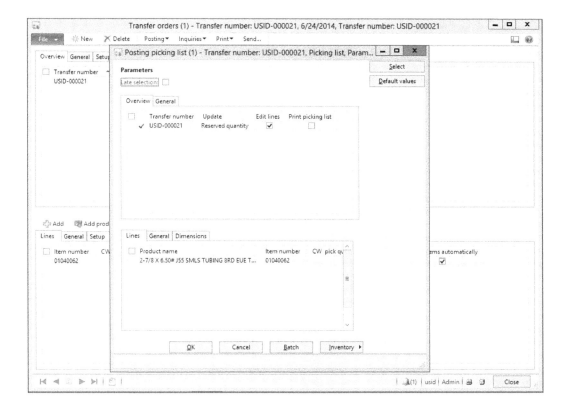

Now when you come into the form, all of the defaults will be applied, and you can just continue on without hitting a road bump.

That is so useful.

OFFICE TRICKS

It's no secret that everyone uses Office to create documents and reports, and that's fine. But if you really want to use Office, then you should take advantage of all the integration that is built into it for Dynamics AX.

Don't just cut and paste your spreadsheets, link them to Dynamics AX. Don't just use Excel as a worksheet to help you with your updates, make it the way that you update Dynamics AX. Don't just copy data to Word documents, make them templates that are automatically updated. Don't just use Project for recording project information, make it a tool that updates Dynamics AX.

In this section we will uncover how you can use some of the integrated Office features to make you a Dynamics AX ninja.

Perform Field Lookups Directly From Excel

The Dynamics AX Add-In for Excel is a great tool for downloading and updating data from Dynamics AX within a tool that everyone is familiar with. But not everyone is familiar with all of the valid values that are allowed for the fields. Don't worry though the Excel Add-In has a nifty lookup function that allows you to find out what valid values are allowed.

No more searching for field values by trial and error.

Perform Field Lookups Directly From Excel

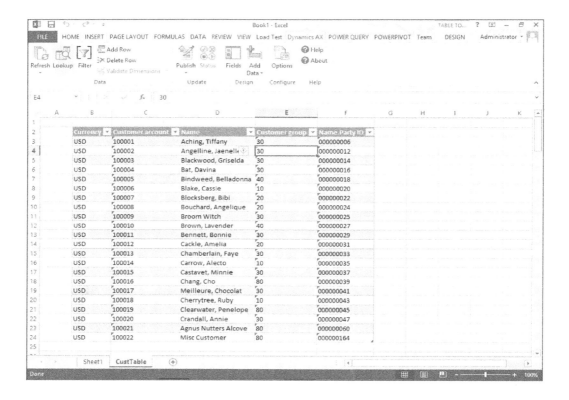

When accessing Dynamics AX data from Excel, select the filed that you want to look up on, and click on the Lookup button within the Data group on the Dynamics AX ribbon bar.

Perform Field Lookups Directly From Excel

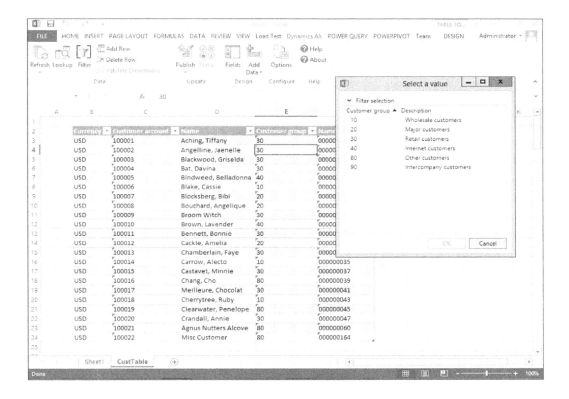

The Dynamics AX Add-In will then open up a dialog box with all of the valid values that you can enter into the field.

All you need to do is select the value, and then click on the OK button.

Make Excel Exports Static By Disabling the Refresh Option

The Export To Excel function within Dynamics AX is a powerful tool, because it gives you a live link back to the database, allows you to add additional fields, and also allows you to refresh the data. But for some people that is just too much power. For those users you can easily turn the Export To Excel from a power tool to a simple screen scrape utility just with a flick of a option flag.

I would never suggest that you do this as an April Fools prank...

Make Excel Exports Static By Disabling the Refresh Option

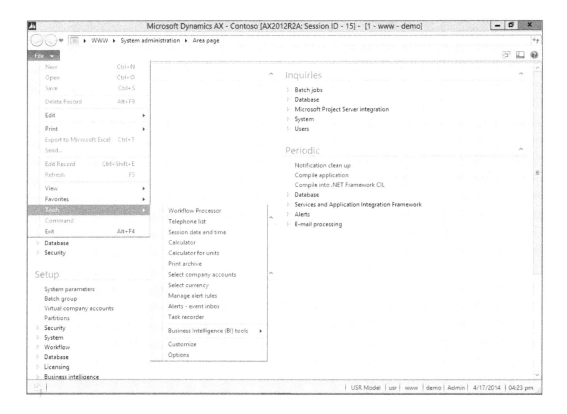

Click on the Files menu, select the Tools submenu, and then click on the Options menu item.

Make Excel Exports Static By Disabling the Refresh Option

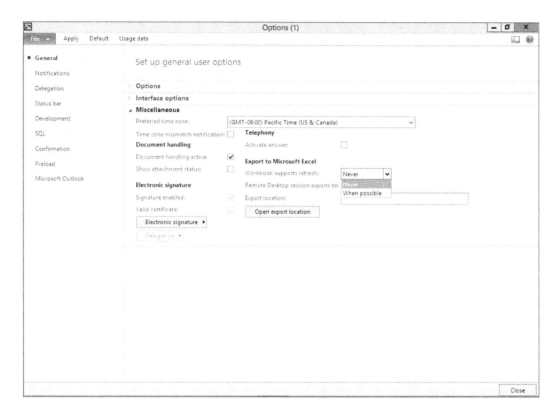

When the Options maintenance form is displayed, select the General page, and change the Workbook Supports Refresh option within the Export to Microsoft Excel group of the Miscellaneous tab from When Possible to Never.

Make Excel Exports Static By Disabling the Refresh Option

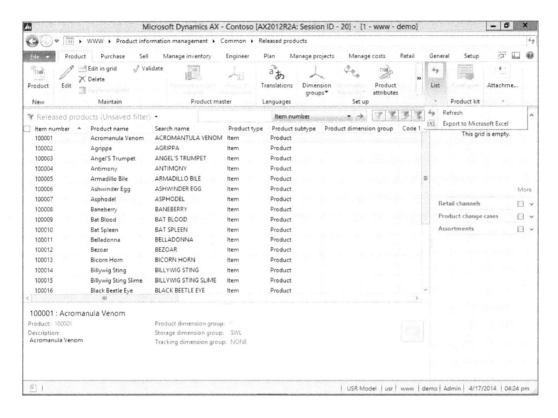

Now just go to any form that you would normally export data from, and click on the Export To Microsoft Excel button.

Make Excel Exports Static By Disabling the Refresh Option

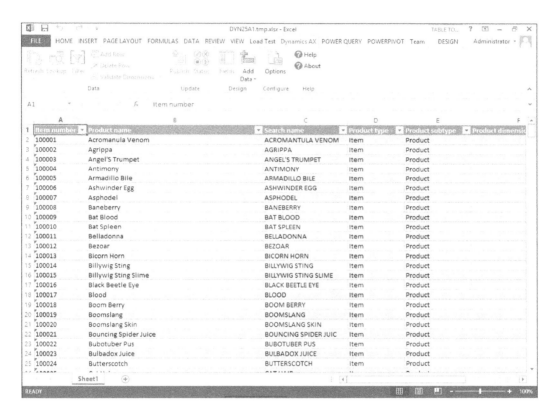

When Excel opens up with your data, you will notice that you are not able to refresh any of the data from within Excel, because this is now just a simple export rather than a live connection.

Creating Document Attachment Templates Using Word

In the perfect world, all documents and reports that are created out of Dynamics AX should be created within Reporting Services, sometimes don't have the time or the resources available to create the reports, so you end up resorting to using other tools like Word or Excel to create quick and dirty versions. I'm not judging you all, because you have to do what you have to do, but if you do use Office as a reporting tool, then there is a feature within Dynamics AX that allows you to save your Word documents as templates and then link data directly from the system into the document, and also automatically save the document that is created as a document attachment. It gives you the best of both worlds – reporting on a shoe string, and also control over the documents.

It's like having your own personal printing press.

Creating Document Attachment Templates Using Word

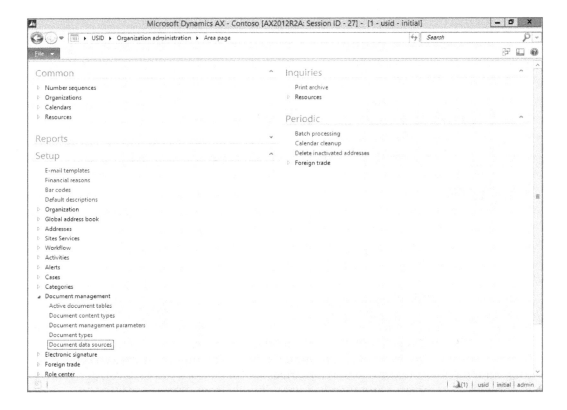

Before we start you need to make sure that you have some data that Word is able to read. To do this, click on the Document Data Sources menu item within the Document Management folder of the Setup group within the Organization Administration area page.

Creating Document Attachment Templates Using Word

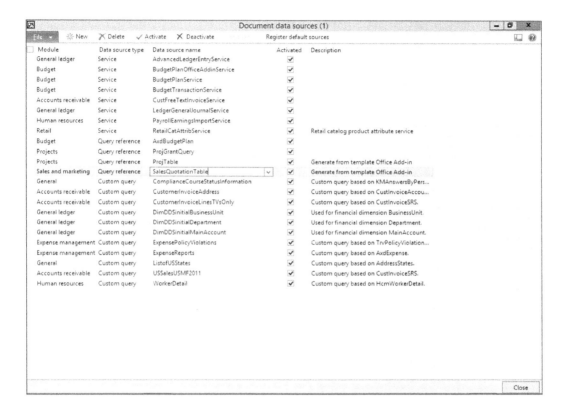

You need to make sure that you have a Query Reference or a Custom Query defined for the main header table of the record that you are going to create the document template for. In this case we are creating a document template for the Sales Quotations so we have a Query Reference defined on the SalesQuotationTable table.

When you are sure that you have the query configured, click on the Close button to exit from the form.

Creating Document Attachment Templates Using Word

Now open up Word and create a new Blank Document.

Creating Document Attachment Templates Using Word

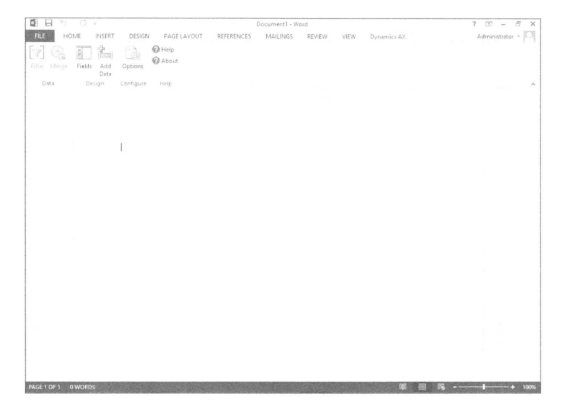

When the blank document is created, click on the Dynamics AX tab within the ribbon bar and then click on the Add Data button within the Design group.

Creating Document Attachment Templates Using Word

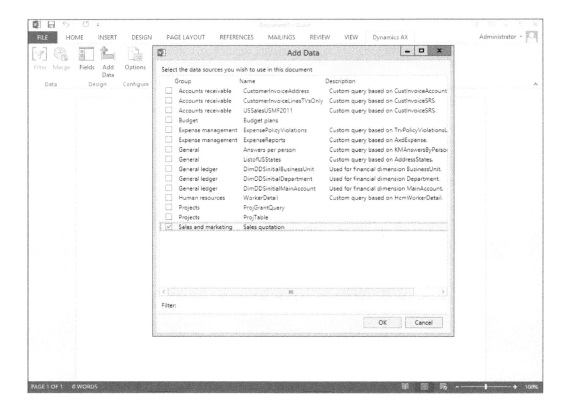

This will open up the Add Data dialog box showing you all of the registered Query References and Custom Queries. Select the main Data Source that you want to use for the document template and then click the OK button.

Creating Document Attachment Templates Using Word

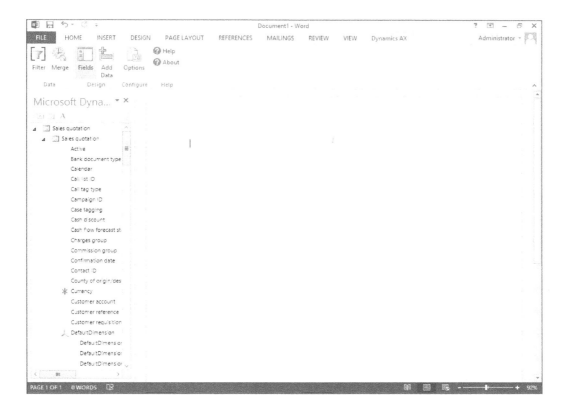

When you return to Word you will notice that the Field Browser is now shown on the left.

Creating Document Attachment Templates Using Word

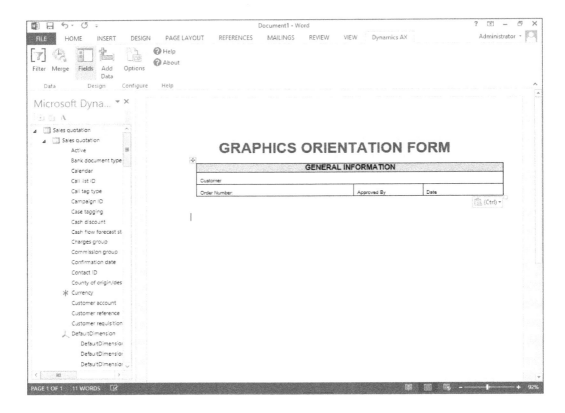

Now start creating your template.

Creating Document Attachment Templates Using Word

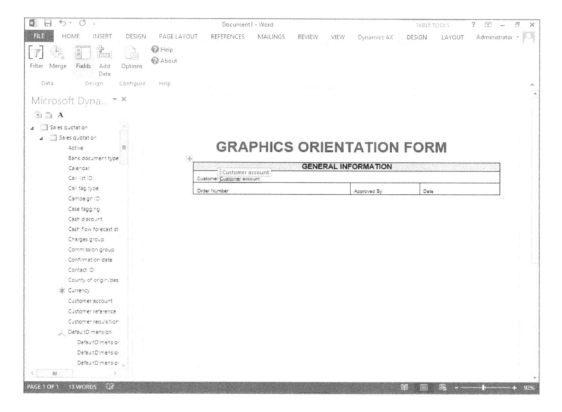

If you want to embed any field values in the word document then you can just drag and drop them from the Field Explorer over to the document.

Creating Document Attachment Templates Using Word

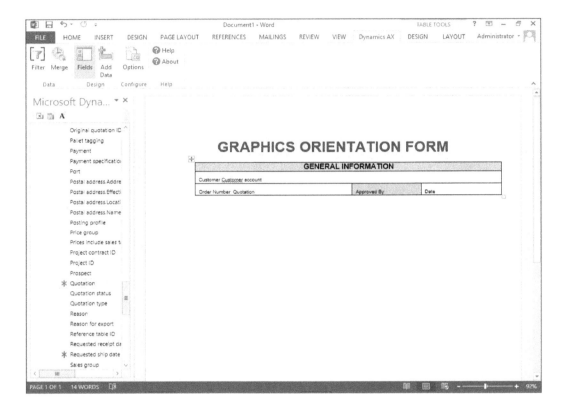

Keep on adding fields until you have all of the field data populated.

Creating Document Attachment Templates Using Word

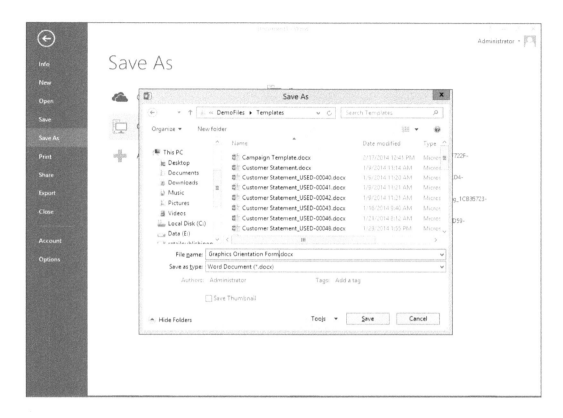

Now save your document away.

Creating Document Attachment Templates Using Word

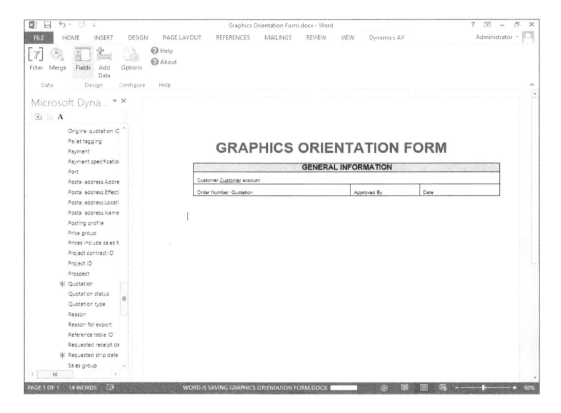

Now that you have finished creating the template, just close down the file.

Creating Document Attachment Templates Using Word

Now we need to save the document to a SharePoint Document Library. If you don't
have one yet, just create a blank Document Library and then note down the URL it
and then click on the Add Document link within the library.

Creating Document Attachment Templates Using Word

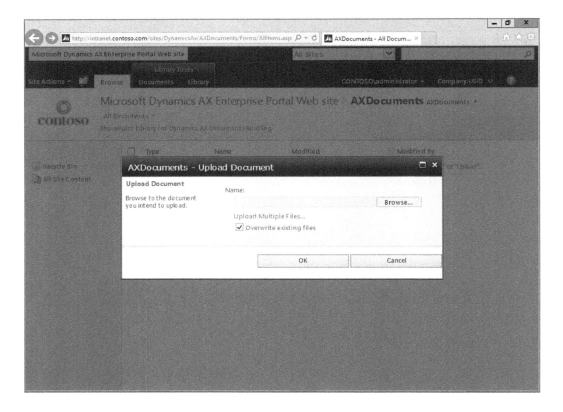

This will open up the Upload Document dialog box. Click on the Browse button to open up the file browser.

Creating Document Attachment Templates Using Word

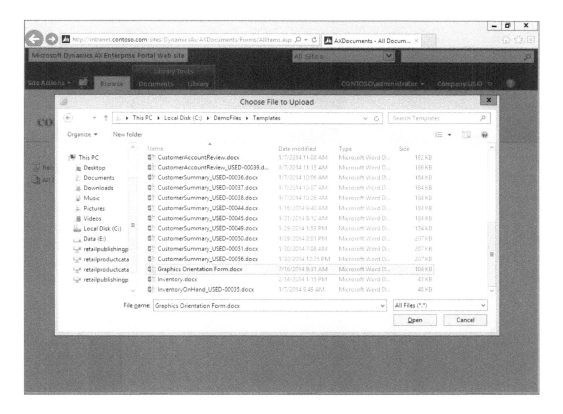

Then navigate to the template file that you just created and click on the Open button.

Creating Document Attachment Templates Using Word

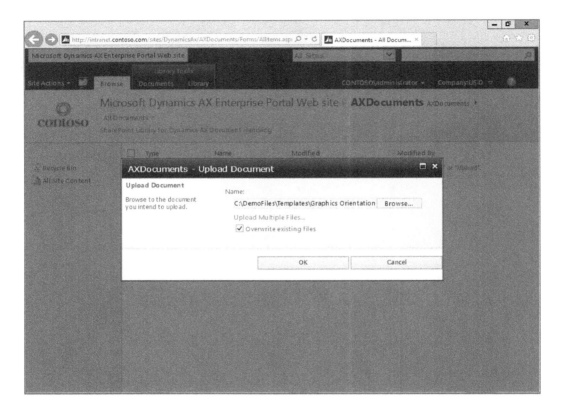

When you return to the Upload Document dialog box, click on the OK button to upload the file to SharePoint.

Creating Document Attachment Templates Using Word

Once you have uploaded the file, just exit out of SharePoint.

Creating Document Attachment Templates Using Word

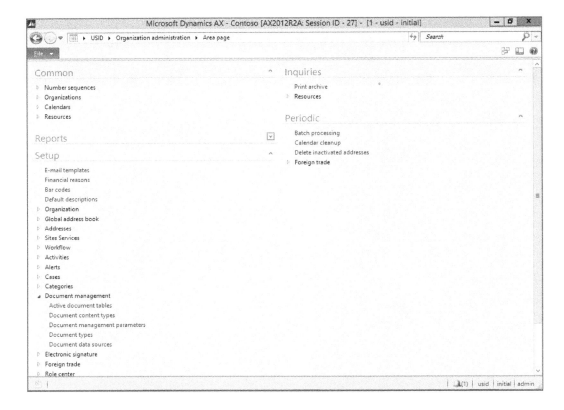

Now we need to create a Template document type that we will use to synchronize with SharePoint and then use to reference all of our document templates. To do this, click on the Document Types menu item within the Document Management folder of the Setup group within the Organization Administration area page.

Creating Document Attachment Templates Using Word

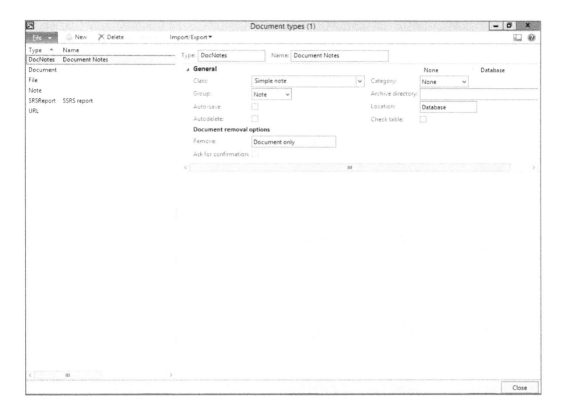

When the Document Types maintenance form is displayed, click on the New button to create a new record.

Creating Document Attachment Templates Using Word

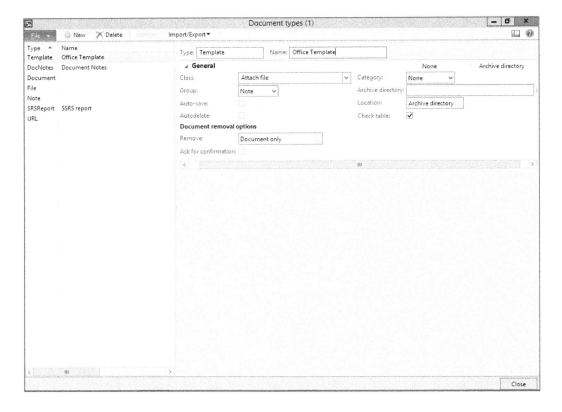

Then give your new record a Type code and also a Name.

Creating Document Attachment Templates Using Word

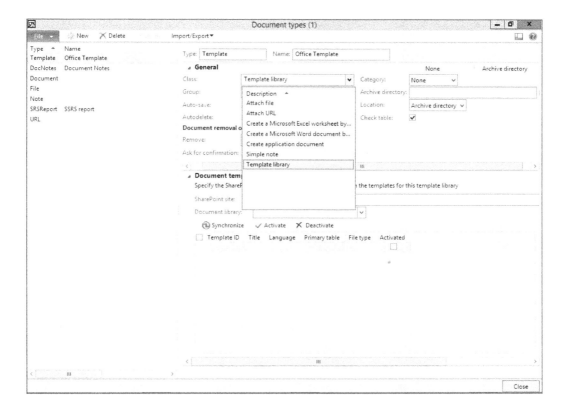

Change the Class to Template Library.

Creating Document Attachment Templates Using Word

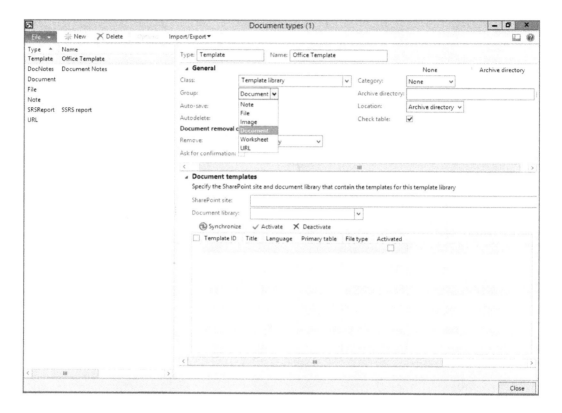

And change the Group to Document.

Creating Document Attachment Templates Using Word

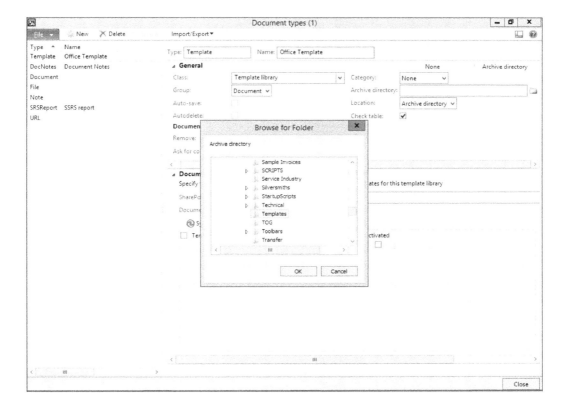

Then click on the folder button to the right of the Archive Directory field and point the Browser to a working directory where you can store all of the template files and then click the OK button.

Creating Document Attachment Templates Using Word

You may have noticed that when you selected the Template Library Class a new tab displayed in the bottom of the form.   Paste in the site URL (without the document library) for the SharePoint Document Library where you uploaded the template into the SharePoint Site field.

Creating Document Attachment Templates Using Word

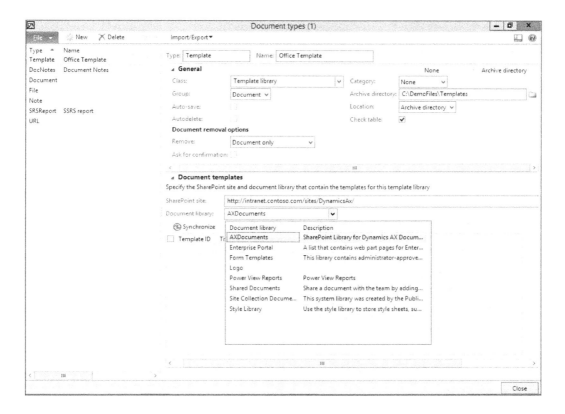

Then from the dropdown, select the Document Library where you stored the template.

Creating Document Attachment Templates Using Word

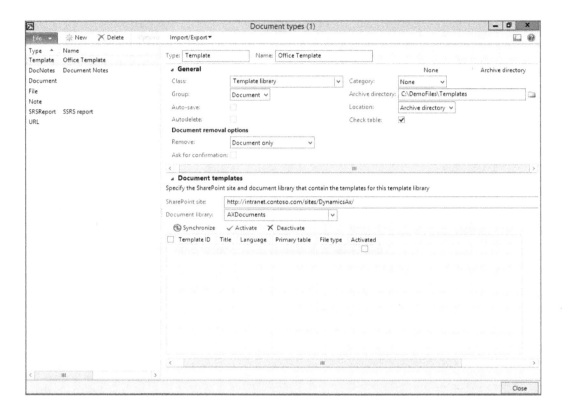

After you have done that, click on the Synchronize button.

Creating Document Attachment Templates Using Word

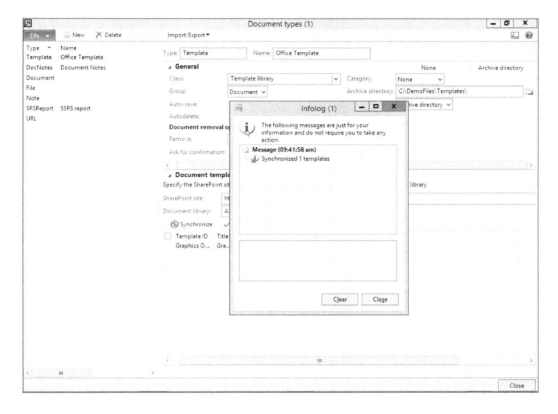

You should get an InfoLog box saying that one (or more) templates were synchronized.

Creating Document Attachment Templates Using Word

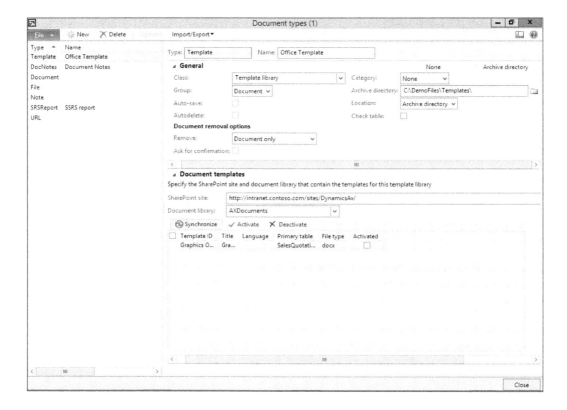

When you return to the Document Types form you will see the Template is now shown.

Creating Document Attachment Templates Using Word

All you need to do is click the Activate button to enable it.

Creating Document Attachment Templates Using Word

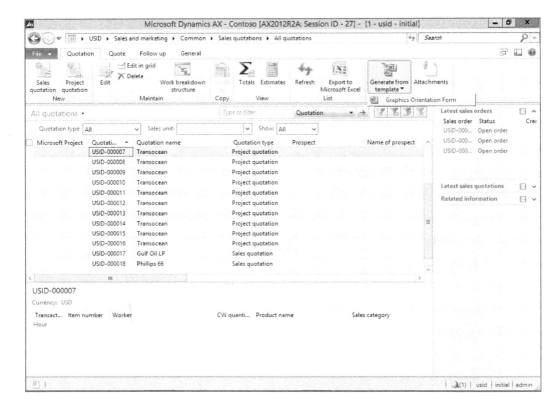

Now when you go to your main form (the Sales Quotations in this case) and click on the Generate From Template button, the Word template will be shown to you.

Creating Document Attachment Templates Using Word

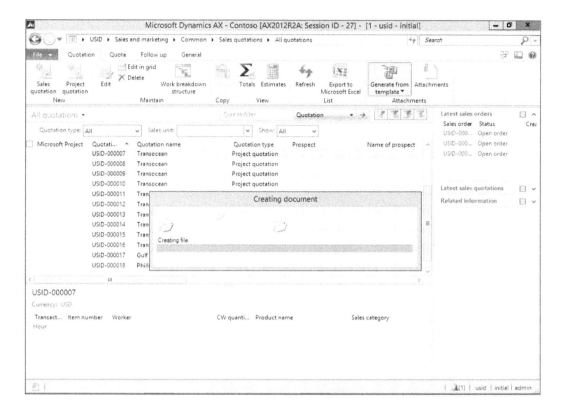

When you click on it, Dynamics AX will diligently use the template that you created to create a new document instance.

Creating Document Attachment Templates Using Word

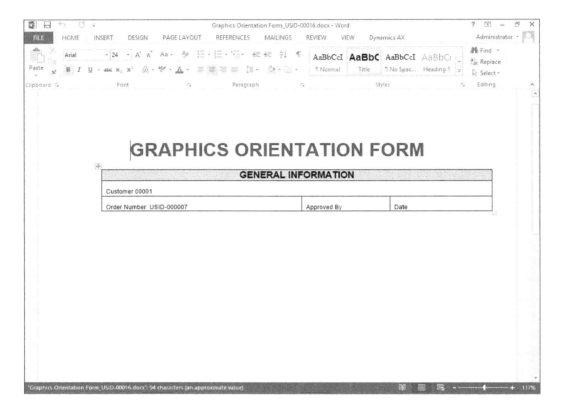

And then it will open up Word for you with the template and also the key fields populated for you.

Creating Document Attachment Templates Using Word

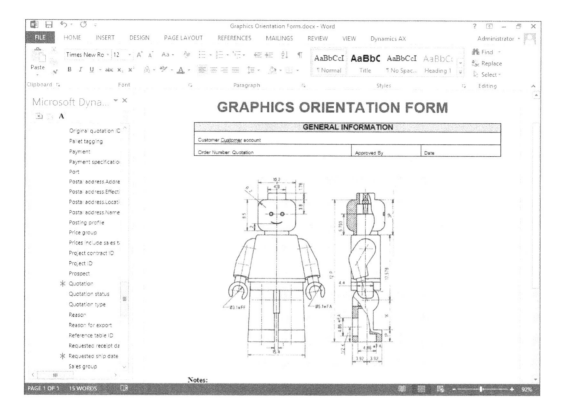

If you want to update the template for everyone, then just return to the original Word template, update it and then save it.

Creating Document Attachment Templates Using Word

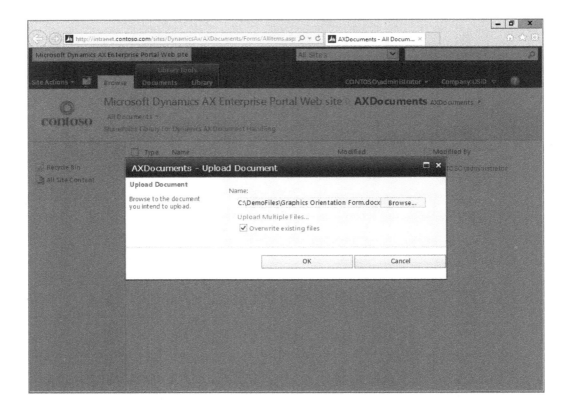

Then return to the SharePoint library and re-upload the template file (overwriting the previous version).

Creating Document Attachment Templates Using Word

And then open up your Document Types, find the template library and click the Synchronize button again.

Creating Document Attachment Templates Using Word

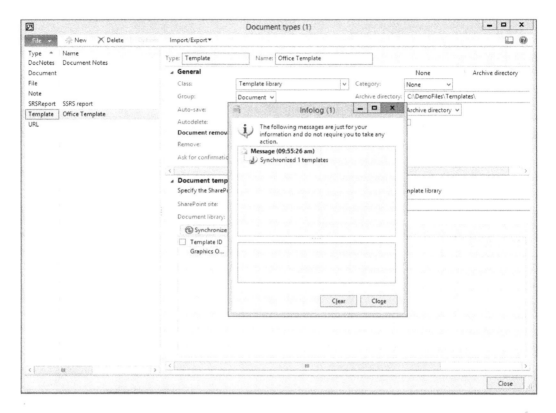

Dynamics AX will find the document for you and update the template it references.

Creating Document Attachment Templates Using Word

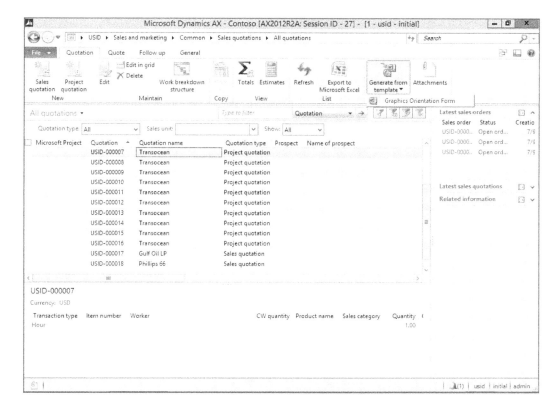

If you go back to your main form and create another document from the template...

Creating Document Attachment Templates Using Word

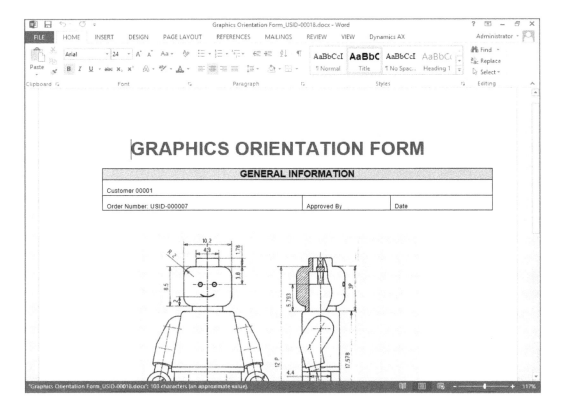

Then it will use the new version of the template that you just uploaded.

Creating Document Attachment Templates Using Word

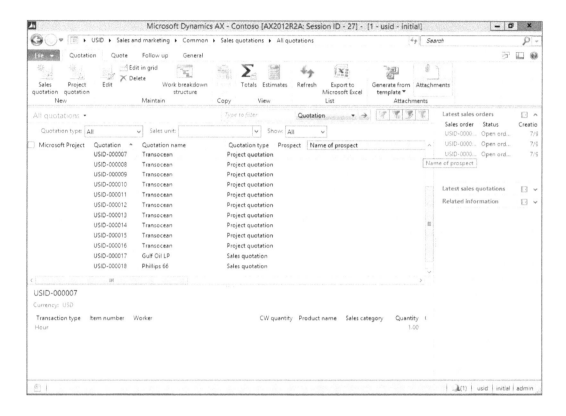

Another benefit of this feature is that all of the documents that you create are tracked and saved as attachments against the record that you created them from. To see them, just click on the Attachments button in the ribbon bar.

Creating Document Attachment Templates Using Word

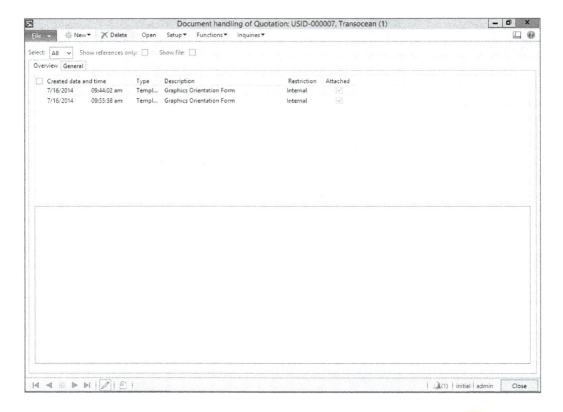

You will see all of the versions of the document that were created. And to see the document itself, just click on the Open button in the menu bar.

Creating Document Attachment Templates Using Word

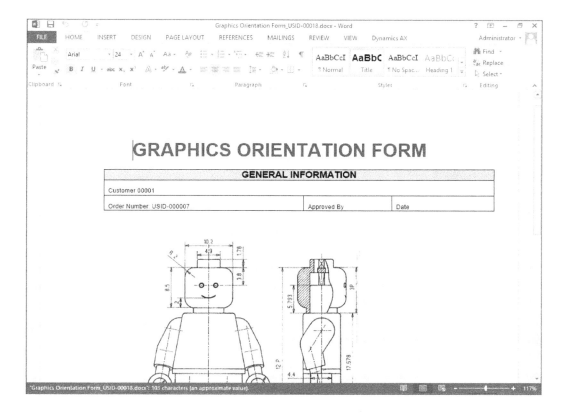

This will open up the Word document that was created by the template.

Rock on!

WORKFLOW TRICKS

Workflow is one of the most misunderstood areas of Dynamics AX, mainly because people think that it's complicated, and requires a developer to set it up and make it work properly. That is far from the case. A lot of the things that you can do with Workflow don't require you to write a single line of come, but add so much accountability to the users and the processes in the system.

In this section we will show some of the ways that you can use the Workflows to streamline your business processes.

Allow Multiple People To Be Involved In Workflow Approval Steps

Not all decisions are made by just one person, there are a lot of times where you need to get multiple people involved as an internal check policy, or maybe you just love making decisions as a group and don't want to leave anyone out. Doing this through workflow within Dynamics AX is a synch as well, because you can include as many people in a single decision process as you like and have them weigh in during the workflow execution. There are also a lot of different ways that you can allow the votes to be counted to speed up the process as well.

Everything is better when it's decided by committee… right?

Allow Multiple People To Be Involved In Workflow Approval Steps

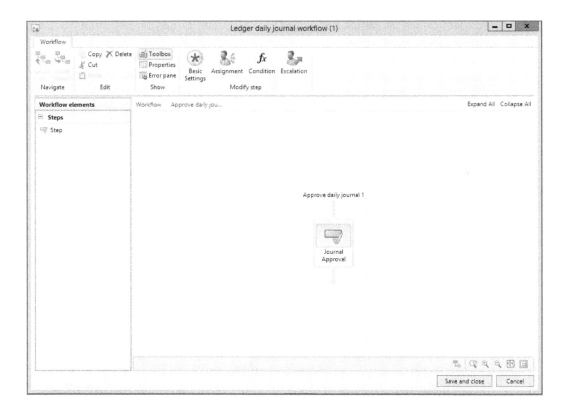

Select the workflow step that you want to allow multiple people to approve and click on the Assignment button within the Modify Step group of the Workflow ribbon bar.

Allow Multiple People To Be Involved In Workflow Approval Steps

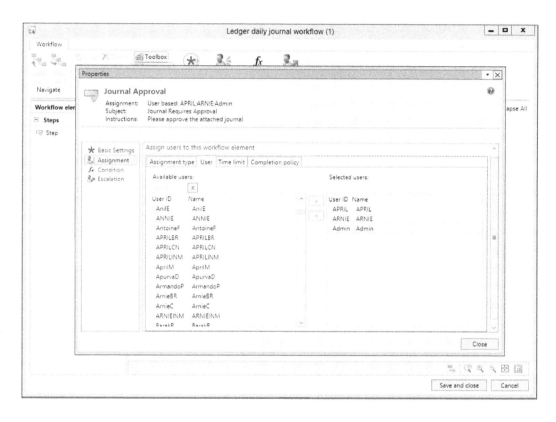

When the Assignment properties are displayed, click on the User tab and add all of the people that you want involved in the workflow step to the Selected Users side of the selection box.

Allow Multiple People To Be Involved In Workflow Approval Steps

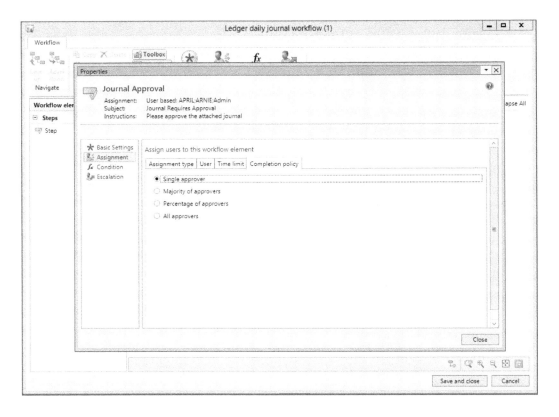

Then switch to the Completion Policy tab.

If you select the Single Approver option, then as soon as one of the approvers either approves or declines this step then the task will be marked as completed.

Allow Multiple People To Be Involved In Workflow Approval Steps

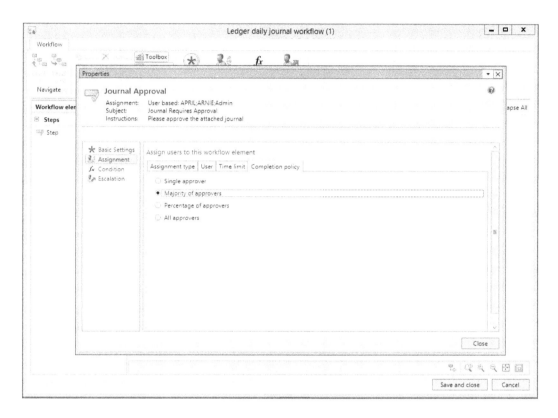

If you select the Majority of Approvers option then you need to have a majority of the users to approve or decline the task before it will continue on. Not all users necessarily have to weigh in.

Note: make sure that you have the numbers for a majority vote so that you don't end up with a hung jury.

Allow Multiple People To Be Involved In Workflow Approval Steps

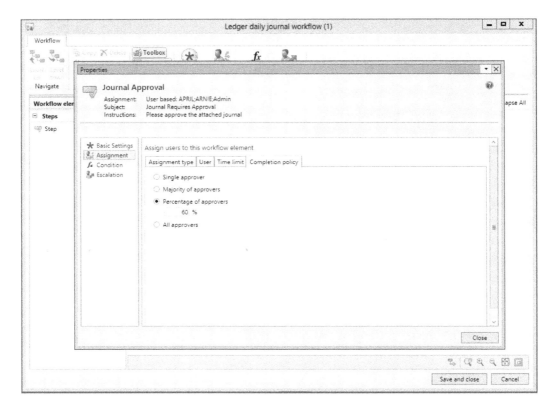

If you select the Percentage of Approvers option you will be allowed to fill in a % value. This is similar to the Majority of approvers option, except you define the watermark to get the step completed.

Allow Multiple People To Be Involved In Workflow Approval Steps

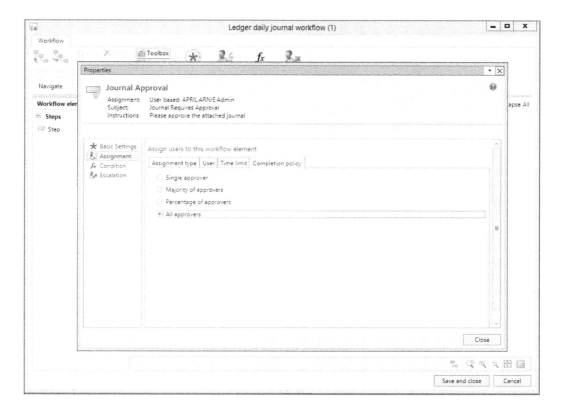

Finally, if you select the All Approvers then all of the people that you selected in the list must approve this task before it continues on.

Once you have selected your completion policy then you can click the close button and your approval step will be updated.

Create Multiple Versions Of Workflows And Choose When To Use Them

Workflows are great, but there are a lot of times that you want to run one version of the workflow in this situation, and another version of the workflow in a different situation. You could take the Sauron approach and create one workflow to rule them all, and embed in conditional tree at the beginning of the workflow that routes you to the right decision tree, or you can just create multiple workflows, and then use the Activation option to tell Dynamics AX when to use the variations of your workflows.

Now you can create an army of workflows that are all unique.

Create Multiple Versions Of Workflows And Choose When To Use Them

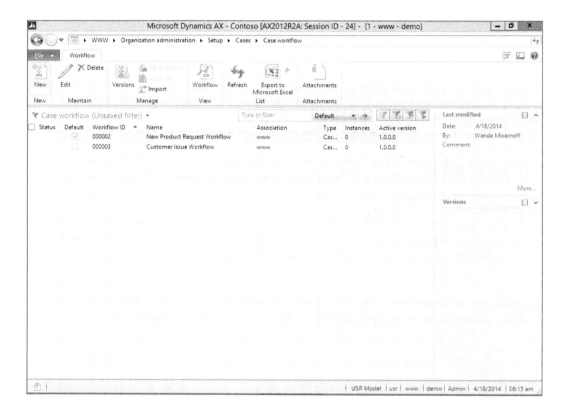

Start off by creating the different workflow processes that you want to use. In this case we have a couple of Case Management workflows that we want to process in different scenarios.

Create Multiple Versions Of Workflows And Choose When To Use Them

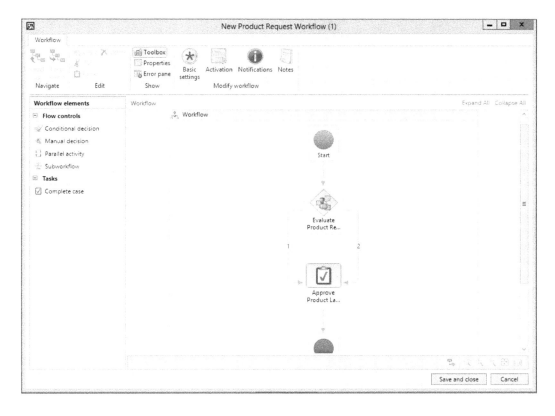

Open up the workflow, and then click on the Properties menu button within the Show group of the Workflow ribbon bar.

Create Multiple Versions Of Workflows And Choose When To Use Them

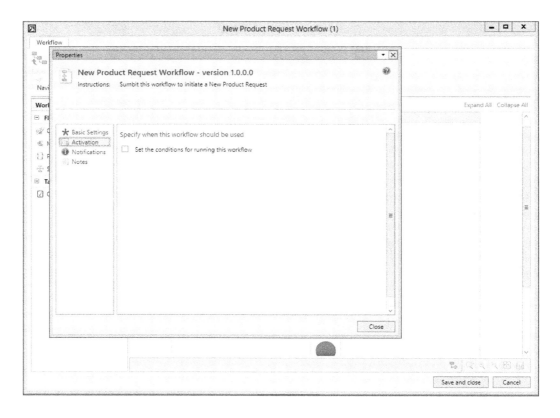

When the Properties maintenance form is displayed, click on the Activation group on the left hand side.

Create Multiple Versions Of Workflows And Choose When To Use Them

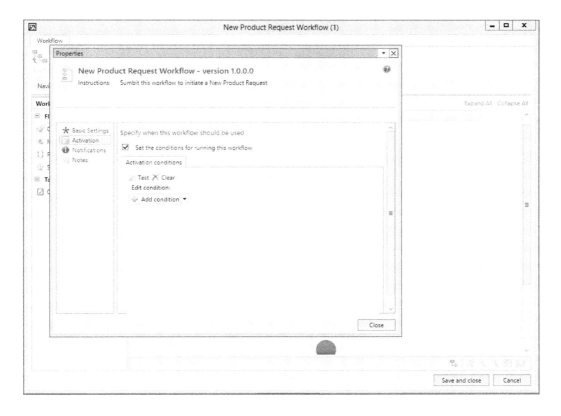

Check the Set the Condition For Running The Workflow check box, to enable the Activation Conditions details to be displayed, and then click on the Add Condition button.

Create Multiple Versions Of Workflows And Choose When To Use Them

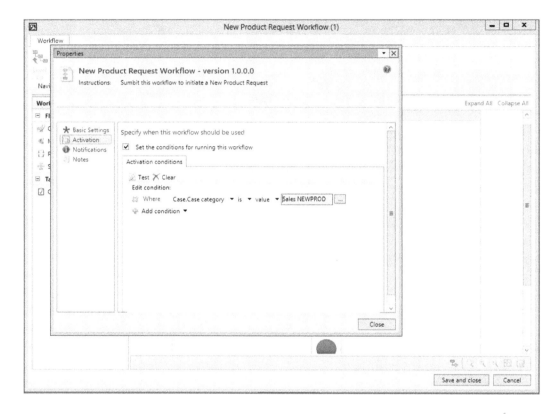

This will create a new condition line where you can select any field element from the Case and also any comparison that you may want to write.

In this case we activate the case only when it is a New Product Request, and then save and activate the workflow.

Create Multiple Versions Of Workflows And Choose When To Use Them

Repeat the process for all of the other workflows.

In this second workflow, we will only run this when it's a Customer Issue, and then close out of the workflow editor.

Create Multiple Versions Of Workflows And Choose When To Use Them

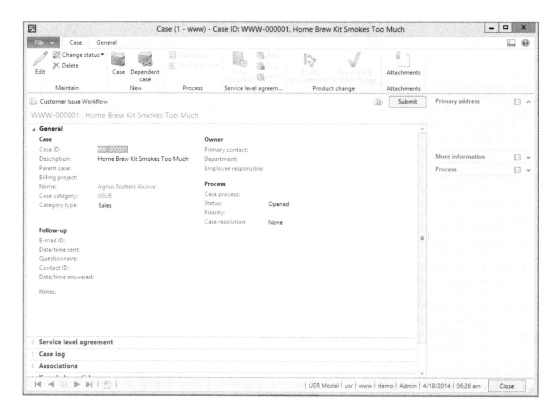

Now when we open up the case, based on the activation rules that we have enabled for the workflow it will pick and choose which one to run.

For Customer Issues, we will run the Customer Issue workflow.

Create Multiple Versions Of Workflows And Choose When To Use Them

For New Product Requests we will run the New Production Request workflow.

Even the submission instructions will be tailored to the type of workflow that you are about to run.

How cool is that?

Add Workflow Feedback Loops To Check Tasks Are Performed

Workflows are great because they automate the assignment of tasks to the right people at the right time like a well-oiled machine. The only thing that they cannot control is that the people actually do the work that they have been asked to do though. If you have bugs within your people processes, then you can add feedback loops into your workflows though that allow you to make sure that all of the fields that you ask the users to update have actually been updated.

Now a failing grade on the task will be caught right away.

Add Workflow Feedback Loops To Check Tasks Are Performed

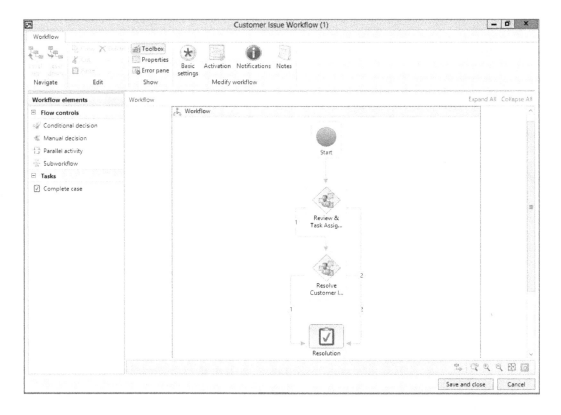

Start off by opening up your workflow within the editor. If this case we have a customer issue case workflow where we are asking someone to assign the task to a user.

Add Workflow Feedback Loops To Check Tasks Are Performed

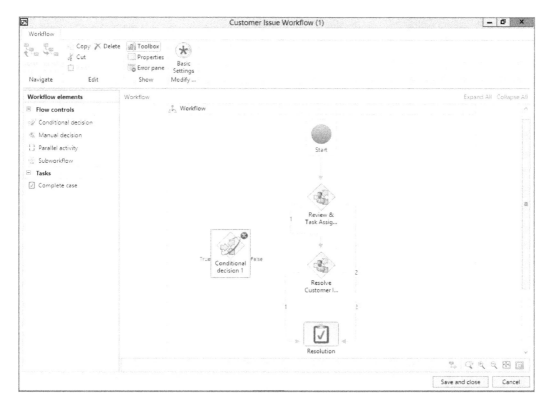

To add a feedback loop, drag the Conditional Decision workflow element onto the workflow canvas, and then click on the Basic Settings button within the Modify group of the Workflow ribbon bar.

Add Workflow Feedback Loops To Check Tasks Are Performed

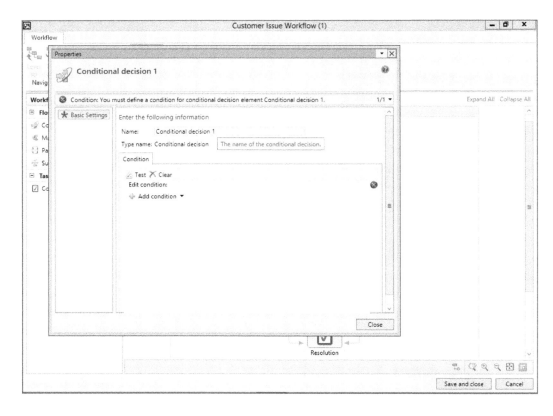

When the Conditional Decision properties are displayed, click on the Add Condition button within the Condition tab.

Add Workflow Feedback Loops To Check Tasks Are Performed

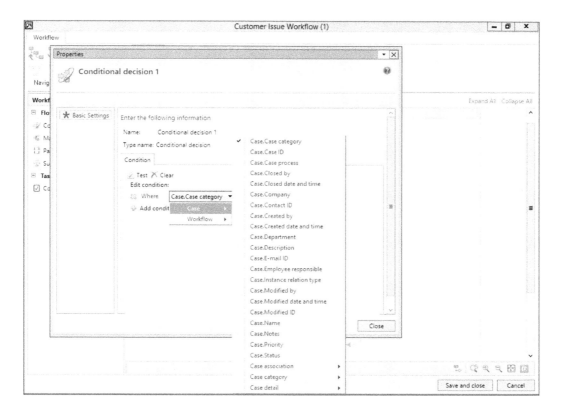

When the new condition is added, click on the field browser and select the field that you want to validate has been updates.

In this case it's the Case.Employee Responsible field.

Add Workflow Feedback Loops To Check Tasks Are Performed

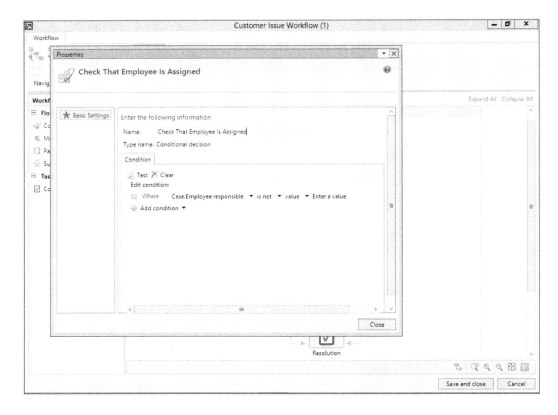

Now change the condition to be true when the field is not empty.

Add Workflow Feedback Loops To Check Tasks Are Performed

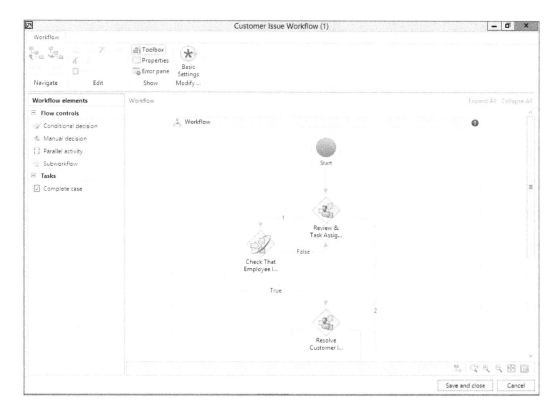

All that is left now is to link up the condition so that when the task is completed, if the field has not been updated, then the workflow returns to the previous task.

Use Workflows To Trap Transactions For Particular Accounts For Review

Although you always want to keep an eye on the transactions that are flowing through Dynamics AX, sometimes there are transactions that you want to keep an even closer eye on. Workflow is a great way to do this, but maybe you don't want to have to initiate a workflow for every transaction, maybe you just want to do it in certain situations. Not a problem, you can tell Dynamics AX when to run the workflow, and in all other cases don't even show the submit button.

It's a devilishly fiendish way to trap transactions.

Use Workflows To Trap Transactions For Particular Accounts For Review

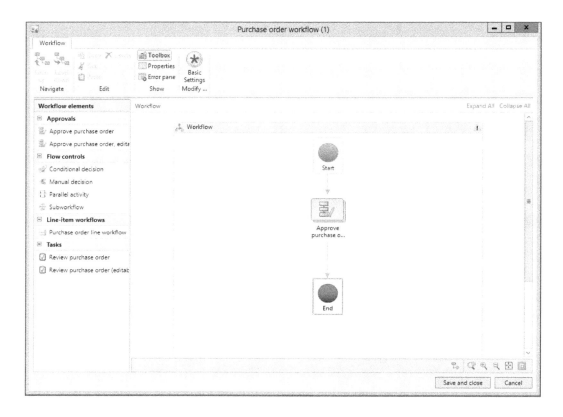

Start off by creating a simple approval workflow.

Use Workflows To Trap Transactions For Particular Accounts For Review

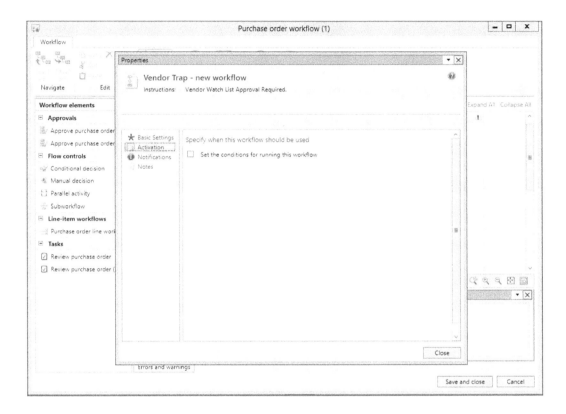

Then click on the Basic Settings within the Modify group of the Workflow ribbon bar, and select the Activation tab.

Use Workflows To Trap Transactions For Particular Accounts For Review

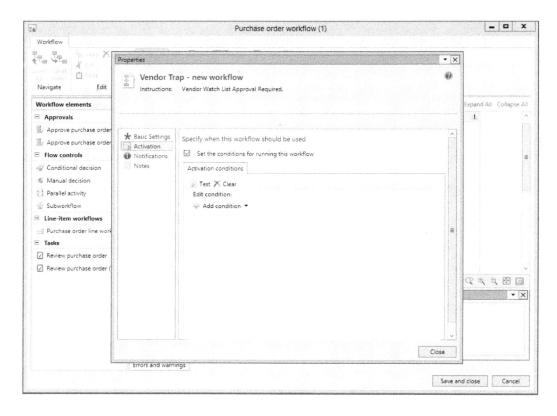

Check the Set the conditions for running the workflow flag to enable the Activation Condition group, and then click on the Add Condition button,

Use Workflows To Trap Transactions For Particular Accounts For Review

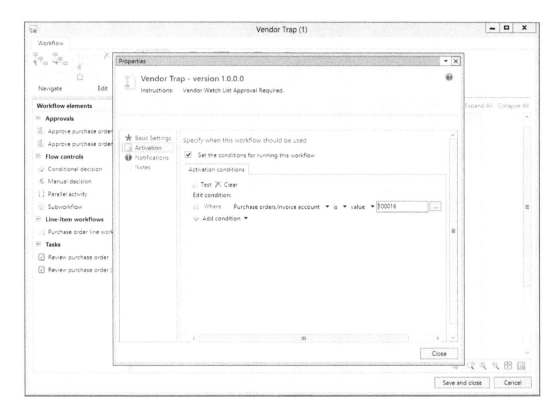

Configure the Condition that you want to perform the workflow for, and then click the Close button to exit from the form.

Note: In this case we are just going to check for one vendor that we want to keep a closer eye on.

Use Workflows To Trap Transactions For Particular Accounts For Review

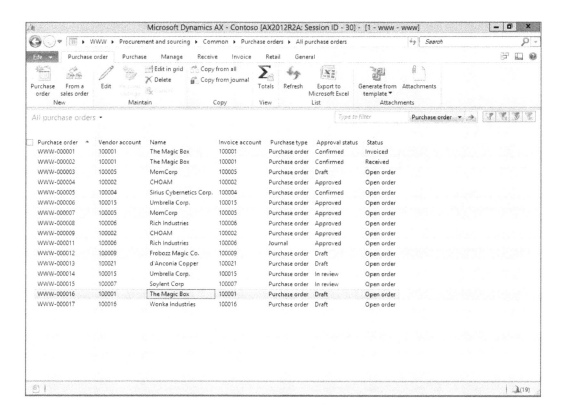

Now when we select a PO for any other vendor than the one that we set the trap for, everything looks normal.

Use Workflows To Trap Transactions For Particular Accounts For Review

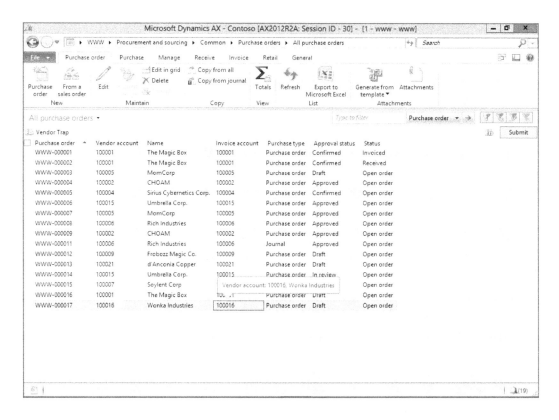

But for our problem Vendor we have to run through an approval workflow before we can confirm the PO.

Use Workflows To Trap Transactions For Particular Accounts For Review

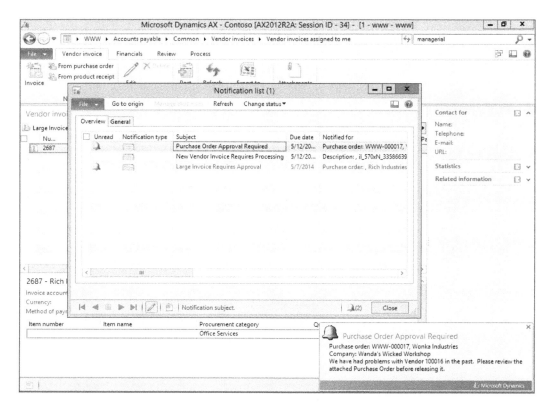

Then workflow notifications will start popping up all over the place.

Streamline Your Workflows By Automatically Performing Tasks Based On Conditions

Workflows are great because they enforce a uniform procedure to your business processes, and make sure people are not sidestepping the standard procedures through creative approval processes. But that doesn't mean that you can't build steps into your workflows that are sidestepped in certain situations. If you don't want a certain task to be performed based on a dollar value, or a coding on the record, then you can use the conditional processing on the workflow tasks to automatically complete it and then continue on to the next step in the workflow.

This way you will always have the users wondering if they are going to have to do something else, or get a free pass through the workflow.

Streamline Your Workflows By Automatically Performing Tasks Based On Conditions

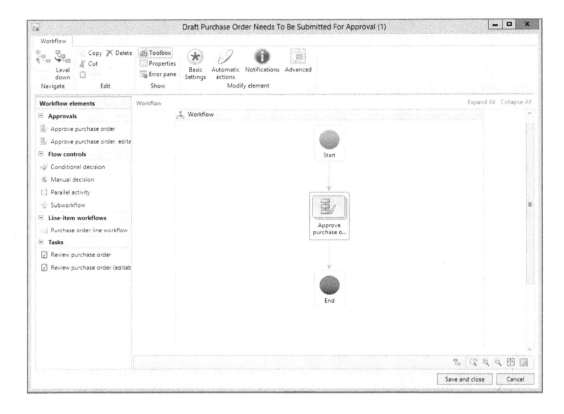

Start off by opening up your workflow that you want to streamline, select the task that you want to make conditional and then click on the Automatic Actions button within the Modify Element group of the Workflow ribbon bar.

Streamline Your Workflows By Automatically Performing Tasks Based On Conditions

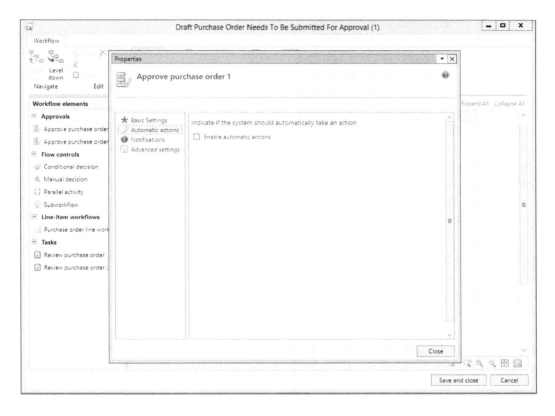

When the Properties maintenance form is displayed, check the Enable Automatic Actions flag within the Automatic Actions page.

Streamline Your Workflows By Automatically Performing Tasks Based On Conditions

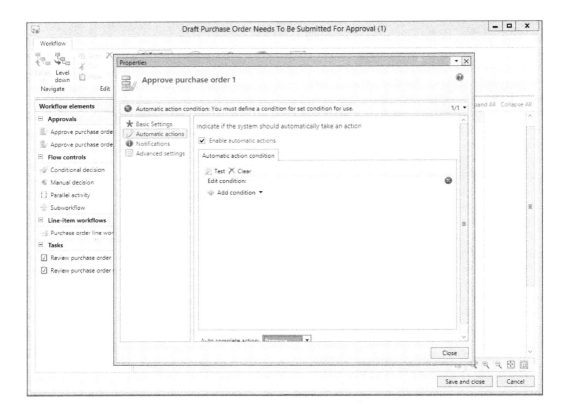

This will enable the condition designer, and you can then click on the Add Condition button.

Streamline Your Workflows By Automatically Performing Tasks Based On Conditions

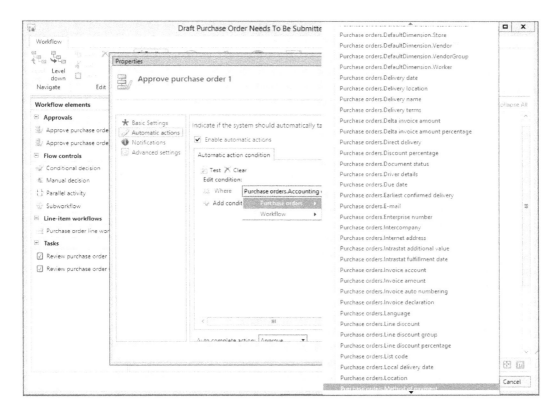

When the condition line is displayed, click on the field box and select the field for the related table that you want to use as your condition.

Streamline Your Workflows By Automatically Performing Tasks Based On Conditions

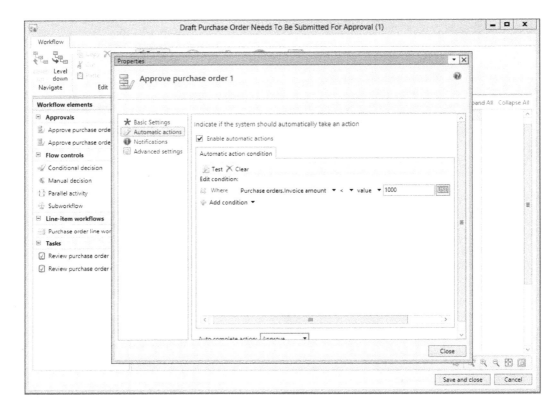

And then specify the rest of the condition clause.

Streamline Your Workflows By Automatically Performing Tasks Based On Conditions

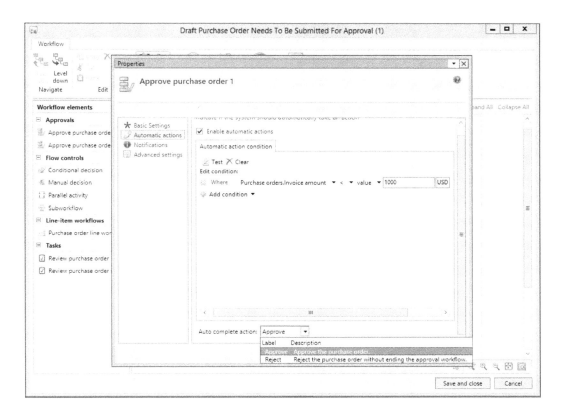

Finally, select the Auto Complete Action that you want to perform when the condition is true.

Note: notice that you don't just have to approve the task, you can also automatically reject the task as well.

Streamline Your Workflows By Automatically Performing Tasks Based On Conditions

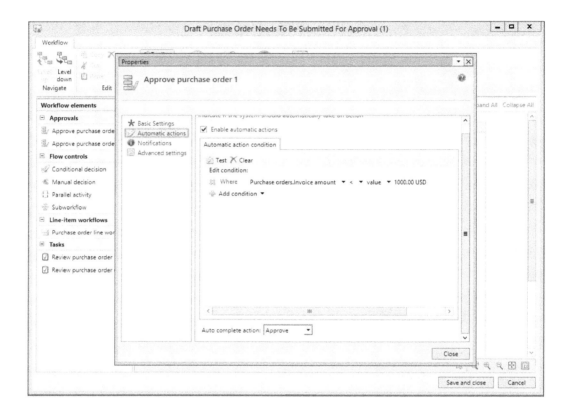

Once you have completed the change, then just exit out of the workflow and save the changes.

Streamline Your Workflows By Automatically Performing Tasks Based On Conditions

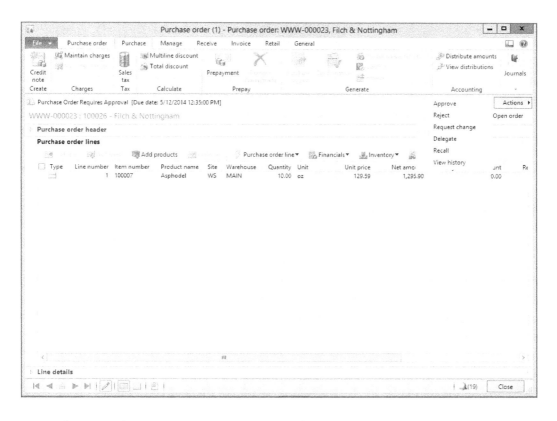

Now if we run through the task that the workflow is related to and the condition is not met everything looks like normal and we have to perform the workflow task.

Streamline Your Workflows By Automatically Performing Tasks Based On Conditions

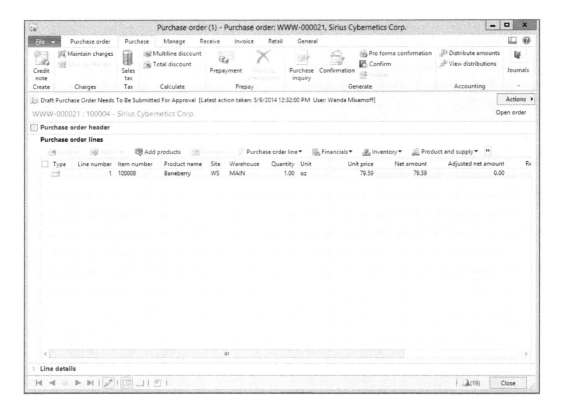

But if the condition is met then the task is skipped.

Streamline Your Workflows By Automatically Performing Tasks Based On Conditions

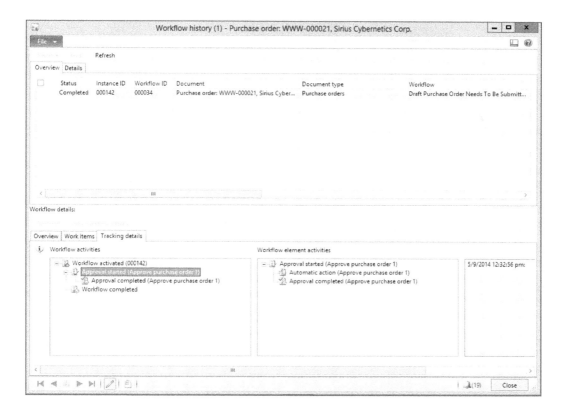

If we look at the workflow history then we will see that the action was automatically performed.

How cool is that?

SYSTEM ADMINISTRATION TIPS

There are a lot of wizards and tools that are included with Dynamics AX that are designed to make the administration and management of the system easier, but they are not there just for the System Administrator, everyone is able to take advantage of them. Features like Alerts, and tools like the Task Recorder are invaluable to everyone.

In this section we will show a few examples of how you can use these administrative tools to save time and make your life generally better.

Add SharePoint Documents Libraries As Menu Links

Storing documents within SharePoint is cool. It allows you to browse through the documents, it allows you to have version control, it allows you to add metadata that you can use to search for documents, it does everything. The problem is that if you work in the AX client all the time, then you have to switch out of the application in order to view all the related documents. Don't worry. If you want to access all of the documents from within Dynamics AX then you can add it to the menu.

Now all of the Axoraphobiacs out there don't have to leave the application all day.

Add SharePoint Documents Libraries As Menu Links

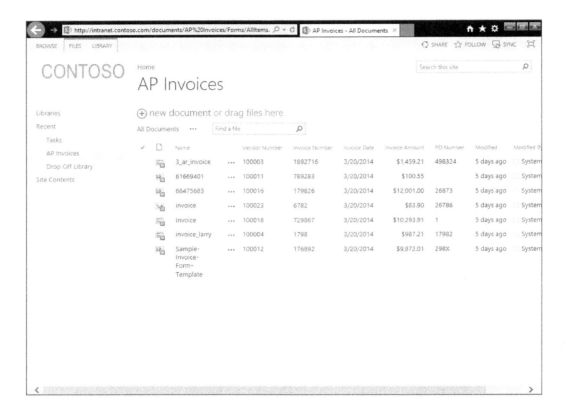

First, start off by finding your document library within SharePoint and note down the URL for the document library.

Add SharePoint Documents Libraries As Menu Links

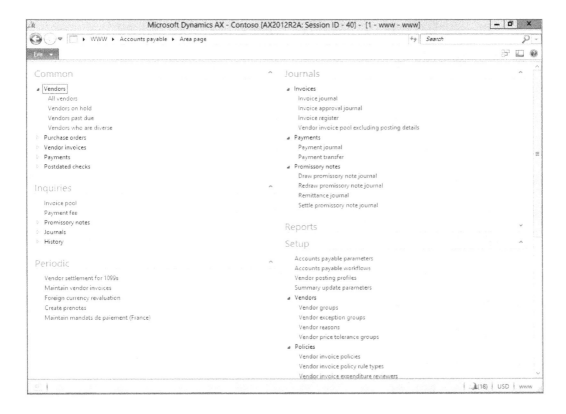

And then find the location where you want to put your link to the Documents...

Add SharePoint Documents Libraries As Menu Links

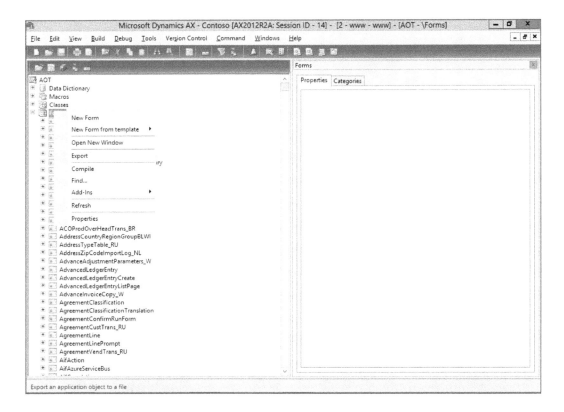

The first step is to create a form that will show the Documents. To do that, open up a new development environment (CTRL+D) right-mouse-click on the Forms group, and select the New Form menu item.

Add SharePoint Documents Libraries As Menu Links

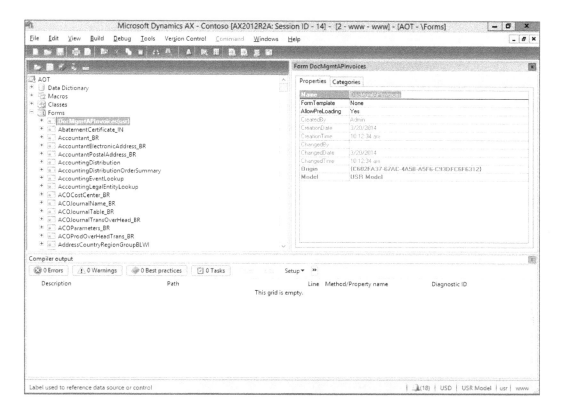

When the new form is created, change the Name in the Properties to something a little more friendly.

Add SharePoint Documents Libraries As Menu Links

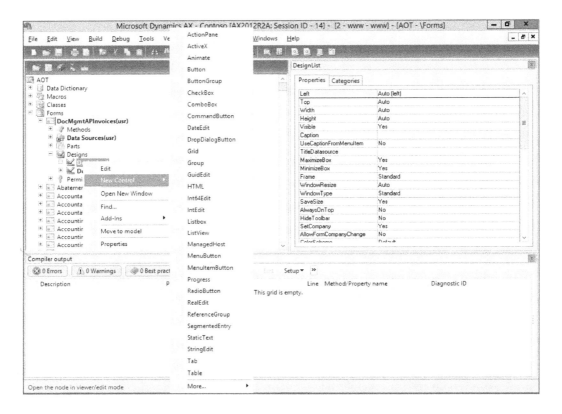

Now we need to add a web browser control to the form. To do that expand out the form details, and expand the Designs group.

Then right mouse click on the Design design click on the New Control submenu, and select the ActiveX menu item.

Add SharePoint Documents Libraries As Menu Links

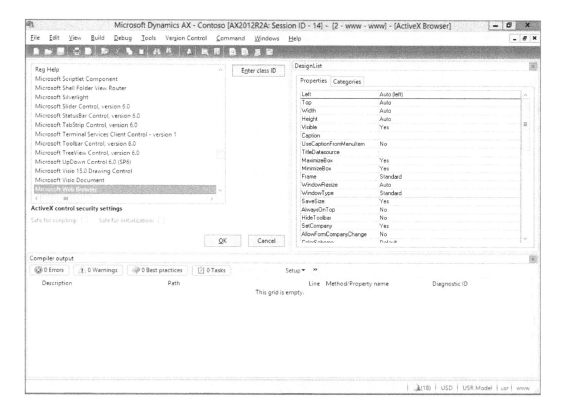

When the ActiveX browser is displayed, scroll down and select the Microsoft Web Browser control and click on the OK button.

Add SharePoint Documents Libraries As Menu Links

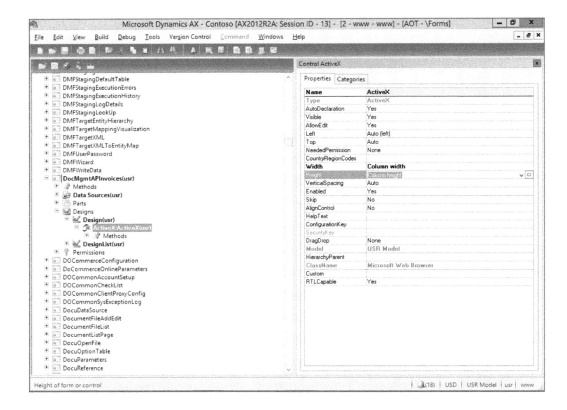

Now you should see that the ActiveX control has been added to the form design.

Change the Width property to Column Width and the Height property to Column Height so that it will expand to take up all of the real-estate in the form.

Add SharePoint Documents Libraries As Menu Links

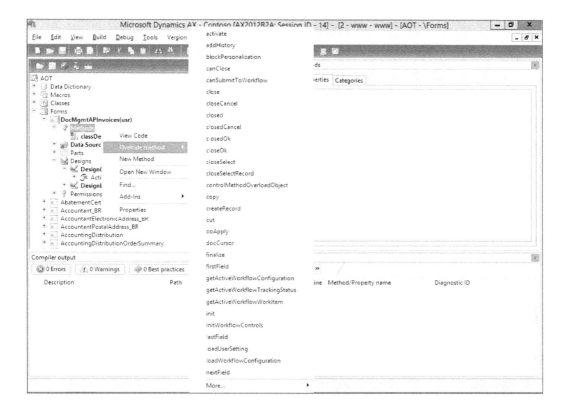

Now we need to make sure that the browser points to our document management library. To do that right-mouse-click on the Methods group, select the Override method menu and click on the Activate method in the sub-menu.

Add SharePoint Documents Libraries As Menu Links

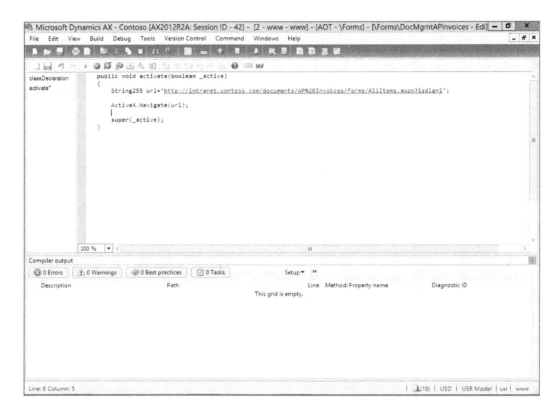

Then add the following lines to the body:

String255 url="http://intranet.contoso.com/documents/AP%20Invoices/Forms/AllItems.aspx?isdlg=1";

ActiveX.Navigate(url);

Notice that the URL is just the URL to the document library.

Add SharePoint Documents Libraries As Menu Links

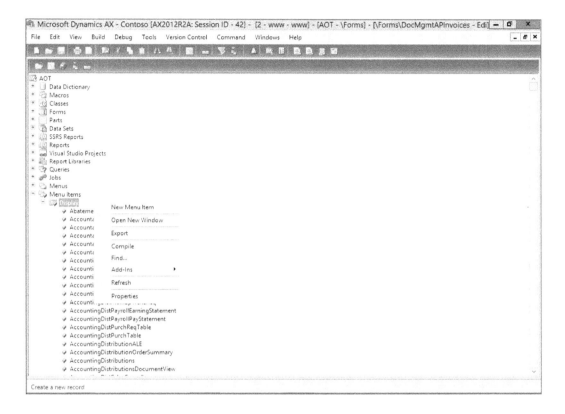

Now we need to add a menu item to open up the form. To do this, expand the Menu Items group, and then right-mouse-click on the Display subfolder and select the New Menu Item menu item.

Add SharePoint Documents Libraries As Menu Links

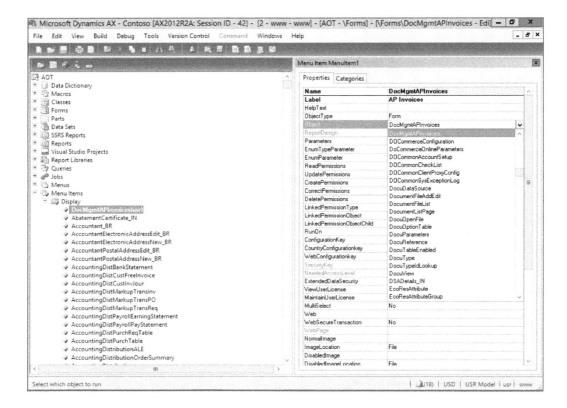

When the new menu item is displayed, give it a more appropriate Name and Label, and then select the new form that you just created from the Object drop down.

Add SharePoint Documents Libraries As Menu Links

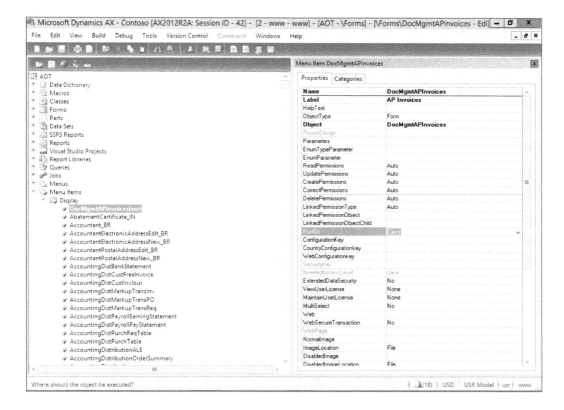

Also, set the RunOn property to Client.

Add SharePoint Documents Libraries As Menu Links

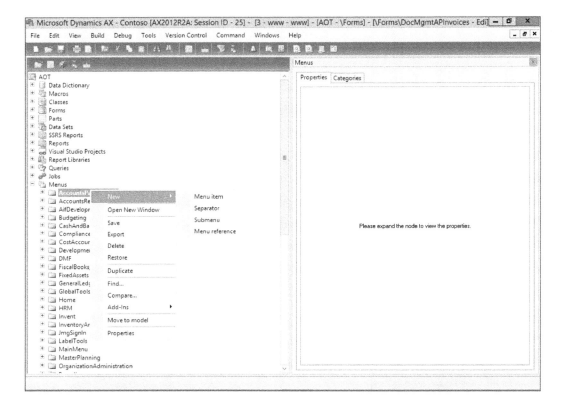

Finally we now need to add the menu item to a menu. To do that, open up the Menus group, and expand the menu that you want to modify (in this case the AccountsPayable).

Right-mouse-click on the menu, and New menu and select the Submenu option.

Add SharePoint Documents Libraries As Menu Links

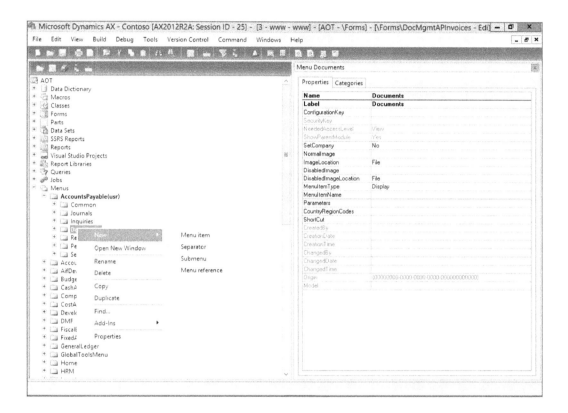

This will create a new submenu group for you that you can call Documents.

Then right-mouse-click on that submenu, and select the New menu, and this time select the Menu Item option.

Add SharePoint Documents Libraries As Menu Links

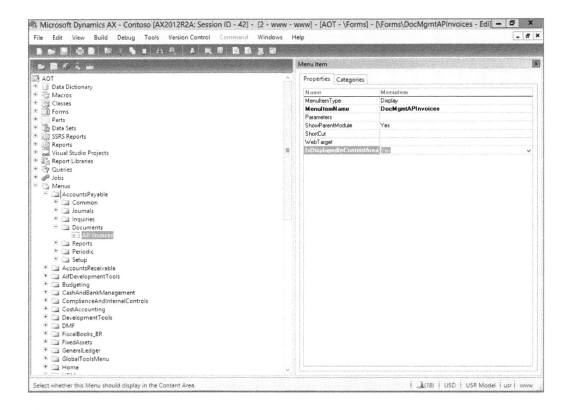

When the menu item is displayed, change the MenuItemName to be the form that you initially created.

Then save your changes and exit from the development environment.

Add SharePoint Documents Libraries As Menu Links

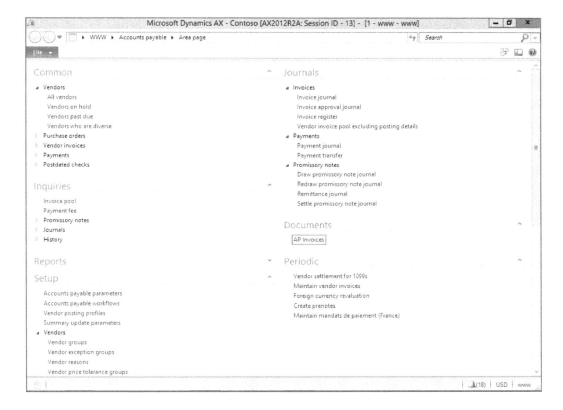

Now when you open up your menu there will be a new link there for your document library...

Add SharePoint Documents Libraries As Menu Links

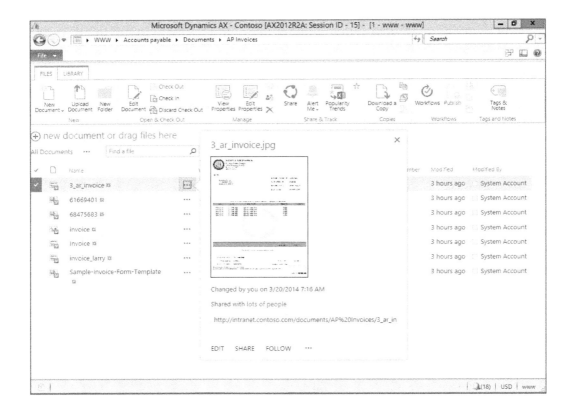

And clicking on it will open up your document library within the Dynamics AX client.

How cool is that.

Copy Data From One Partition To Another Using The Data Import Export

Creating new partitions is a great way to create new instances of Dynamics AX without the overhead of creating new databases, and installing new AOS servers, because it piggybacks on the existing infrastructure you have. But it also means that you need to set up all of the data in the partition because it start's off as a blank system... or do you? Dynamics AX has an inbuilt export and import function that allows you to export out all of the data in one partition and then import it into another.

Duplication has never been so easy.

Copy Data From One Partition To Another Using The Data Import Export

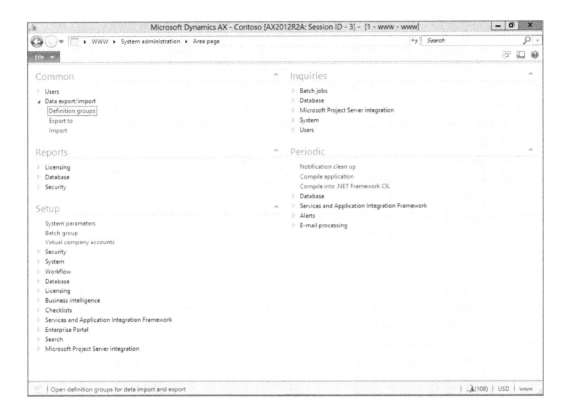

The first step in the process is to create an export from your original database partition. To do this click on the Definition Groups menu item within the Data Export/Import folder of the Common group within the System Administration area page.

Copy Data From One Partition To Another Using The Data Import Export

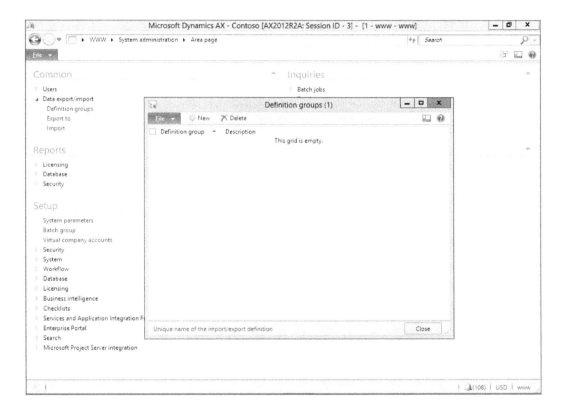

When the Definition Groups maintenance form is displayed, click on the New button within the menu bar to create a new record.

Copy Data From One Partition To Another Using The Data Import Export

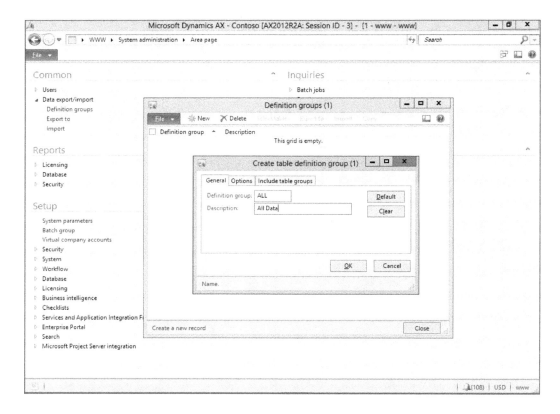

When the **Create Table Definition Group** dialog box is displayed, assign your record a Definition Group code and Description.

Copy Data From One Partition To Another Using The Data Import Export

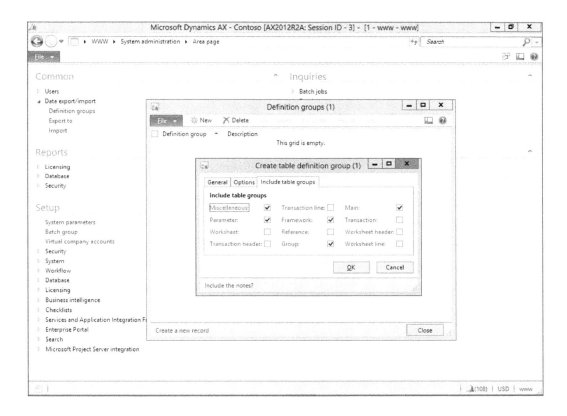

Then switch to the Include Table Groups tab within the dialog box. This will show you all of the different types of data that you want to export. By default all of the codes and controls are marked to be exported, which would allow you to create a export template for a new company partition.

Copy Data From One Partition To Another Using The Data Import Export

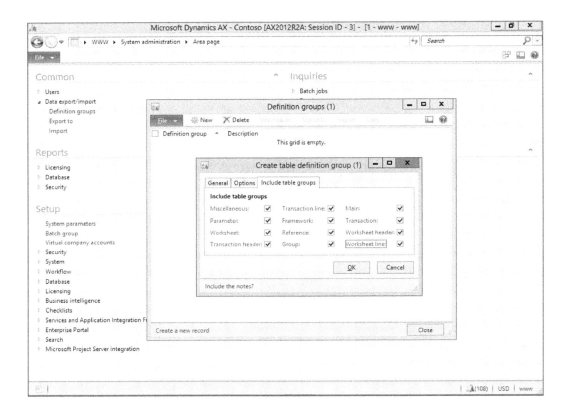

In this case though we will select all of the table groups so that we can export the entire database and all of the transactions.

When you have selected the table groups that you want to export, just click the OK button to finish the setup.

Copy Data From One Partition To Another Using The Data Import Export

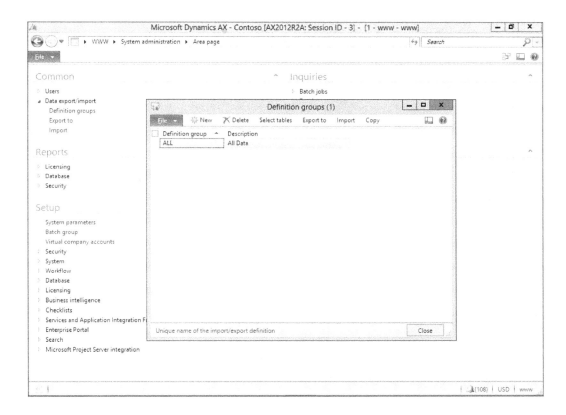

Now we can create an export file. To do this, click on the Export button within the menu bar of the Definition Groups maintenance form.

Copy Data From One Partition To Another Using The Data Import Export

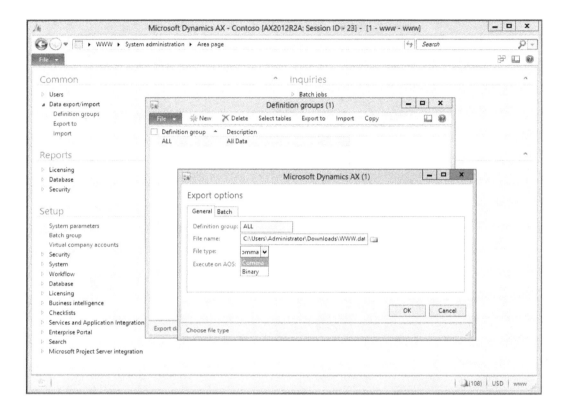

When the Export Options dialog box is displayed, click on the folder icon to the right of the File Name field and define a new file and location for the export.

Also, select the File Type of export that you want to perform. This can either be Comma for simple exports, or Binary for when you have a database that you want to retain carriage returns etc. in the data.

Copy Data From One Partition To Another Using The Data Import Export

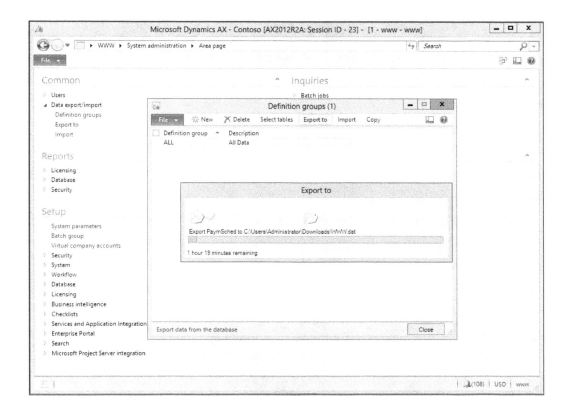

Now just wait for the export to complete.

Copy Data From One Partition To Another Using The Data Import Export

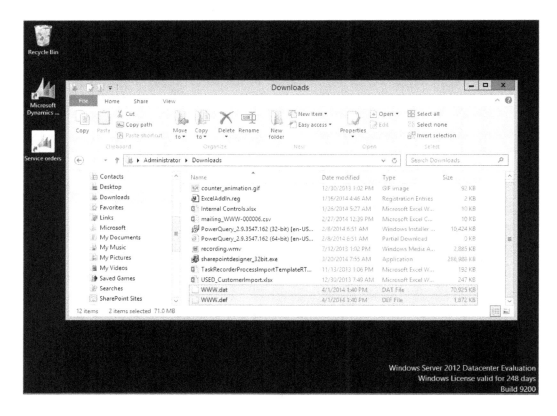

After the export has completed, you should see a .dat, and .def file within you export folder containing all of the information from the company.

Copy Data From One Partition To Another Using The Data Import Export

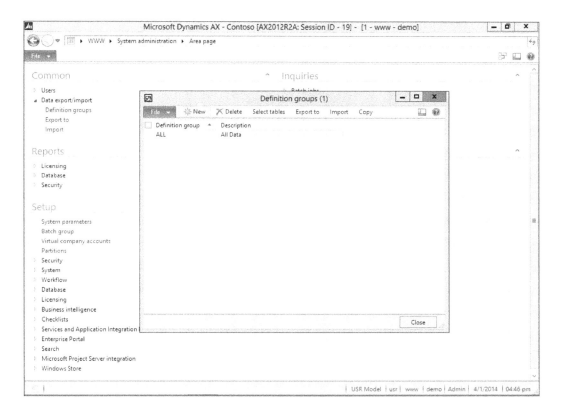

Now we can import all of the data into our empty target partition. To do that open up the target partition, and then create a definition group that matches the one that we used within the source database for the export.

Copy Data From One Partition To Another Using The Data Import Export

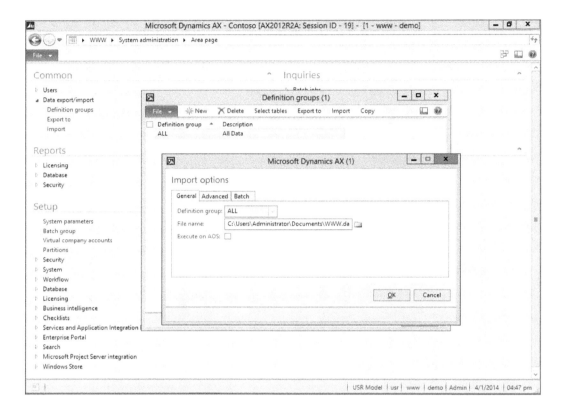

Then click on the Import button within the menu bar of the Definition Groups maintenance form, point the File Name to your file that you created during the export, and click on the OK button.

Copy Data From One Partition To Another Using The Data Import Export

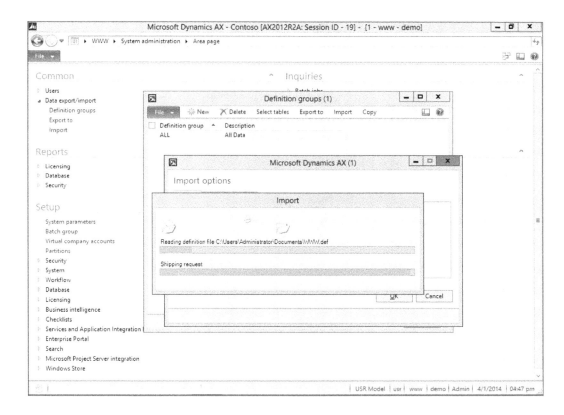

The import will first analyze the data within the export file and check for possible problems.

Copy Data From One Partition To Another Using The Data Import Export

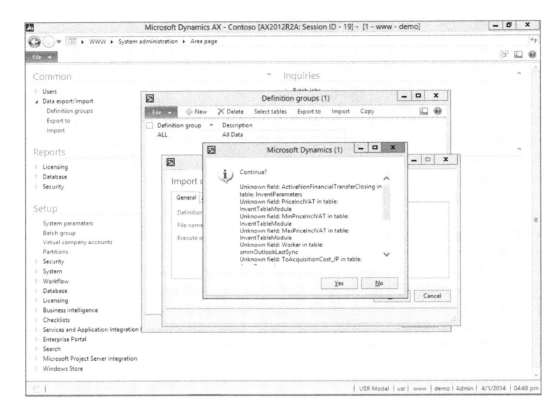

You may get a couple of dialog boxes that indicate that there are fields or parameters that don't exist in the target database, buy just throw caution to the wind, and click on the Yes button.

Copy Data From One Partition To Another Using The Data Import Export

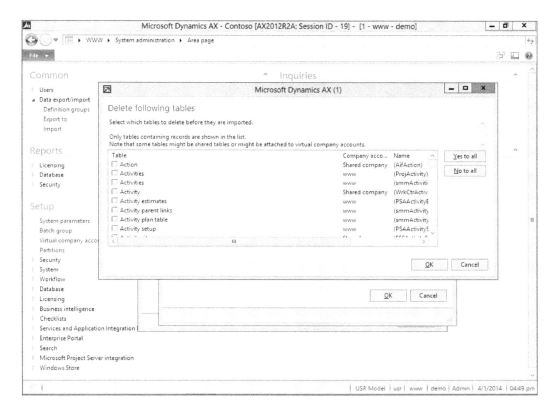

Also the Import will ask you if you want to clean out some of the tables. Don't select any of them, because Dynamics AX will merge the data in the common tables like UOM etc. for you. Continue by clicking on the OK button.

Copy Data From One Partition To Another Using The Data Import Export

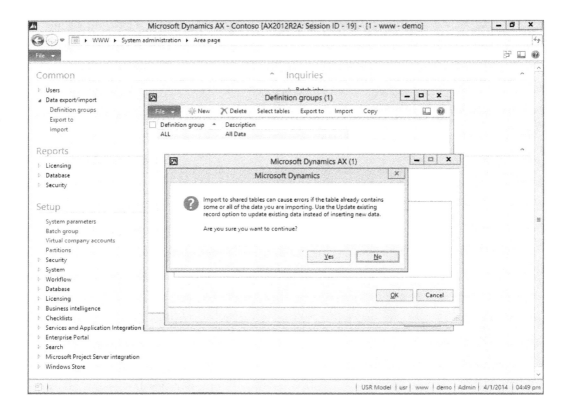

When the merge confirmation box is displayed, click on the Yes button.

Copy Data From One Partition To Another Using The Data Import Export

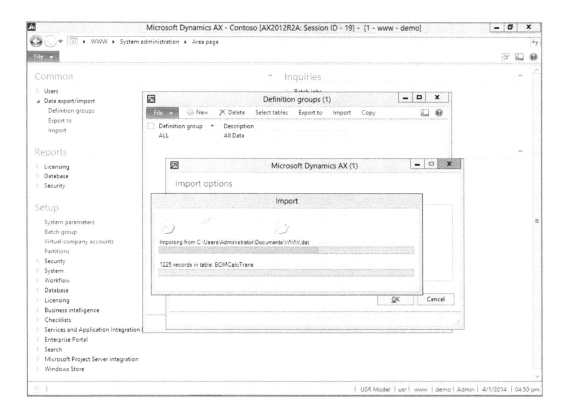

Then just let Dynamics AX do all of the hard work for you.

Copy Data From One Partition To Another Using The Data Import Export

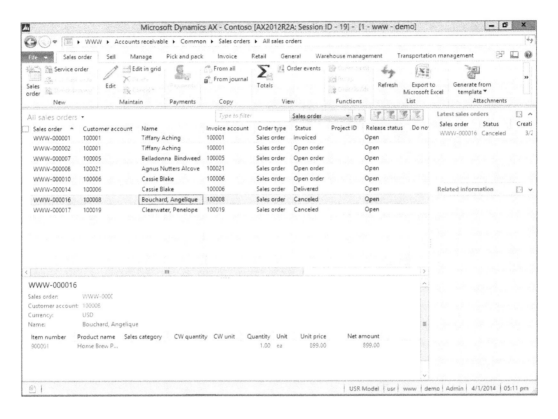

When it finishes you will see all of your data is now set up in your new partition.

That was a way simpler way to load a demo within R3 than I was originally thinking that I would have to do it ☺

Assign User Permissions through Active Directory Groups

Access to all of the roles have to be configured within Dynamics AX, but that does not mean that all of the users have to be managed there as well. If you want, you can link all of the security roles to Active Directory Groups, and then within Active Directory, when you assign the users to the groups, then Dynamics AX will automatically inherit these, even if the user is not explicitly added to the system.

Now you can manage all security access through Active Directory and simplify your security administrators life.

Assign User Permissions through Active Directory Groups

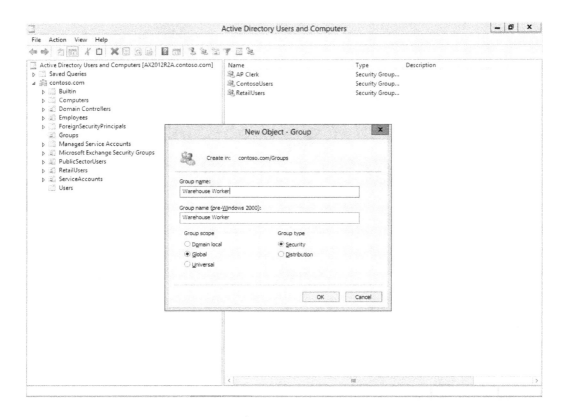

First create a new user group within Active Directory

Assign User Permissions through Active Directory Groups

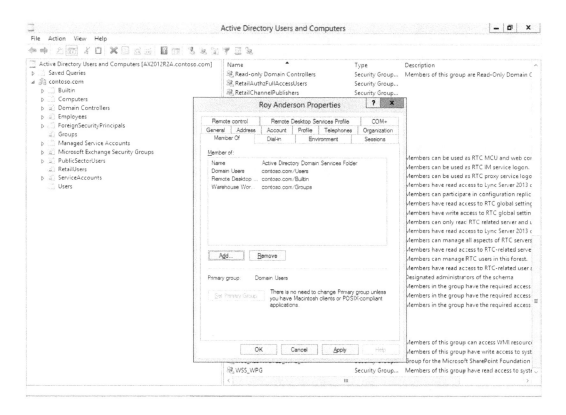

Then assign your user to the Active Directory Group.

Assign User Permissions through Active Directory Groups

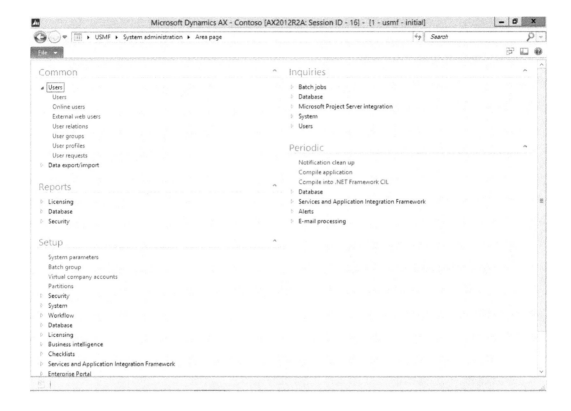

To add the Active Directory Group to the Dynamics AX users, click on the Users menu item within the Users folder of the Common group within the System Administration area page.

Assign User Permissions through Active Directory Groups

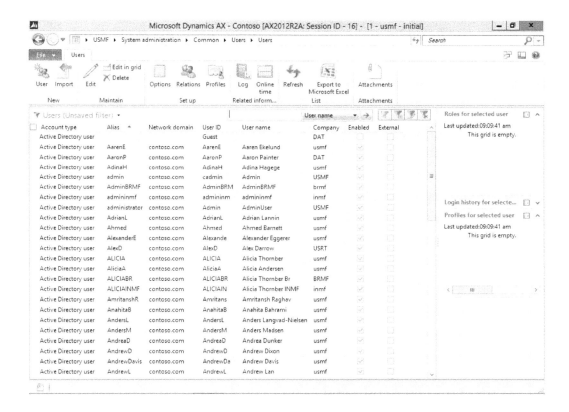

When the Users maintenance form is displayed, click on the User menu button within the New group of the Users ribbon bar.

Assign User Permissions through Active Directory Groups

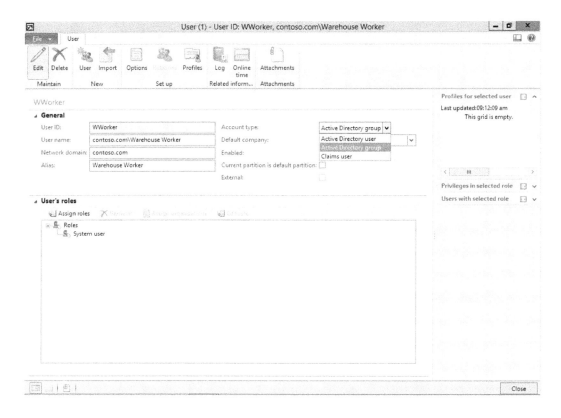

Give your new User record a User ID, set the User Name, Network Domain, and Alias to match the security group that you created within Active Directory and then change the Account Type to be Active Directory User.

Assign User Permissions through Active Directory Groups

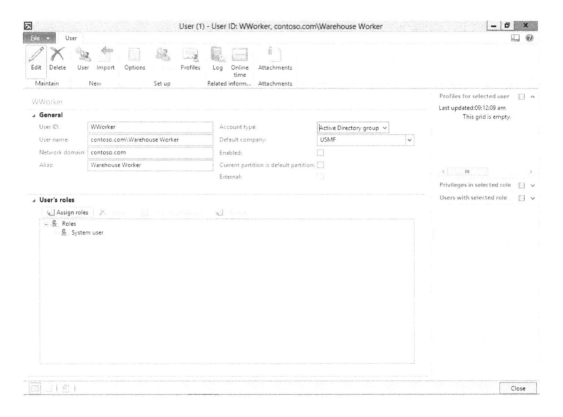

Then click the Assign Roles menu button within the User Roles tab to link your security roles with the group.

Assign User Permissions through Active Directory Groups

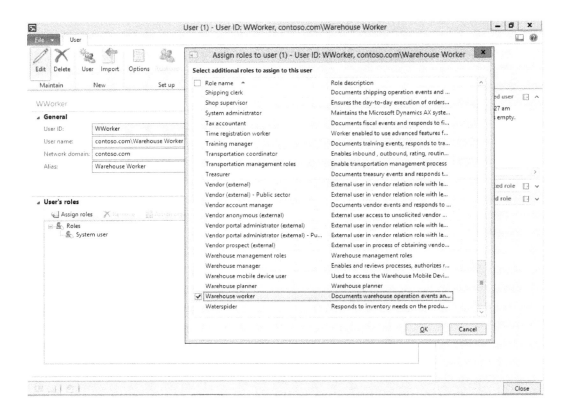

When the Assign Roles To User dialog box is displayed, select the user roles that you want associated with the group and then click on the OK button to assign them to the user group.

Assign User Permissions through Active Directory Groups

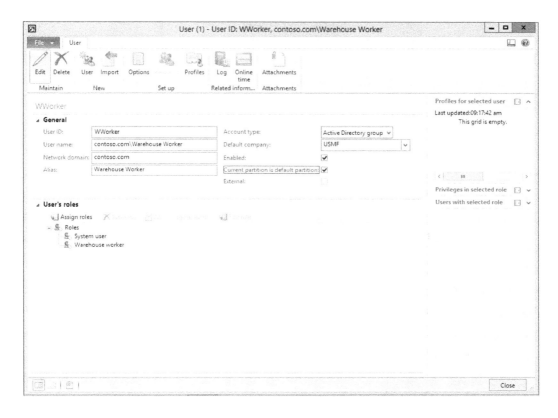

Finally, check the Enabled checkbox on the user group and then click on the Close button to exit the form.

Assign User Permissions through Active Directory Groups

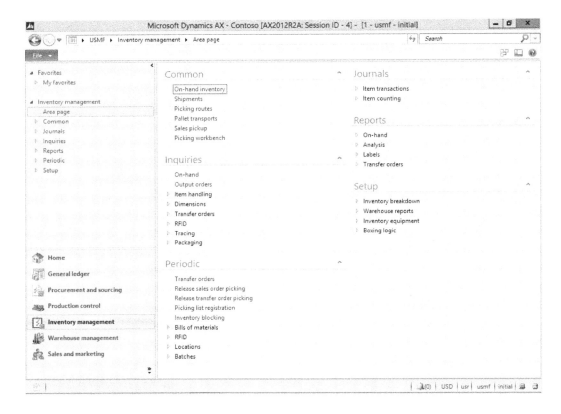

Now if you log into Dynamics AX using the user that you assigned to the user group within Active Directory they will inherit the security roles of the group, even though they have not been explicitly set up within Dynamics AX as a user.

How easy is that!

Restrict User Access To Certain Companies Through Roles

The multi-company capability within Dynamics AX is one of the major selling points of the application, because you can easily switch between organizations with just a click of a button. But that does not mean that you want everyone to have free reign to perform transactions in any company, or even to see some of the other company data. If you want to simplify the users choices just to one or more select companies then that's not a problem though, you can do that easily through the user administration.

It's like putting your users on house arrest.

Restrict User Access To Certain Companies Through Roles

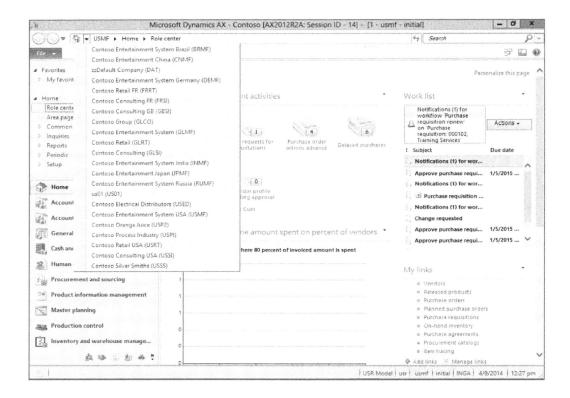

Start off by finding the user that you want to restrict access to just a select number of companies.

Restrict User Access To Certain Companies Through Roles

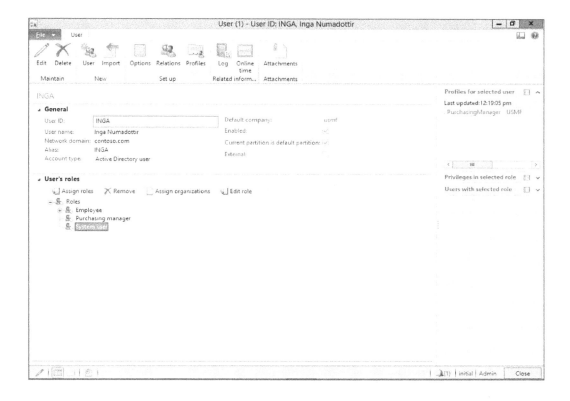

Now open up the user profile, and click on the Assign Organizations menu button within the User's Roles tab.

Restrict User Access To Certain Companies Through Roles

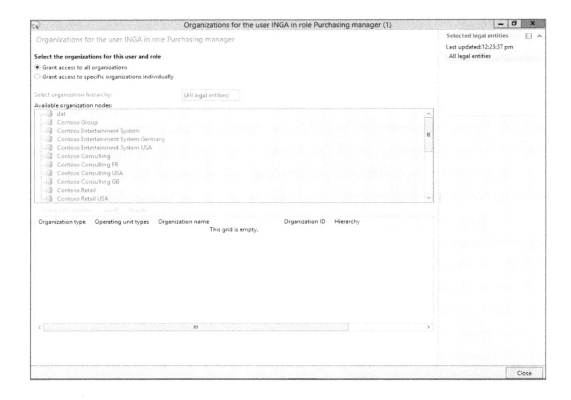

When the Organizations for the User * maintenance form is displayed, you will see that the user has full access to all of the companies within the system.

To restrict access, click on the Grant Access o Specific Organizations Individually radio button.

Restrict User Access To Certain Companies Through Roles

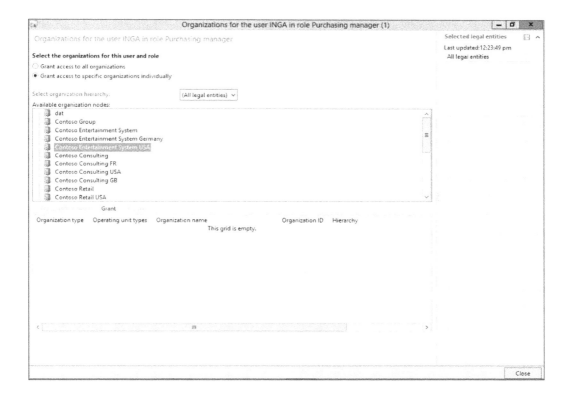

This will allow you to select from the Available Organization Nodes. Select Organization that you want to grant the user access to, and then click on the Grant button.

Restrict User Access To Certain Companies Through Roles

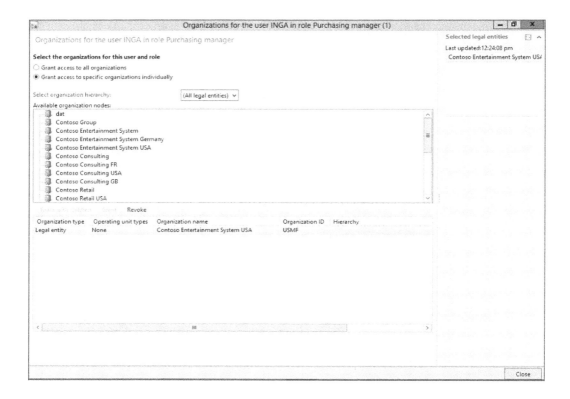

You can repeat this process for any additional Organizations that you want them to have access to and then click on the Close button to exit the form.

Restrict User Access To Certain Companies Through Roles

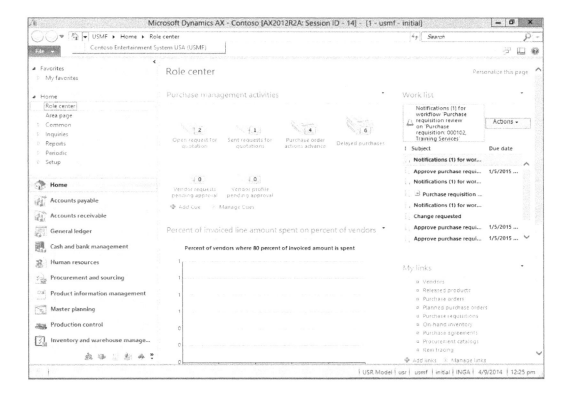

The next time the user logs in, they will only see the organization that you have granted them access to.

Import Data Using The Data Import Export Framework

Although Excel is a great way to import base data into Dynamics AX, sometime you need to bring in the big guns and that's where the Data Import Export Framework applies. This is a new module that makes importing data into Dynamics AX so much simpler, especially when importing complex data types that include multiple dependent tables. All you need to do is check the data that you want to import and the D.I.E.F. will do the rest for you.

On a side note, "dief" in Dutch actually means "thief". Is this a coincidence, or is it a reminder that the D.I.E.F. stealing data seem so simple?

Import Data Using The Data Import Export Framework

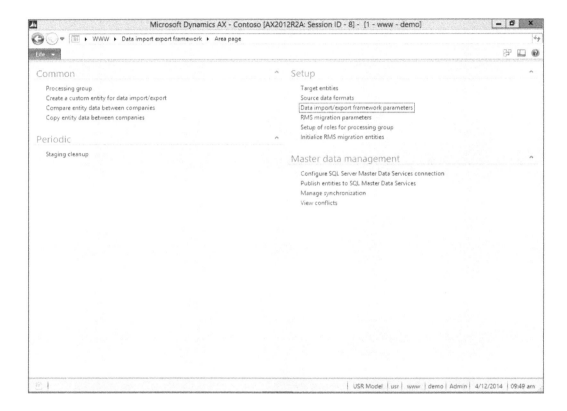

First we need to make sure that the Data Import Export Framework is configured. To do this, click on the Data Import/Export Framework Parameters menu item within the Setup group of the Data Import Export Framework area page.

Import Data Using The Data Import Export Framework

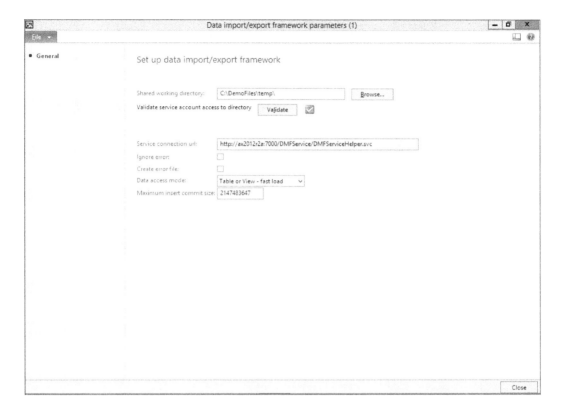

When the Data Import/Export Framework Parameters maintenance form is displayed, make sure that you have a Shared Working Directory has been defined. If you don't have one yet, just specify a working directory, and then click on the Validate button to make sure that you have the correct access to the folder.

Then click on the Close button to exit from the form.

Import Data Using The Data Import Export Framework

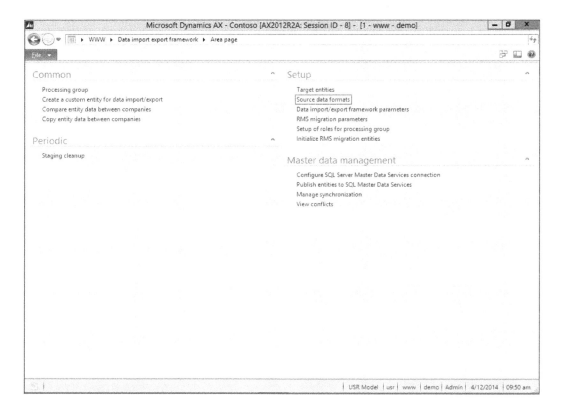

Next we need to make sure that we have a data format defined that we will be using for our import files. To do that, click on the Source Data Format menu item within the Setup group of the Data Import Export Framework area page.

Import Data Using The Data Import Export Framework

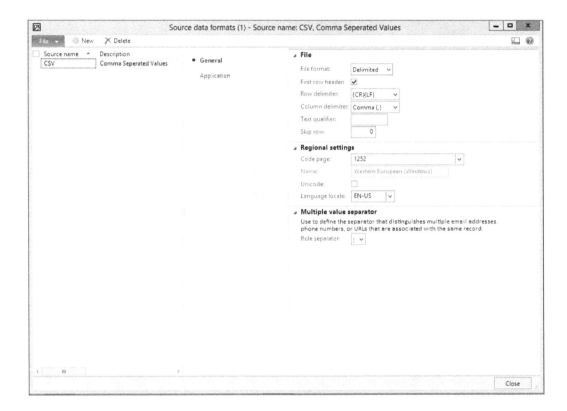

When the Source Data Formats maintenance form is displayed, make sure that you have some import formats defined. In this case we have a CSV format defined.

If you have not got any formats defined ye, just click on the New button in the menu bar to create a new record and specify your import preferences.

After you have configured your import format then just click on the Close button to exit from the form.

Import Data Using The Data Import Export Framework

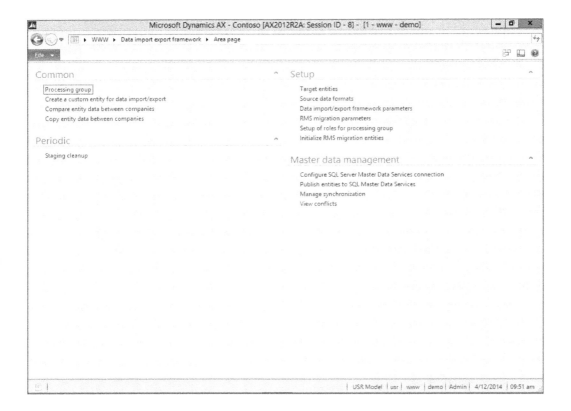

Now we can start importing data. To do that, just click on the Processing Group menu item within the Common group of the Data Import Export Framework area page.

Import Data Using The Data Import Export Framework

When the Processing Group maintenance form is displayed, click the New button in the menu bar to create a new record, and then assign your record a Group Name and Description.

Once you have created your new Processing Group, click on the Entities button within the menu bar to start adding your import entities to your Processing Group.

Import Data Using The Data Import Export Framework

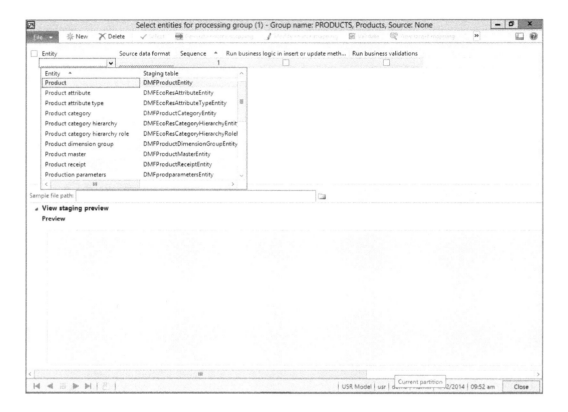

When the Select Entities For Processing Group maintenance form is displayed, click on the New button in the menu bar to create a new record, and then from the Entity dropdown, select he type of data you want to import – in this case we will import products.

Import Data Using The Data Import Export Framework

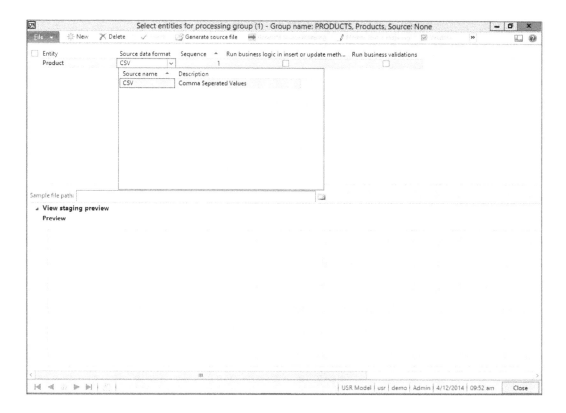

Then select the Source Data Format that you want to use for the import.

Import Data Using The Data Import Export Framework

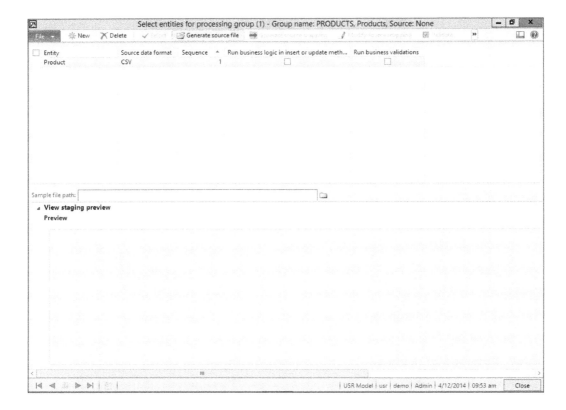

Next we need to specify the data that we want to import. To do this click on the Generate Source File button within the menu bar.

Import Data Using The Data Import Export Framework

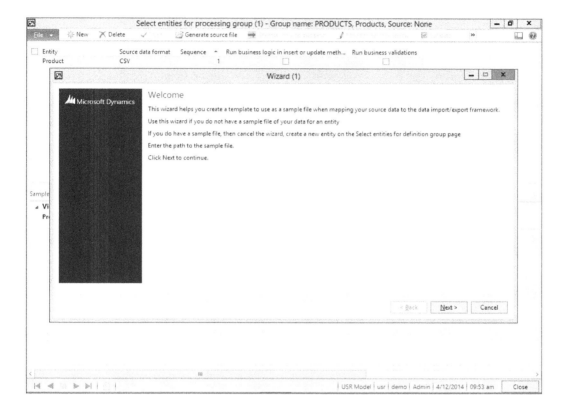

This will start up a wizard to guide you through the process. Click on the Next button to start the process.

Import Data Using The Data Import Export Framework

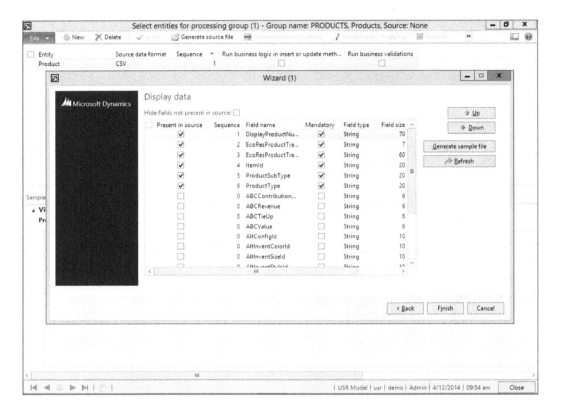

When the Display Data page of the wizard is displayed, you can select any of the fields that have been mapped to your Entity, and also rearrange the order to your liking.

Once you have chosen all of the fields that you want, click on the Generate Sample File button.

Import Data Using The Data Import Export Framework

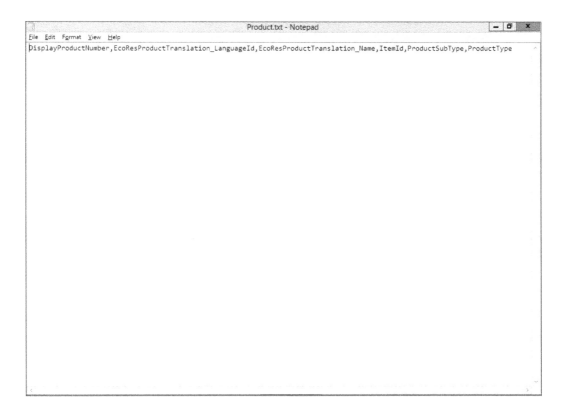

This will create a new blank template for you based on the Source Data Format that you chose.

Import Data Using The Data Import Export Framework

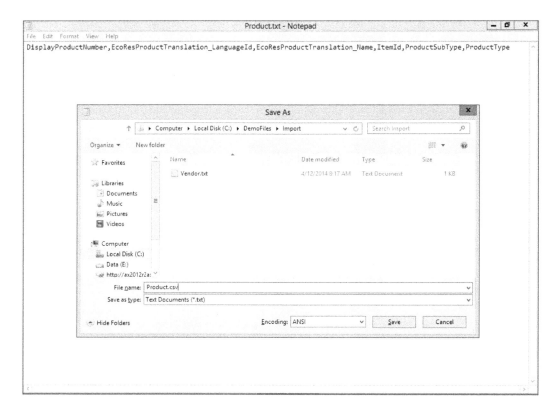

Save the file away to a working folder, we will need this in a second.

Import Data Using The Data Import Export Framework

When you return to the Select Entities For Processing Group maintenance form, point the Sample File Path to point to the sample file that you just created.

Import Data Using The Data Import Export Framework

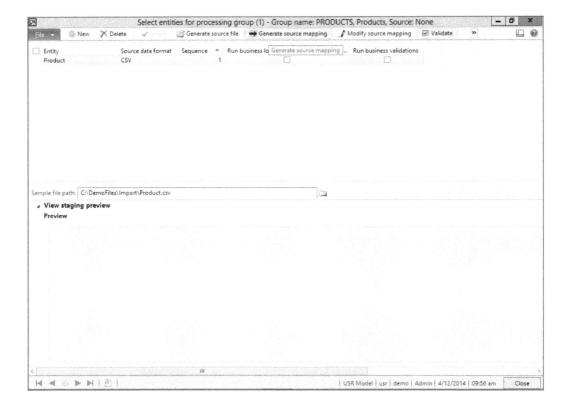

Now we need to link all of the fields that we chose to import to all of the actual entities. To do that, click on the Generate Source Mapping button within the menu bar.

Import Data Using The Data Import Export Framework

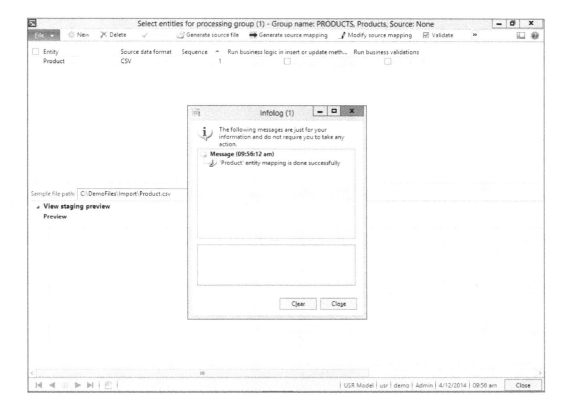

This should result in a pretty uneventful message saying that the mapping was successful.

Import Data Using The Data Import Export Framework

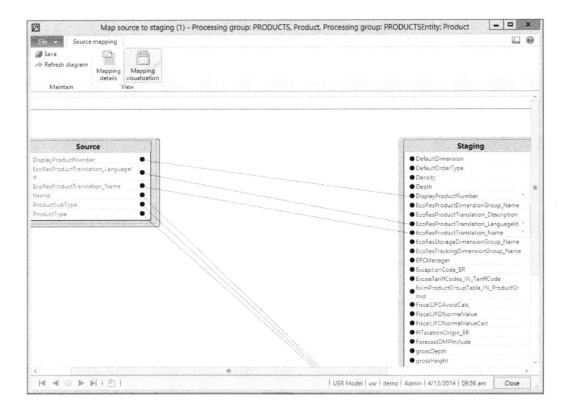

If you click on the Modify Source Mapping button in the menu bar, then you will see what Dynamics AX has really done – link all of the source fields to the import staging table.

Import Data Using The Data Import Export Framework

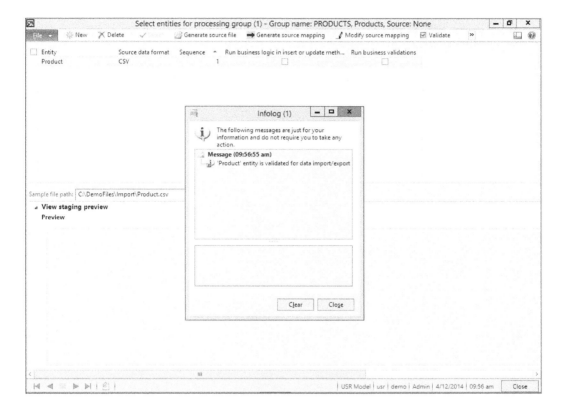

If you want to make doubly sure that everything is working, then click on the Validate button within the menu bar and you should have no errors.

Import Data Using The Data Import Export Framework

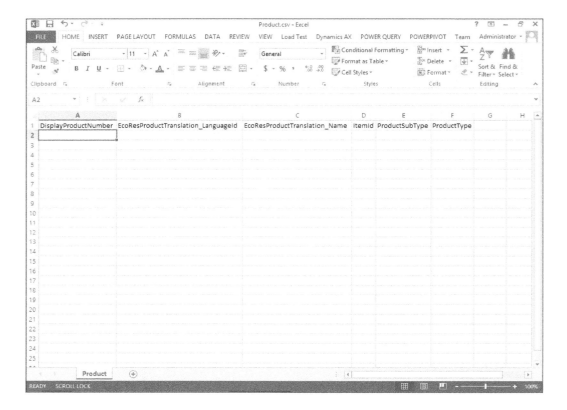

Now open up the sample import file that you created.

Import Data Using The Data Import Export Framework

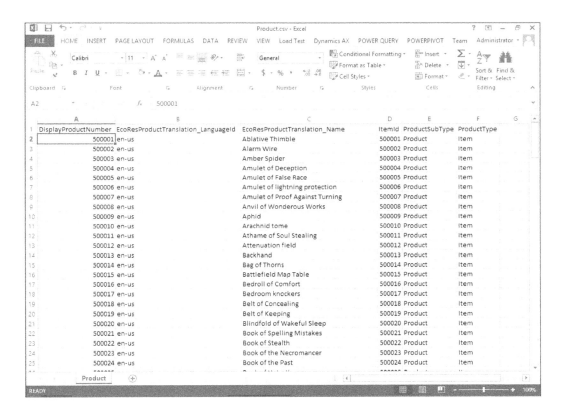

All you need to do is paste in all of your data and save the file.

Import Data Using The Data Import Export Framework

Now you can preview the data that you put in the import file by clicking on the Preview Source File menu button within the Select Entities For Processing Group maintenance form.

Import Data Using The Data Import Export Framework

In the Preview area you will be able to see all of the data.

Click on the Close button to save your entities.

Import Data Using The Data Import Export Framework

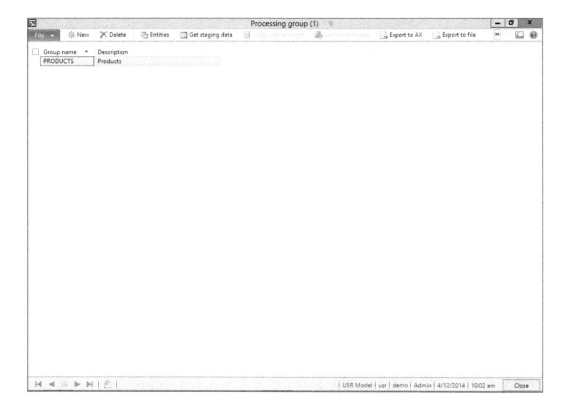

When you return to the Processing Group maintenance form, click on the Get Staging Data menu item to start the import process.

Import Data Using The Data Import Export Framework

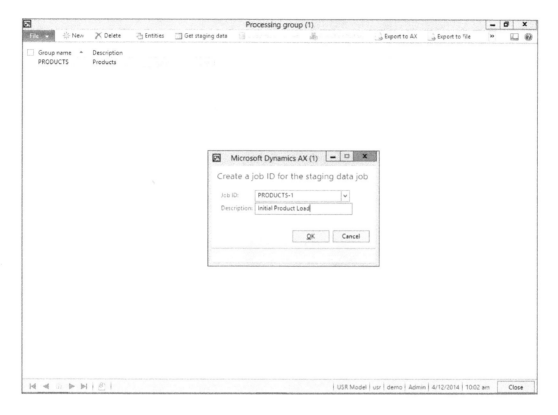

When the Create Job dialog box is displayed, give your import process a description and then click on the OK button.

Import Data Using The Data Import Export Framework

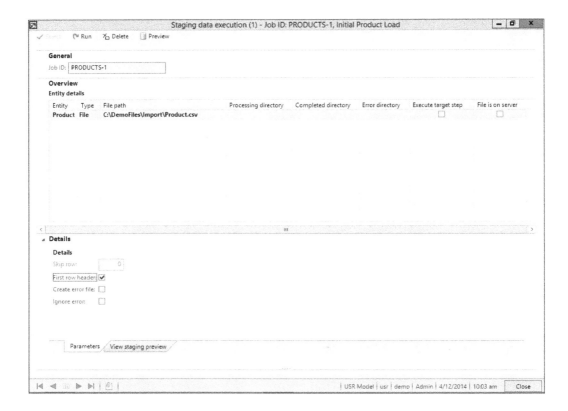

When the Staging Data Extraction dialog box is displayed, you can test your data by clicking on the Preview button within the menu bar.

Import Data Using The Data Import Export Framework

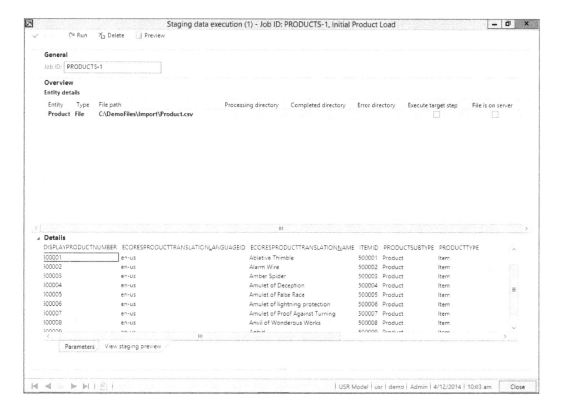

After a second or two, you will be able to look at the View Staging Preview detail tab on the form and see all of the data has been staged for you.

Import Data Using The Data Import Export Framework

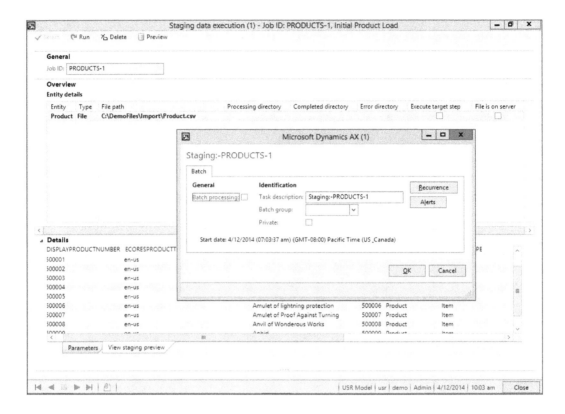

To start the real import, click on the Run button within the menu bar. When the Staging dialog box is displayed, just click on the OK button.

Import Data Using The Data Import Export Framework

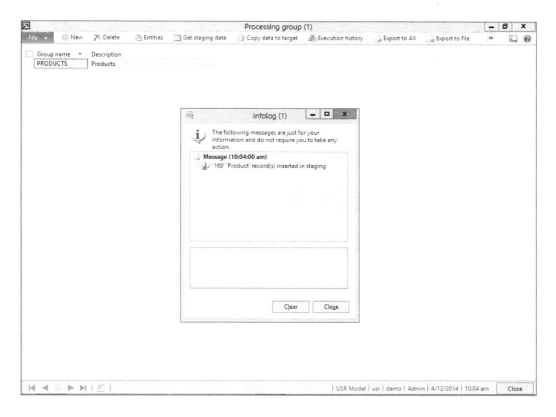

You should get a notification of the number of records that have been staged.

Import Data Using The Data Import Export Framework

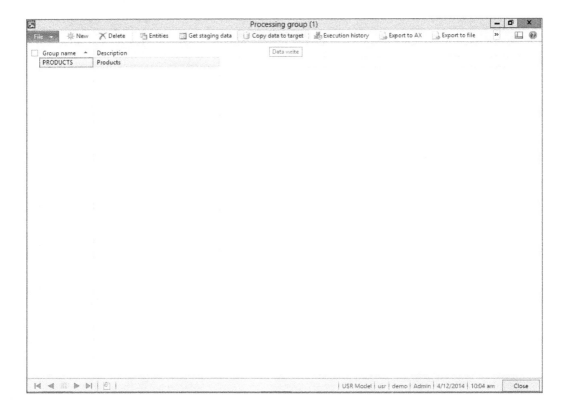

To update the real tables within Dynamics AX, just click on the Copy Data To Target button within the menu bar.

Import Data Using The Data Import Export Framework

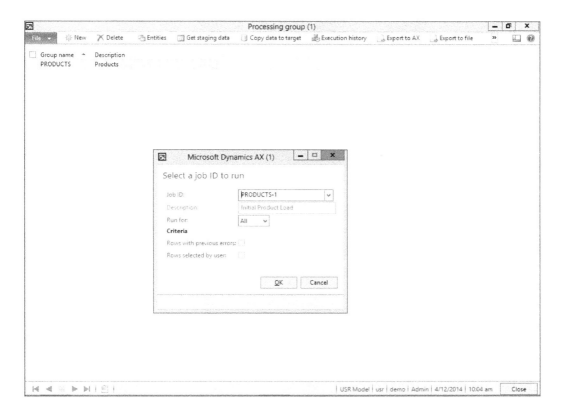

When the Select a Job To Run dialog box is displayed, select the job that you just created, and then click on the OK button.

Import Data Using The Data Import Export Framework

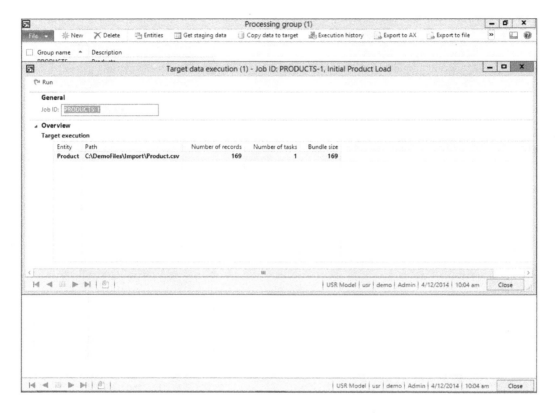

This will open up a Target Data Extraction dialog box. Just click on the Run button within the menu bar.

Import Data Using The Data Import Export Framework

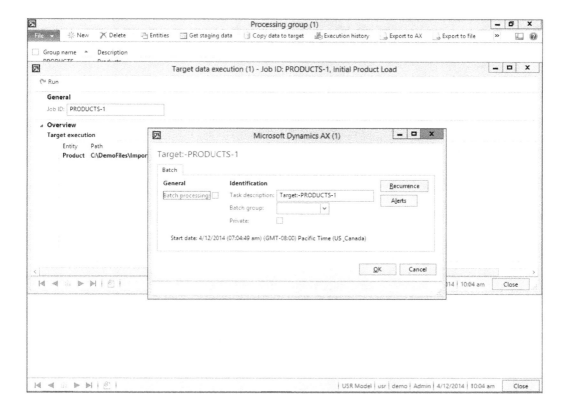

Then click on the OK button to start the import.

Import Data Using The Data Import Export Framework

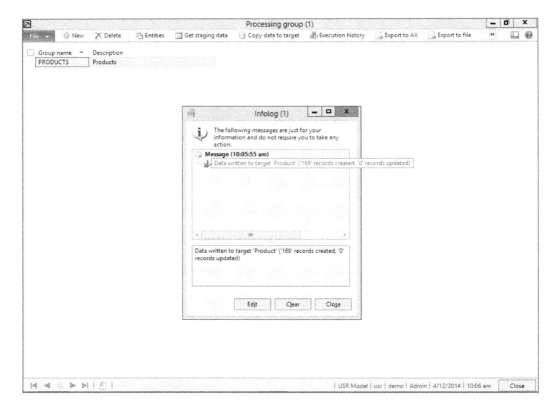

The Data Import Export Framework will do all of the hard work for you.

Import Data Using The Data Import Export Framework

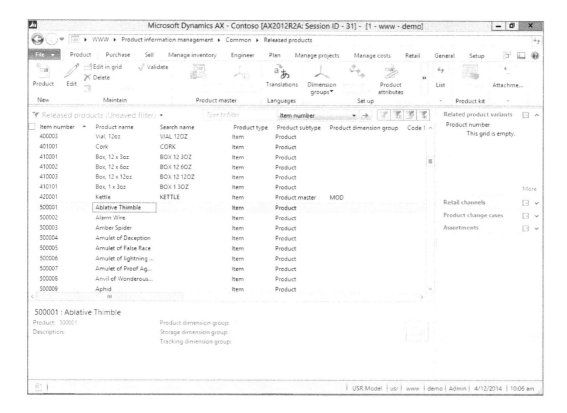

Now when you look at your table within Dynamics AX all of your new data will be ready for you to use.

How cool is that.

Restrict Field Access By Security Role

The roles within Dynamics AX are pre-configured to restrict users from accessing areas that they usually don't need to use, but you don't have to stop there. You can tweak the security even more by restricting access to the field level data that shows up on the forms through the security role maintenance feature, allowing you to give people read only access, or not even show the field in the case of sensitive information. As an added benefit, if you restrict access this way, then the users will not be able to access the data through the reports, or through the Excel add-in.

If your users are already paranoid that they don't see all of the data, then redacting access this way may push them over the edge.

Restrict Field Access By Security Role

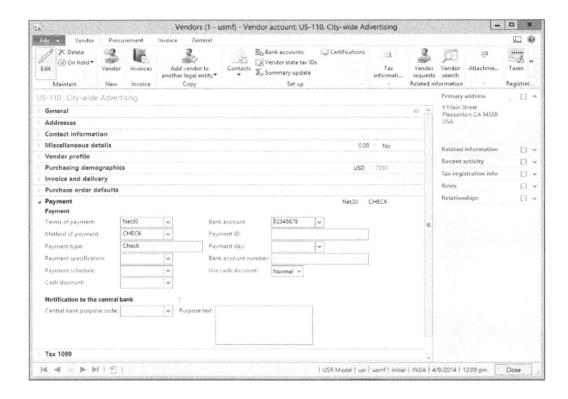

Start off by finding the field that you want to restrict access to. In this case we want to stop particular users from maintaining the Vendors Bank Account.

Restrict Field Access By Security Role

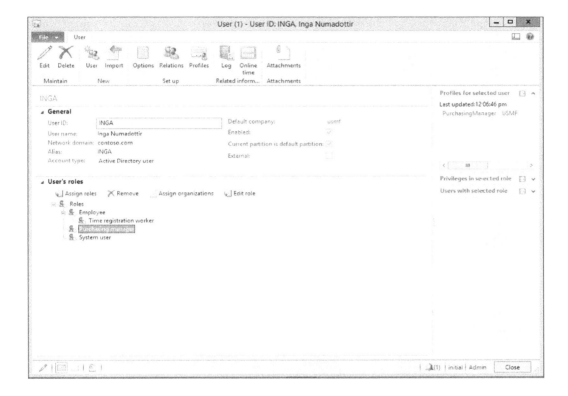

Then find the Role that you want to restrict access through – in this example we are cheating a little and finding the Role through the user account, an then clicking on the Edit Role button within the User Roles tab.

Restrict Field Access By Security Role

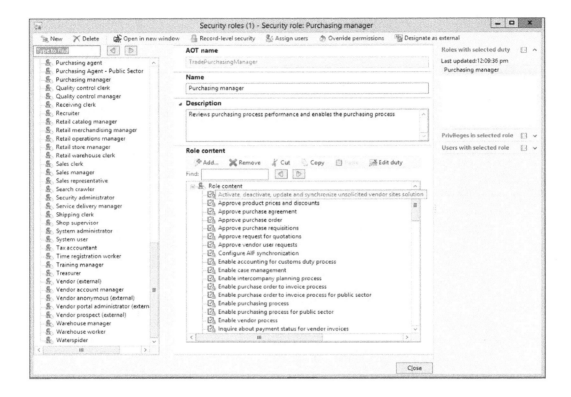

When the Security Roles maintenance form is displayed, click on the Override Permissions button within the menu bar.

Restrict Field Access By Security Role

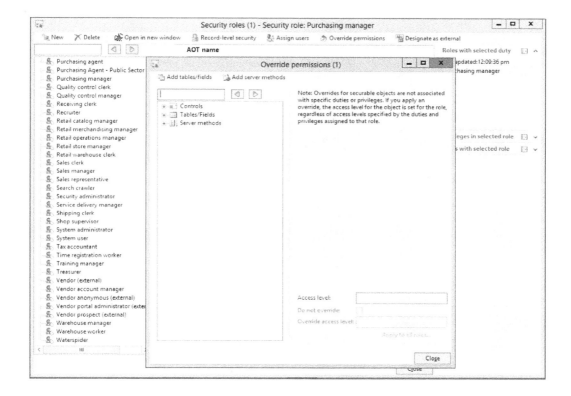

This will open up the Override Permissions form. To override the permissions on a table, click on the Table/Fields node.

Restrict Field Access By Security Role

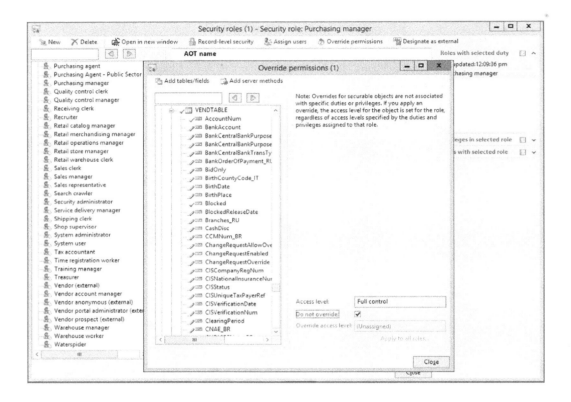

This will allow you to browse all of the tables within Dynamics AX. Select the table that you want to restrict access to (in this case the VendTable) and expand it so that you can see all of the fields.

To override the permissions by field, select the parent table and then uncheck the Do Not Override checkbox.

Restrict Field Access By Security Role

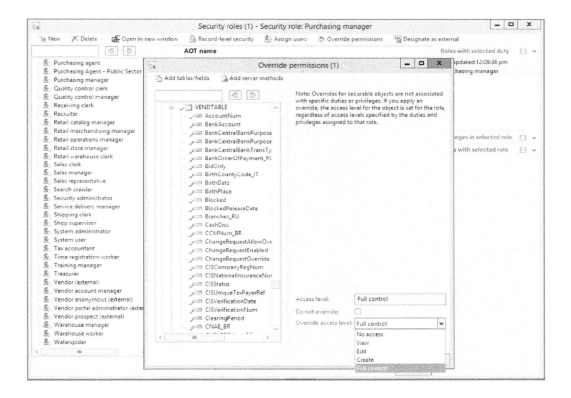

This will allow you to override the general access to the table if you like. In this example though we will leave it with the Full control access level because we want to override the access to an individual field.

Restrict Field Access By Security Role

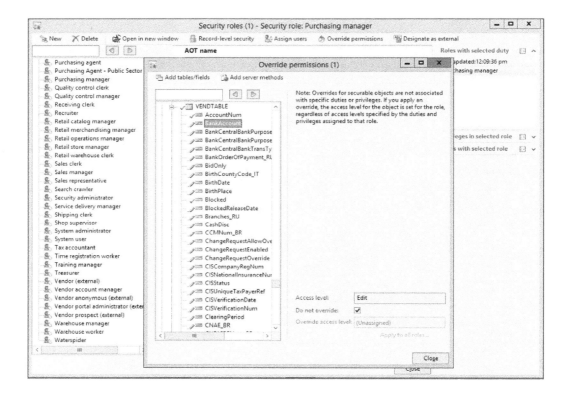

Now select the field that you want to restrict access to, and uncheck the Do Not Override checkbox.

Restrict Field Access By Security Role

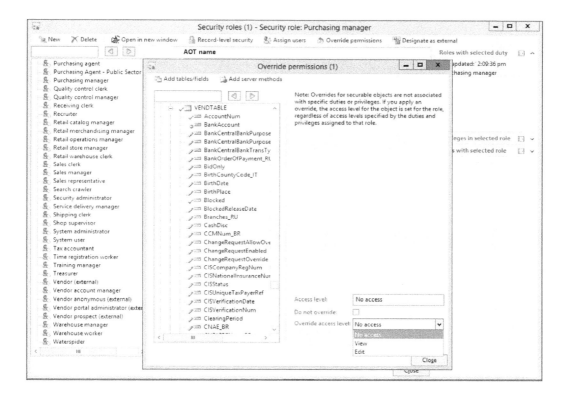

Now you can change the access rights to that field by selecting the option from the Override Access Level dropdown box. You can set it to No Access, View, or Edit.

Restrict Field Access By Security Role

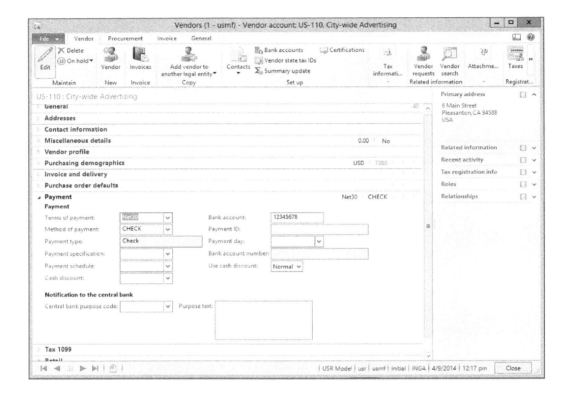

Now when the user returns to the form, they are not able to change the field if they belong to that security role.

Access Denied.

Copy Data Between Companies Quickly Using The Data Import Export Framework

The Data Import Export Framework module is not just for getting data in and out of Dynamics AX through import and export files, it also has a nifty feature that allows you to copy data within your companies, so if you are configuring a new legal entity for testing or production purposes, and want to populate it with information from another existing company, you can replicate the data in a matter of minutes.

It's like having your own personal Sketch-A-Graph, but not as much fun...

Copy Data Between Companies Quickly Using The Data Import Export Framework

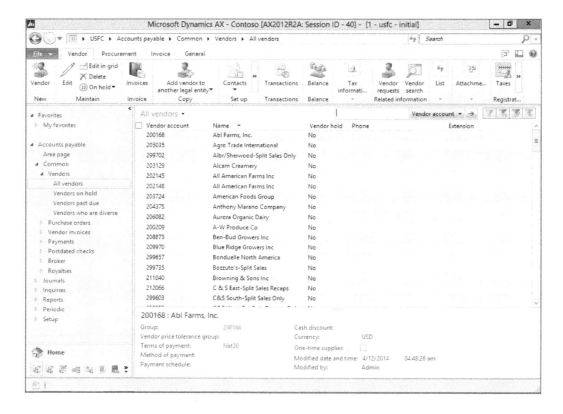

Just to set the stage for this example, we have one company that has a number of vendors loaded into one company.

Copy Data Between Companies Quickly Using The Data Import Export Framework

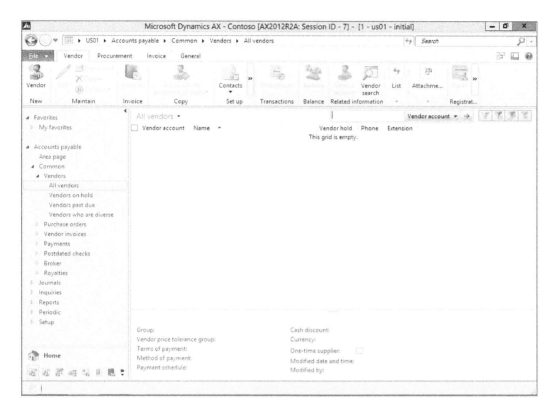

And in another company the cupboards are bare…

Copy Data Between Companies Quickly Using The Data Import Export Framework

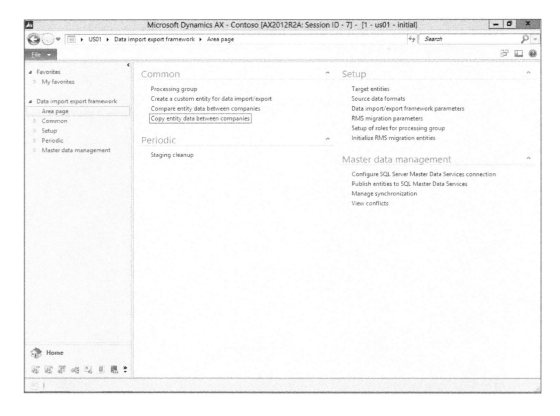

To copy the data between the companies, click on the Copy Entity Data Between Companies menu item within the Common group of the Data Import Export Framework area page.

Copy Data Between Companies Quickly Using The Data Import Export Framework

When the Copy Processing Group list page is displayed, click on the New button in the menu bar to create a new transfer.

Copy Data Between Companies Quickly Using The Data Import Export Framework

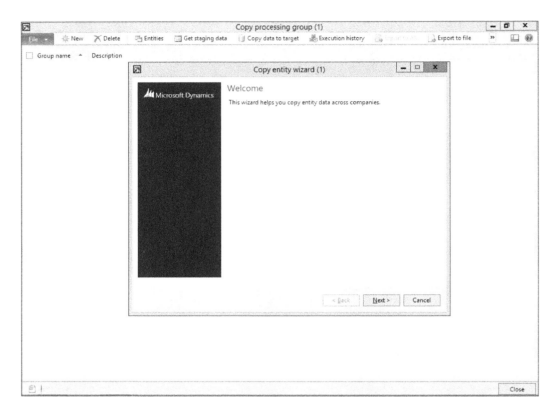

This will start off a Copy Entity Wizard. Click the Next button to start the process.

Copy Data Between Companies Quickly Using The Data Import Export Framework

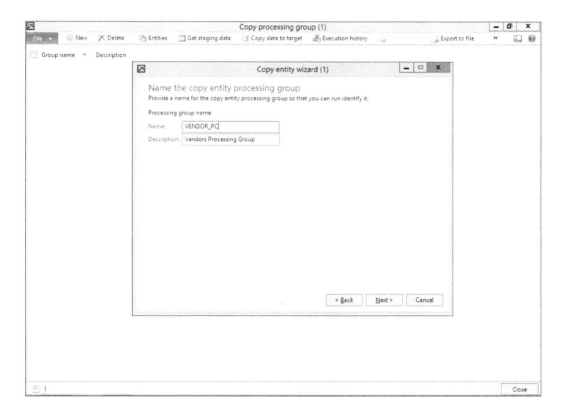

When the Name The Copy Entity Processing Group page is displayed, give your record a Name and Description and then click on the Next button.

Copy Data Between Companies Quickly Using The Data Import Export Framework

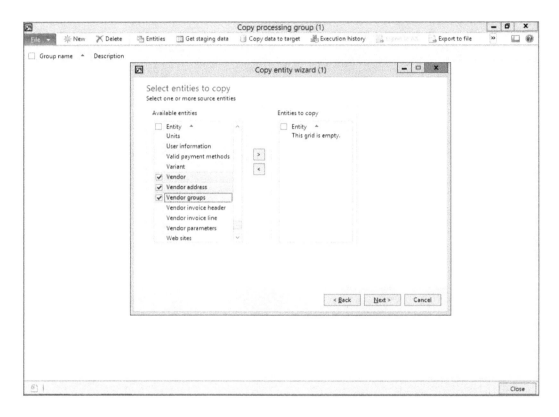

On the Select Entities To Copy page, select the Entities that you want to copy over from the Available Entities list box and then click on the > button to move them to the Entities To Copy side of the form.

In this case we are just selecting the Vendors, but if you wanted to populate an entirely new company with data from the existing one, then you could select everything if you liked.

Copy Data Between Companies Quickly Using The Data Import Export Framework

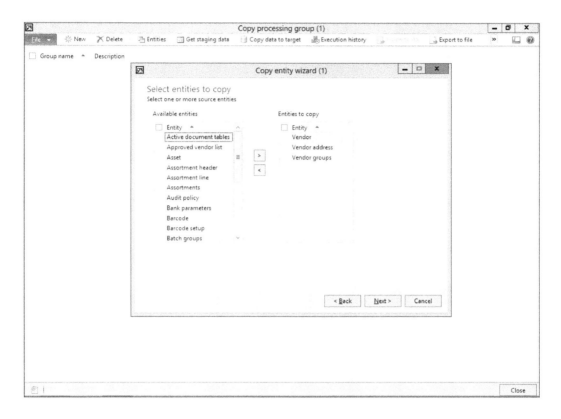

When you have selected the Entities To Copy, click on the Next button to continue on.

Copy Data Between Companies Quickly Using The Data Import Export Framework

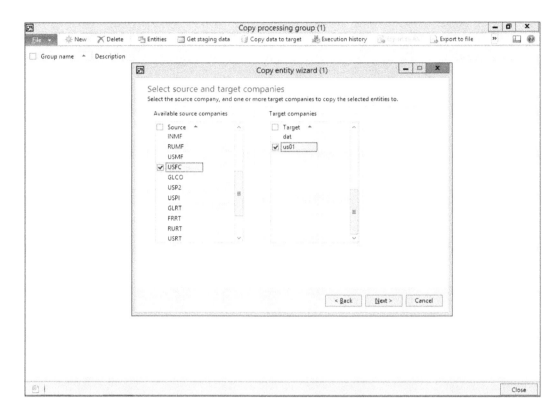

On the Set Source And Destination Companies page, select the company that you want to copy from on the left hand side with the Available Source Companies, and also select the Target Companies on the right hand side where you wont to copy the data to.

Then click on the Next button.

Copy Data Between Companies Quickly Using The Data Import Export Framework

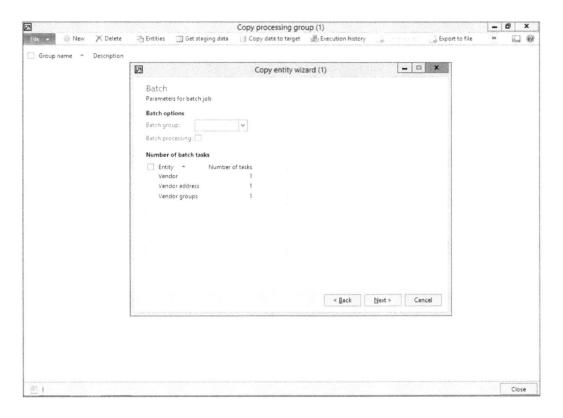

If this is going to be a large update then you can specify the Batch details on the next page, but in this case we just click the Next button.

Copy Data Between Companies Quickly Using The Data Import Export Framework

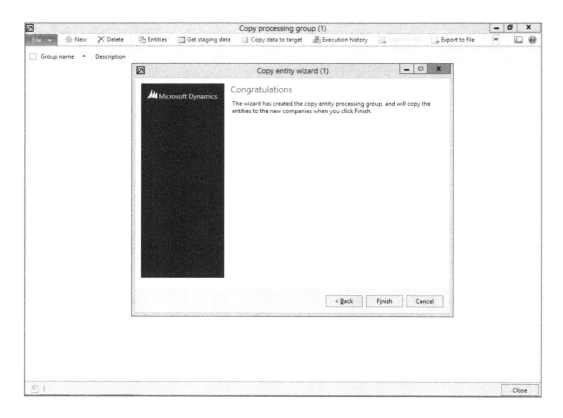

Now we have finished the configuration of the Copy Processing Group, we can click the Finish button to kick off the process.

Copy Data Between Companies Quickly Using The Data Import Export Framework

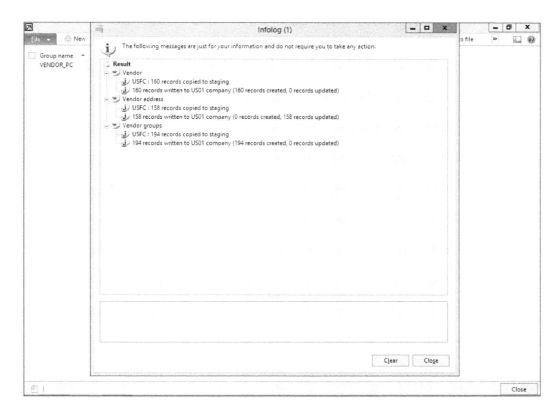

After a short while, you will get a notification that the records have been copied within the two entities...

Copy Data Between Companies Quickly Using The Data Import Export Framework

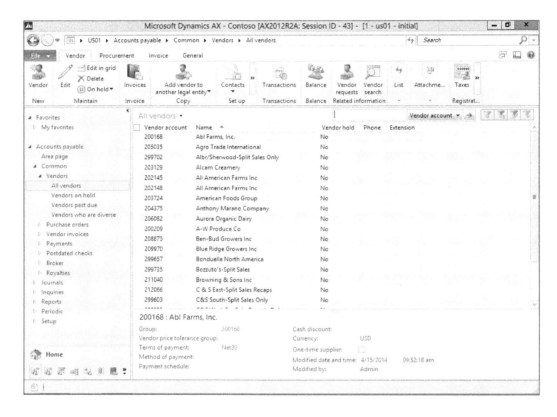

And if you look in the company that was missing the data, you will see all of the new data that you have created.

Now that's a heck of a lot easier than retyping in the data for sure.

Add Quick Links To Websites As Ribbon Bar Buttons

There are probably a lot of reference websites that you always go to during your day that you use in conjunction with Dynamics AX. Although it is not a big deal to open up your browser and type in the website address, you may want to make your life just a little bit easier and add the links to the pages directly within the Dynamics AX form that you are usually in when you need it. That way you are just a click away from the site rather than a couple of clicks and a lot of typing.

Although I wouldn't suggest that you add Farm Town as a link no matter how many crops you still have to harvest...

Add Quick Links To Websites As Ribbon Bar Buttons

First, find the website that you want to open from the Dynamics AX ribbon bar.

Add Quick Links To Websites As Ribbon Bar Buttons

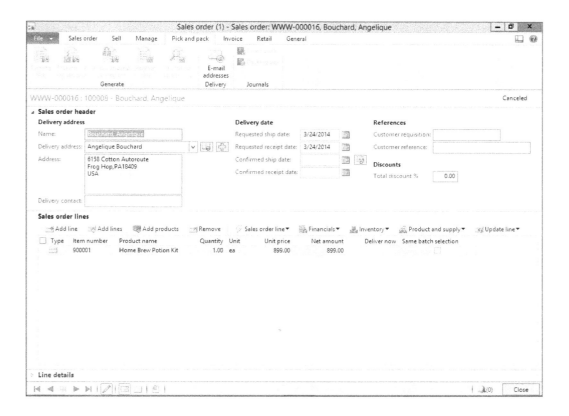

Then find the form that you want to add a link to the website from.

Add Quick Links To Websites As Ribbon Bar Buttons

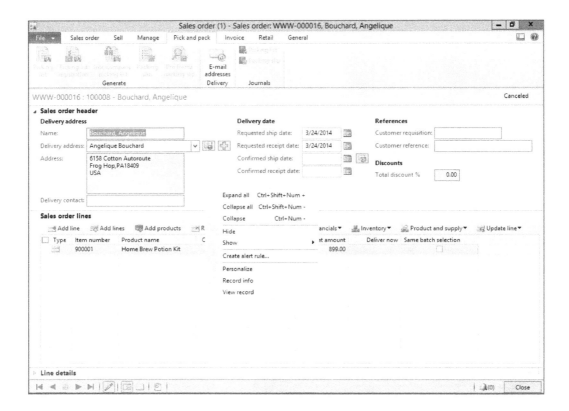

Now we need to edit the form. A quick trick to find the form in AOT is to right-mouse-click on the form and select the Personalize option.

Add Quick Links To Websites As Ribbon Bar Buttons

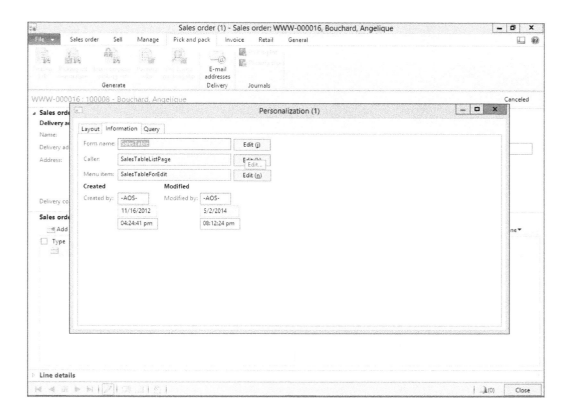

When the Personalization form is displayed, switch to the Information tab, and click on the Edit button to the right of the Form Name.

Add Quick Links To Websites As Ribbon Bar Buttons

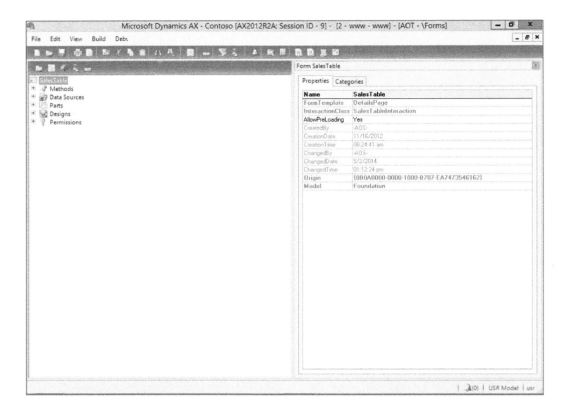

This will open up AOT and take you straight to the form that you need to modify.

Add Quick Links To Websites As Ribbon Bar Buttons

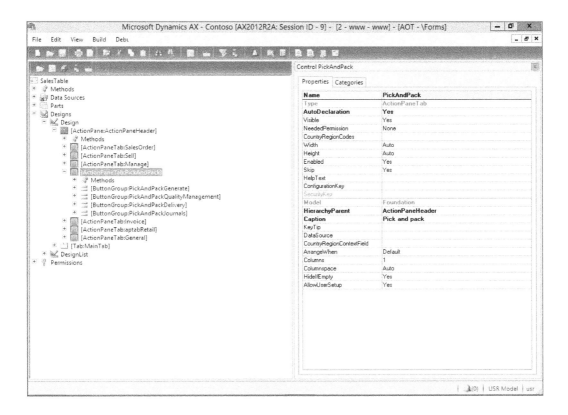

Expand out the Design section and the ActionPane (a.k.a. the ribbon bar) and find the ribbon that you want to add the button to.

Add Quick Links To Websites As Ribbon Bar Buttons

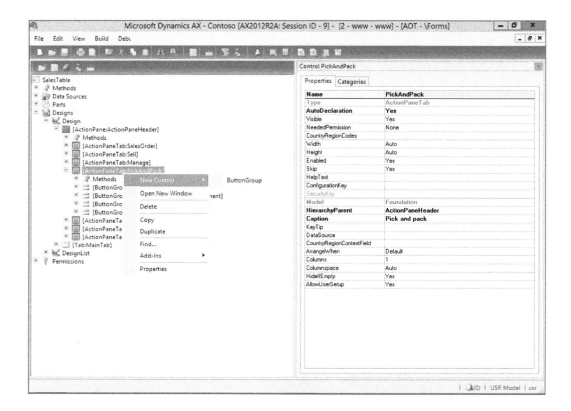

Right-mouse-click on the ActionPane, select the New Control sub-menu, and then select the ButtonGroup menu item.

Add Quick Links To Websites As Ribbon Bar Buttons

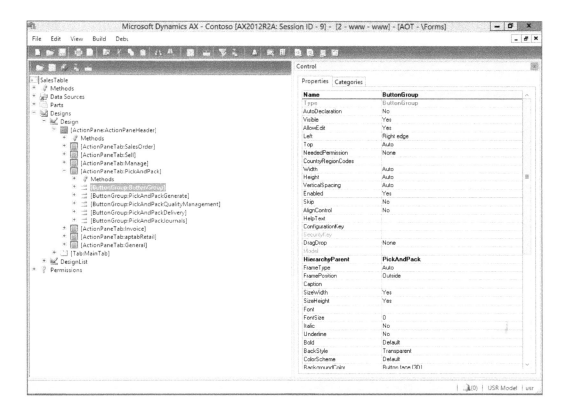

This will add a new Button Group to the ribbon bar.

Add Quick Links To Websites As Ribbon Bar Buttons

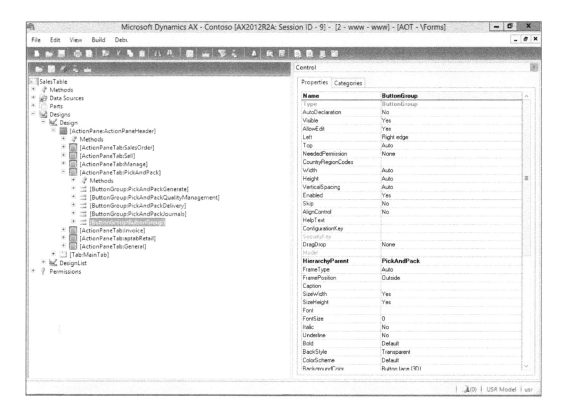

Hold down the ALT key and then use the Down Arrow key to move the button group to the bottom of the list.

Add Quick Links To Websites As Ribbon Bar Buttons

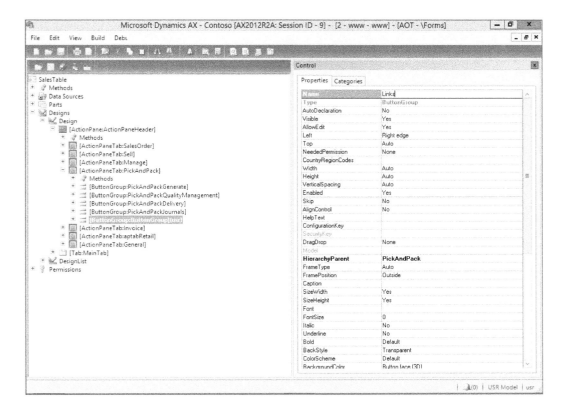

Now we need to tidy up the button group. Start off by giving it a better Name value within the Properties panel.

Add Quick Links To Websites As Ribbon Bar Buttons

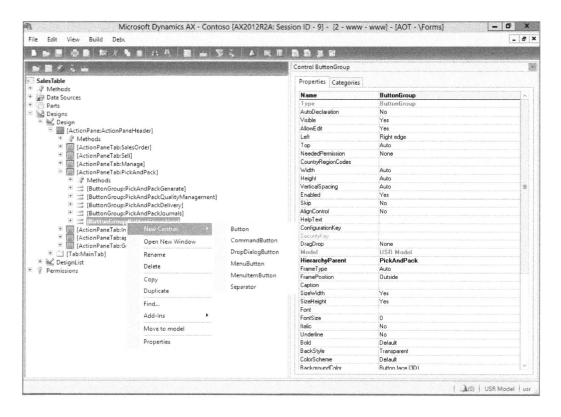

Then right-mouse-click on the Button Group and select the New Control sub menu, and then select the Button menu item to create the button.

Add Quick Links To Websites As Ribbon Bar Buttons

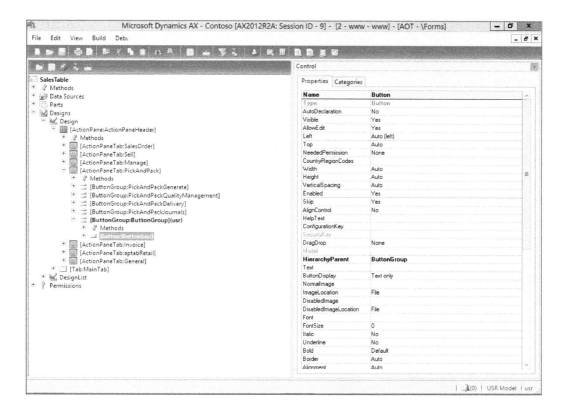

Now you will have a new Button control.

Add Quick Links To Websites As Ribbon Bar Buttons

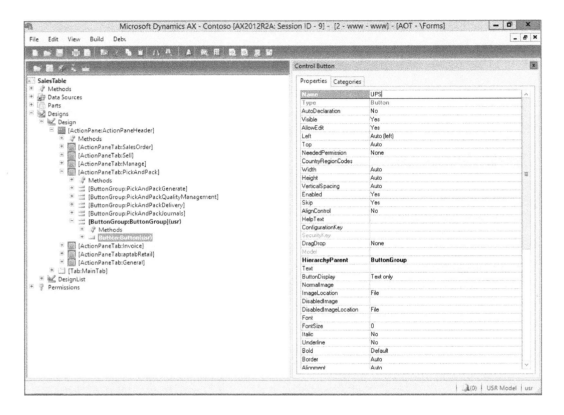

Change the Name for the button in the properties panel.

Add Quick Links To Websites As Ribbon Bar Buttons

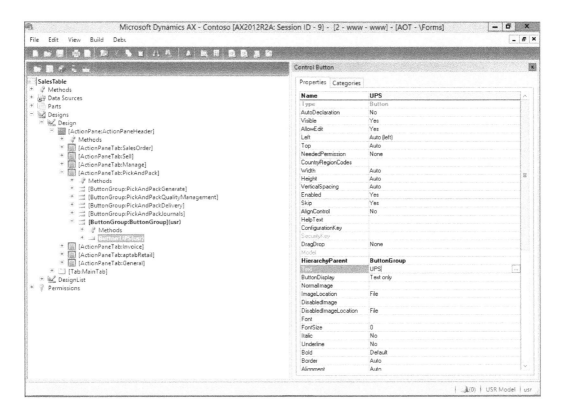

Then change the Text that will show for the button.

Add Quick Links To Websites As Ribbon Bar Buttons

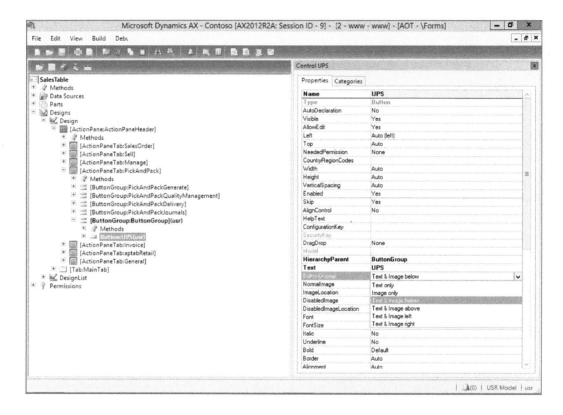

Change the ButtonDisplay property to Text & Image Below.

Add Quick Links To Websites As Ribbon Bar Buttons

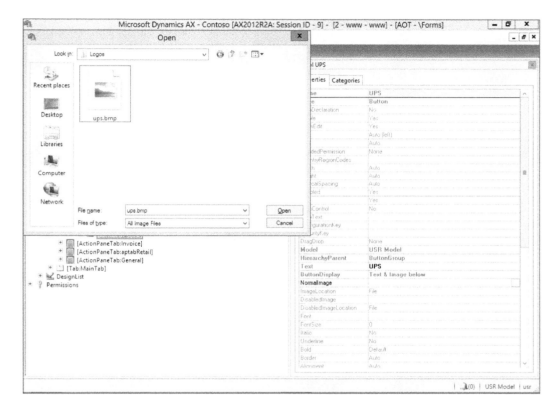

Then click on the ... button to the right of the NormalImage property and select an icon for the button.

Add Quick Links To Websites As Ribbon Bar Buttons

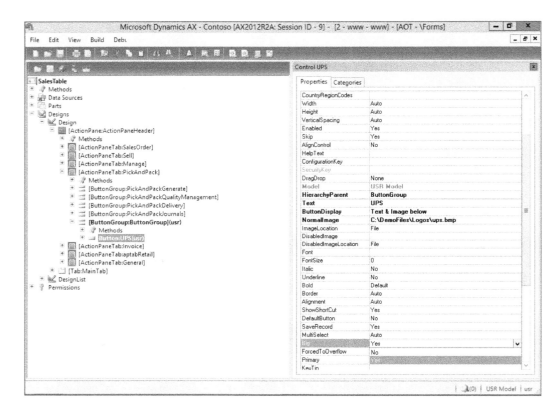

Finally, we want a big image, so change the Big property to Yes.

Add Quick Links To Websites As Ribbon Bar Buttons

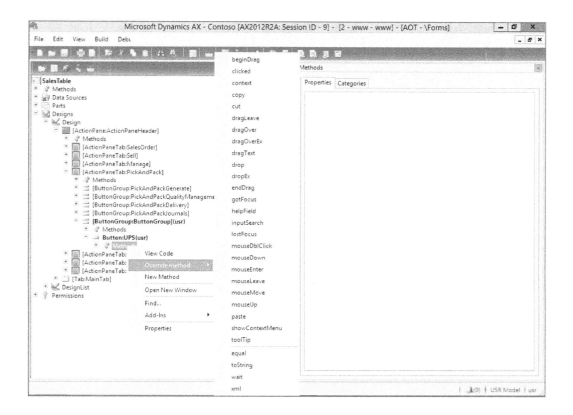

Now expand the Button control, right-mouse-click on the Methods node, select the Override Method submenu, and then select the Clicked method so that we can tell it what to do when the button is clicked.

Add Quick Links To Websites As Ribbon Bar Buttons

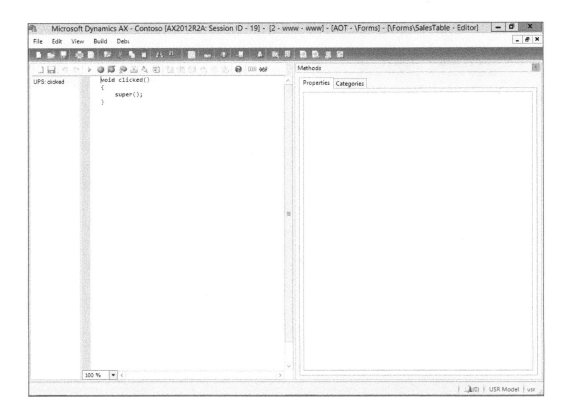

This will open up the method code editor.

Add Quick Links To Websites As Ribbon Bar Buttons

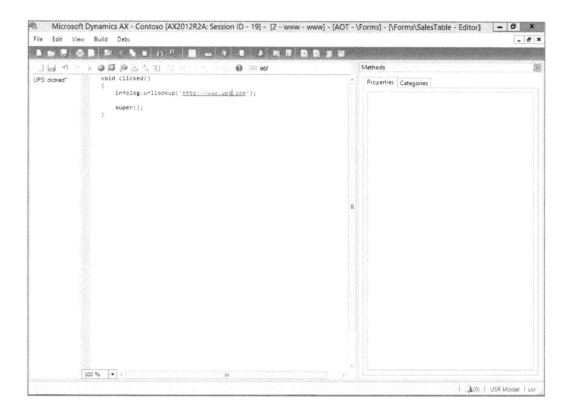

Just add the following code to the beginning of the method:

Infolog.urllookup(http://yourwebsiteaddress);

After you have done that you can close the editor.

Add Quick Links To Websites As Ribbon Bar Buttons

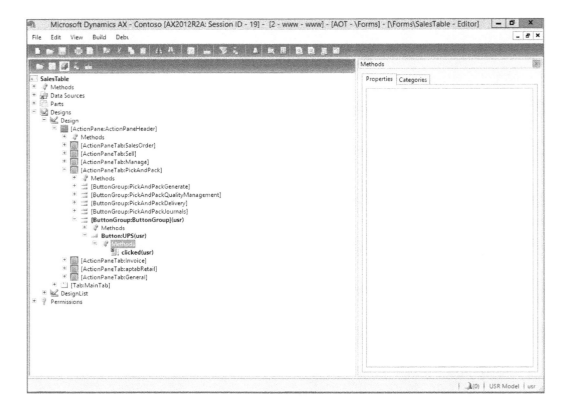

Now all that is left to do is to save the changes and close the form.

Add Quick Links To Websites As Ribbon Bar Buttons

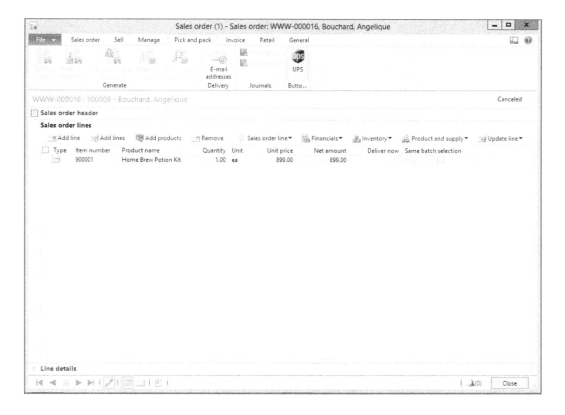

Now when you open up your form, there is an icon there for your website.

Add Quick Links To Websites As Ribbon Bar Buttons

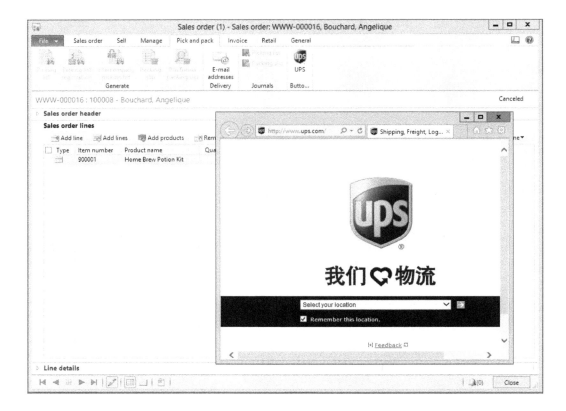

If you just click on it then Dynamics AX will open up your default browser and go straight to the site that your specified.

That is cool!

Deliver Blog Feeds Directly To Your Role Centers

Blogs are a great source of information, and come in many shapes and sizes ranging from external blogs that you may periodically access for inspiration and information, to internal blogs that you may have set up within your organization that give the employees updates on the happening within the company. For the more important blogs, you may want to add them to your Dynamics AX Role Center page so that they are delivered directly to you.

It's like your own personal newspaper delivery minus the neighbor that steals it before you get up.

Deliver Blog Feeds Directly To Your Role Centers

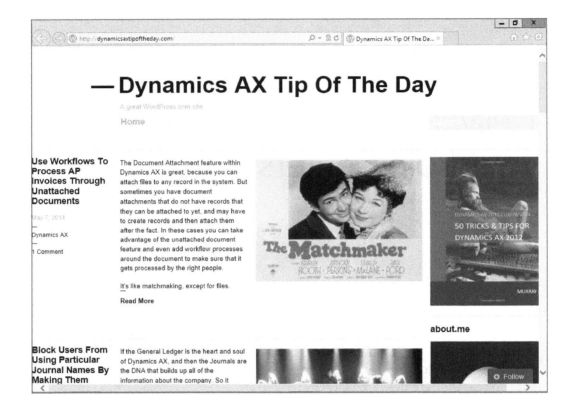

First start off with the blog that you want to link to your role center.

Deliver Blog Feeds Directly To Your Role Centers

Then find the RSS feed for the blog.

Tip: Usually you can find this by adding rss or feed to the end of the website URL.

Deliver Blog Feeds Directly To Your Role Centers

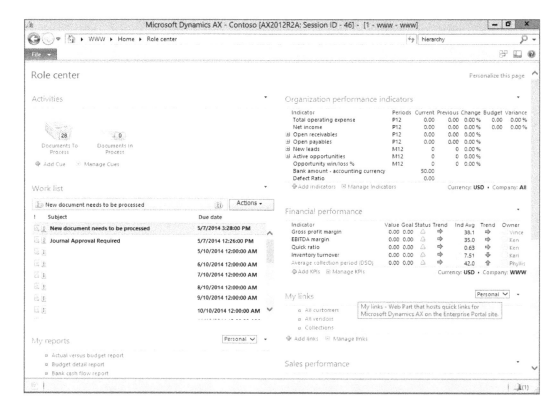

Now open up Dynamics AX and open up your Role Center home page.

Then click on the Personalize This Page link in the top right of the form.

Deliver Blog Feeds Directly To Your Role Centers

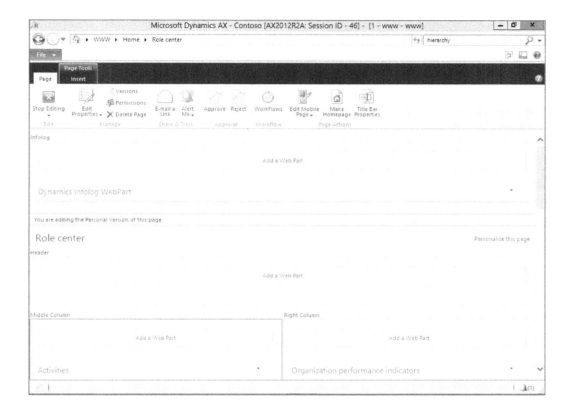

This will open the page up in personalization mode. You will notice some of the sections have a Add A Web Part link in them. Click on the one in the area that you want to add your blog post link.

Deliver Blog Feeds Directly To Your Role Centers

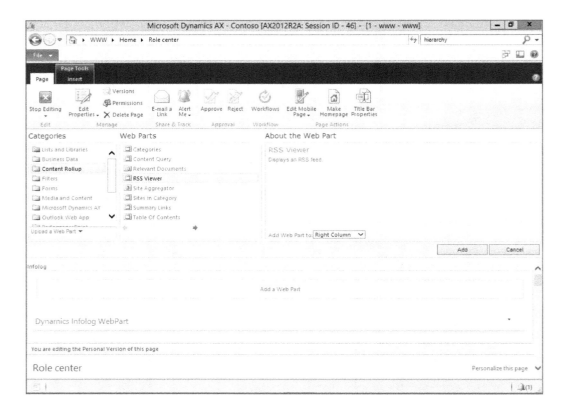

When the web part browser is displayed, select the Content Rollup Category, select the RSS Viewer from the Web Parts list and then click on the Add button.

Deliver Blog Feeds Directly To Your Role Centers

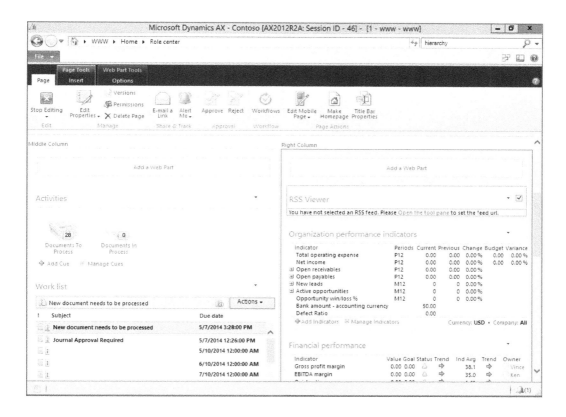

When you return to the Role Center page you will see that a new control has been added to the form, but it is not configured. Click on the Open The Tools Pane link.

Deliver Blog Feeds Directly To Your Role Centers

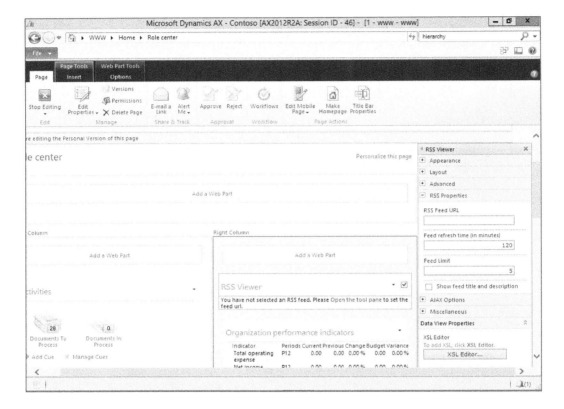

This will open up the properties panel for the RSS Viewer web part on the right.

Deliver Blog Feeds Directly To Your Role Centers

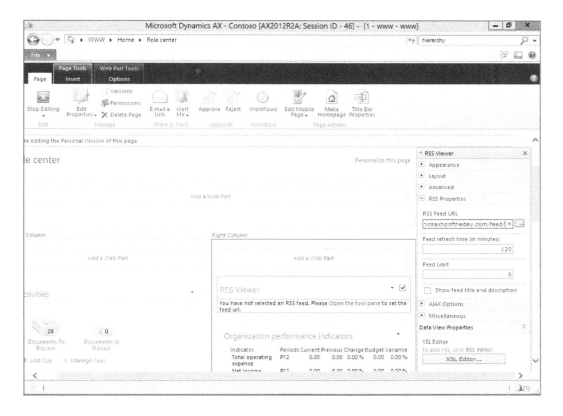

Within the RSS Properties group, paste in the URL for the RSS feed that you discovered earlier on.

Deliver Blog Feeds Directly To Your Role Centers

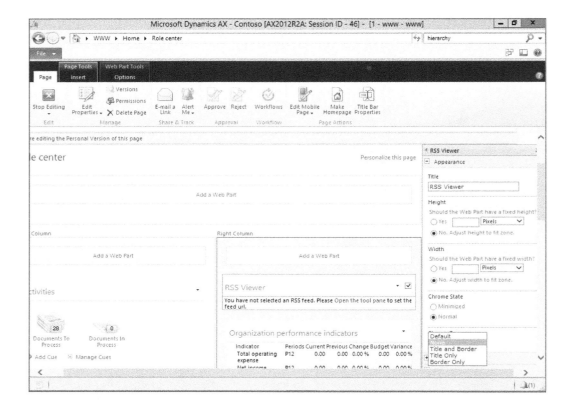

Then within the Appearance group, change the Chrome State property to None. This will just remove the title from the web part which makes lit look tidier.

Deliver Blog Feeds Directly To Your Role Centers

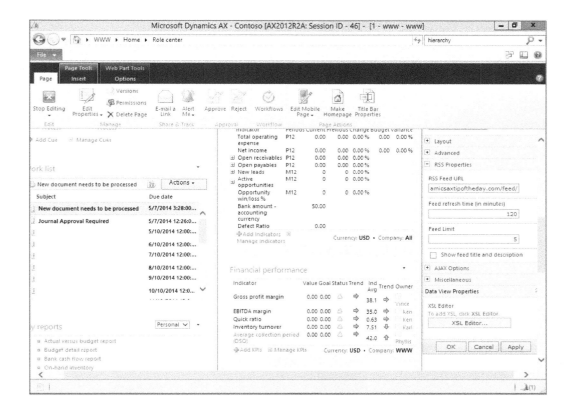

The default view of the blog post will look a little bland, so we will spiff it up a little by changing the format. To do this scroll right down to the bottom, and click on the XSL Editor button.

Deliver Blog Feeds Directly To Your Role Centers

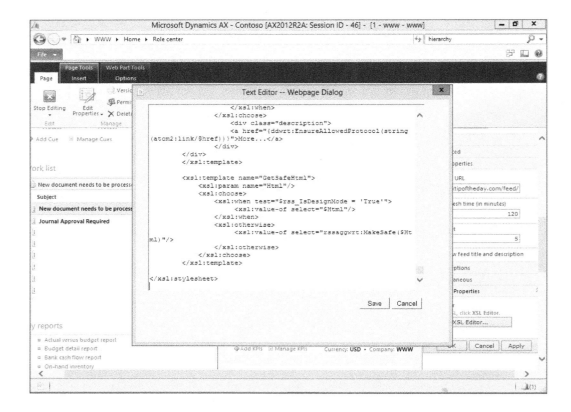

This will open up a Text Editor for the XSL.

Deliver Blog Feeds Directly To Your Role Centers

```
<?xml version="1.0" encoding="UTF-8"?>
<xsl:stylesheet version="1.0"
xmlns:xsl="http://www.w3.org/1999/XSL/Transform">
<xsl:output method="html" indent="yes"/>
<xsl:param name="TITLE"/>
<xsl:template match="rss">
  <div style="background:#ffffff; padding:0; font-size:14px;">
    <xsl:for-each select="channel/item">
      <xsl:if test="position() &lt;= 1">
        <a href="{link}" target="_new" style="background:#ffffff; padding:0;
font-size:24px;">Tip Of The Day<br/><xsl:value-of select="title"/></a><br/>
          <xsl:value-of disable-output-escaping="yes" select="description"/><br/>
      </xsl:if>
    </xsl:for-each>
  </div>
</xsl:template>
<xsl:template match="description"><xsl:value-of select="."/><br/></xsl:template>
</xsl:stylesheet>
```

Paste in the following code into the text editor.

Deliver Blog Feeds Directly To Your Role Centers

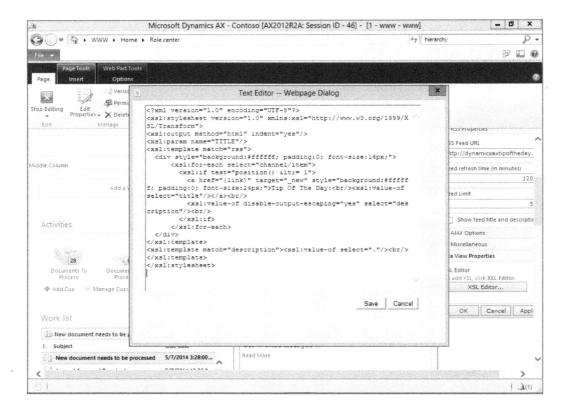

Once you have done that, just click on the Save button to update the style sheet.

Deliver Blog Feeds Directly To Your Role Centers

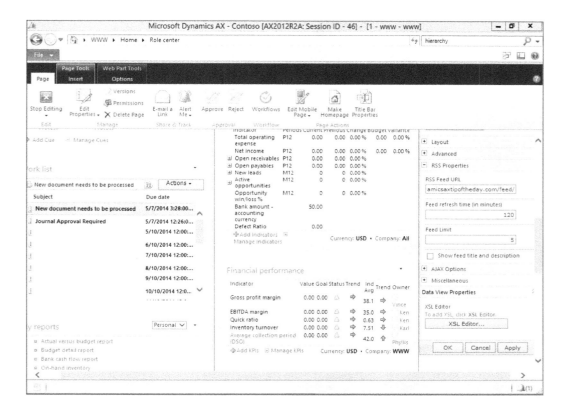

And then click on the OK button to save your changes.

Deliver Blog Feeds Directly To Your Role Centers

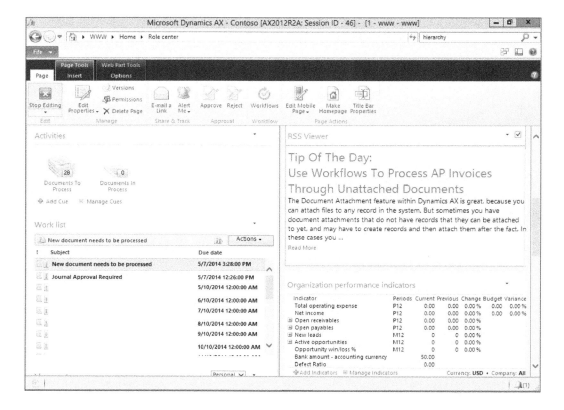

When the role center is updated you will notice that the blog post has been retrieved and is displayed in the designer mode.

All that you need to do now is click on the Stop Editing button within the Edit group of the Page ribbon bar.

Deliver Blog Feeds Directly To Your Role Centers

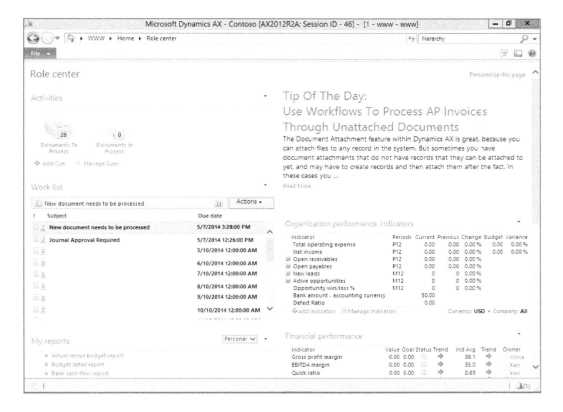

Now you have an ultra-cool link directly to one of your favorite blog sites.

Make Users Feel Special By Creating New Role Centers For Their Unique Roles

Dynamics AX comes pre-packaged with over 40 standard role centers for a lot of the normal user types that you would expect to see within an organization – CFO, Salesperson, AP Clerk, etc. Chances are though you probably have roles within your organization that don't quite fit into those roles. You can either try to assign those users to one of the roles that most closely fits, or you can just create a new role centers especially for those users.

Say no to being generic.

Make Users Feel Special By Creating New Role Centers For Their Unique Roles

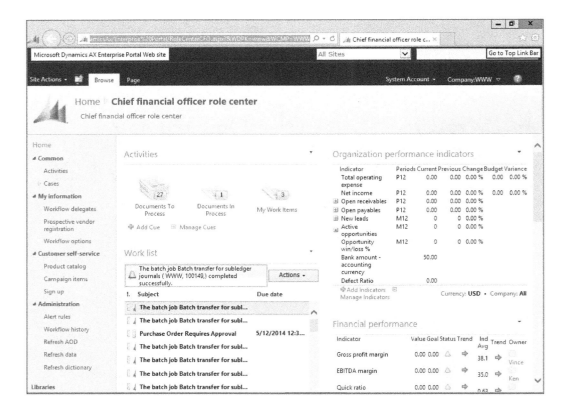

Start off by browsing to one of your default Role Center pages.

Make Users Feel Special By Creating New Role Centers For Their Unique Roles

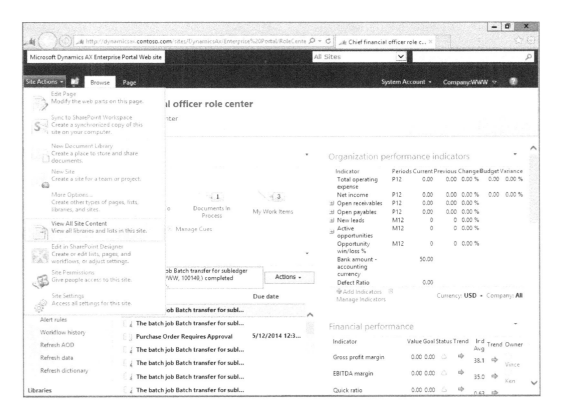

Then from the Site Actions menu, click on the View All Site Content menu item.

Make Users Feel Special By Creating New Role Centers For Their Unique Roles

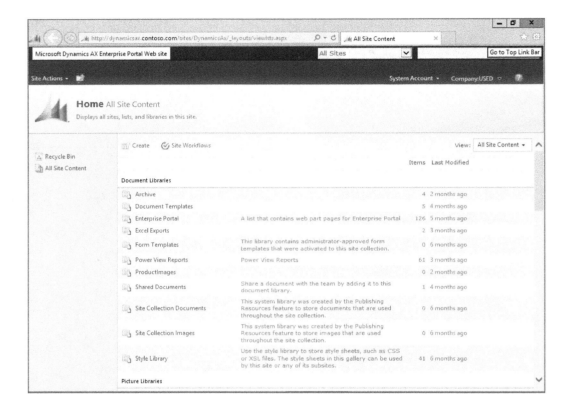

When the Site Contents page is displayed, click on the Enterprise Portal document library.

Make Users Feel Special By Creating New Role Centers For Their Unique Roles

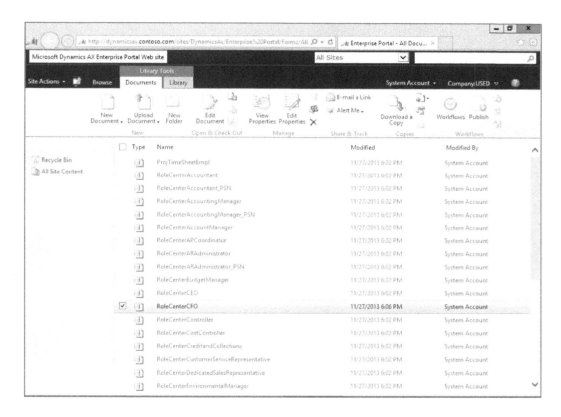

When the Enterprise Portal library is displayed, you will be able to see all of the default Role Center templates. They are easy to spot and all begin with RoleCenter.

Make Users Feel Special By Creating New Role Centers For Their Unique Roles

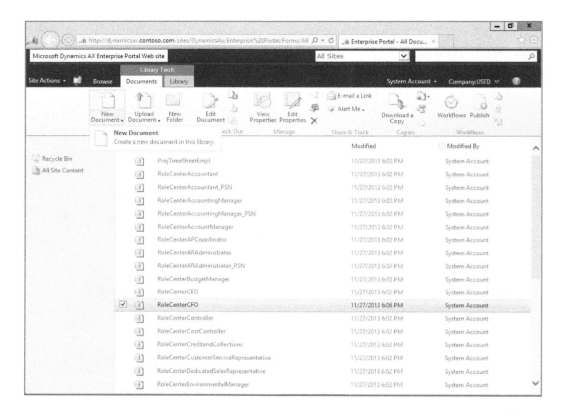

To create a new Role Center template click on the New Document menu item within the Documents tab on the ribbon bar.

Make Users Feel Special By Creating New Role Centers For Their Unique Roles

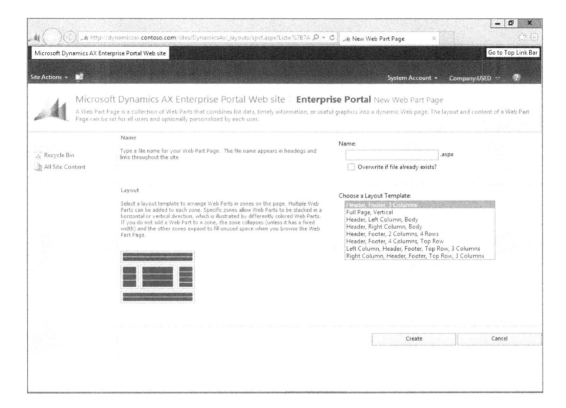

This will open up the New Web Part Page creation page.

Make Users Feel Special By Creating New Role Centers For Their Unique Roles

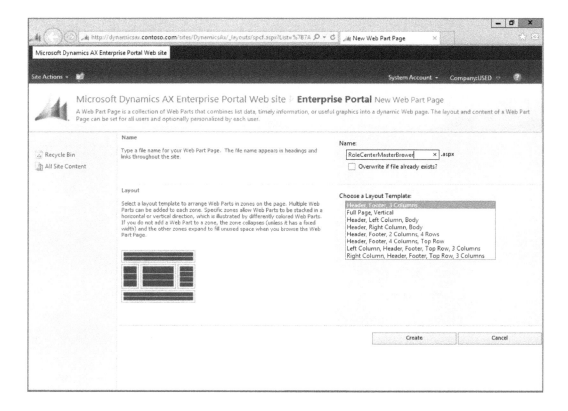

Give your Role Center Template a Name and then click on the Create button.

Note: You can change the layout of the template, but it is best just to use the default.

Make Users Feel Special By Creating New Role Centers For Their Unique Roles

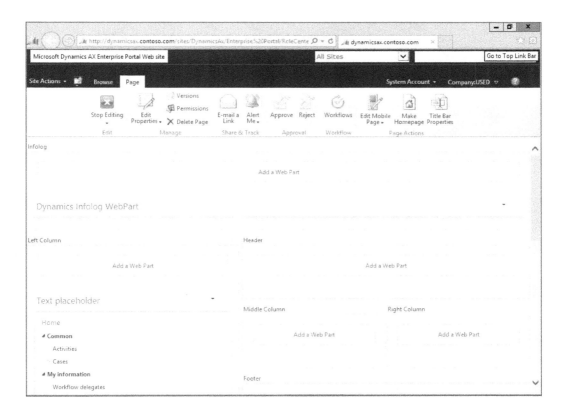

After the new Role Center Template is created, you will be taken into the edit mode for the page. To tweak the page, click on the Add a Web Part link on any of the columns.

Make Users Feel Special By Creating New Role Centers For Their Unique Roles

This will open up the Web Part browser above the page. Select any of the standard web parts delivered with SharePoint and also Dynamics AX that you want to add to the page, and then click the Add button.

Make Users Feel Special By Creating New Role Centers For Their Unique Roles

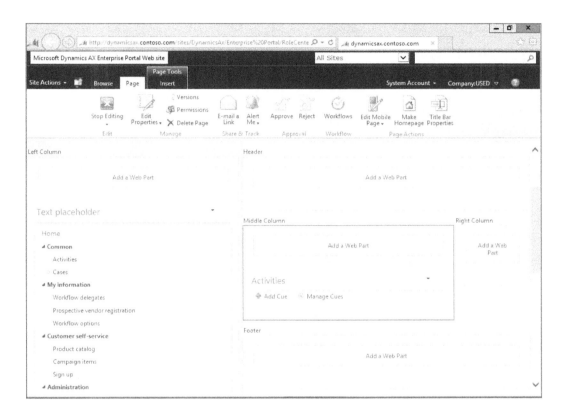

In this case we added the Cues control to the page.

Make Users Feel Special By Creating New Role Centers For Their Unique Roles

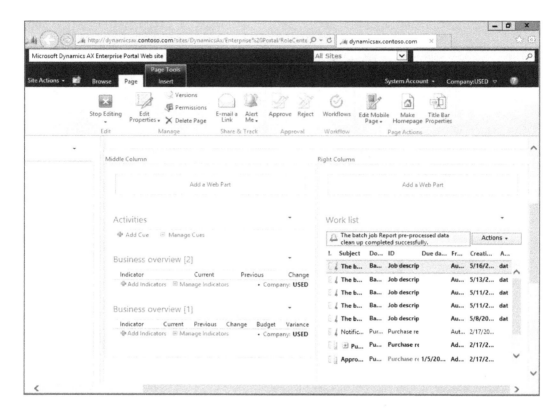

You can continue adding Web Parts until you are satisfied with the template. Then click the Stop Editing button on the ribbon bar.

Make Users Feel Special By Creating New Role Centers For Their Unique Roles

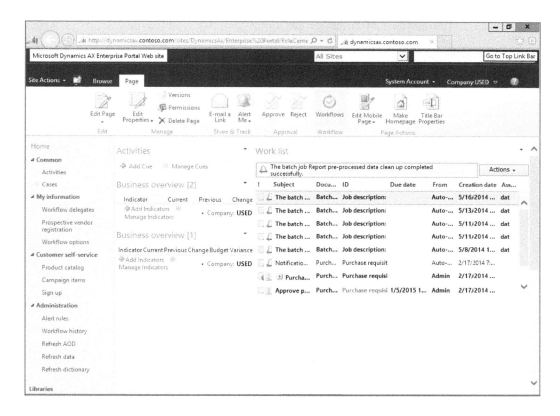

This will take you back to the view mode and you are done with the template creation.

Make Users Feel Special By Creating New Role Centers For Their Unique Roles

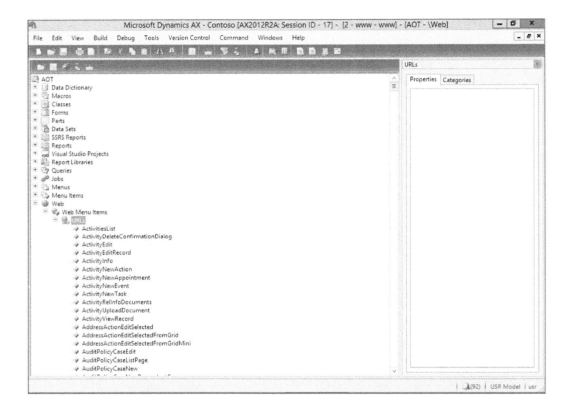

The next step is to create a menu item for the Role Center within AOT. To do this you can go directly into the AOT tree and drill down into the URLs node within the Web Menu Items folder of the Web group.

Make Users Feel Special By Creating New Role Centers For Their Unique Roles

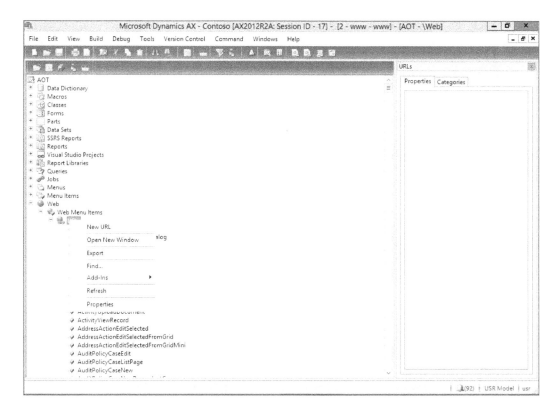

Right-mouse-click on the URLs node and select the New URL menu item from the context menu.

Make Users Feel Special By Creating New Role Centers For Their Unique Roles

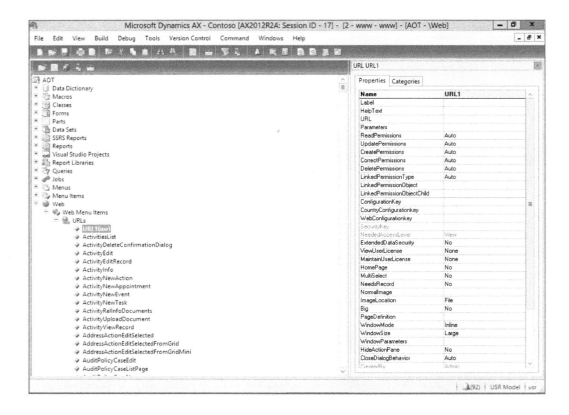

This will create a new URL record for you that we will configure to point to the Role Center that you just created.

Make Users Feel Special By Creating New Role Centers For Their Unique Roles

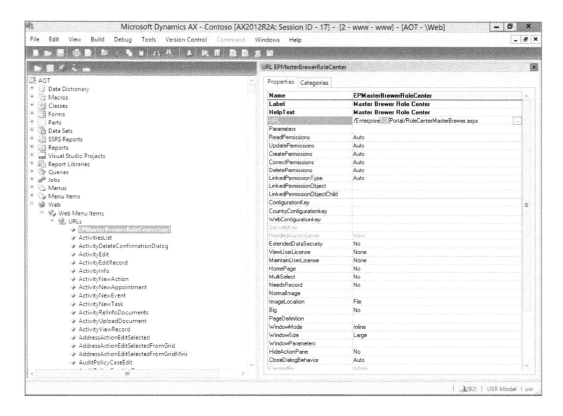

Give the URL object a Name, Label, and Help Text.

Within the URL property, type in the relative path for the Role Center that you created. It will probably be:

/Enterprise Portal/RoleCenterName.aspx

Make Users Feel Special By Creating New Role Centers For Their Unique Roles

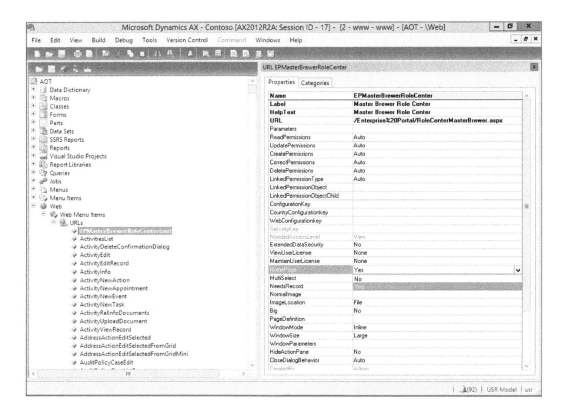

Also, make sure that you set the HomePage field to Yes. If you don't do this then the Role Center will open up in another window.

Make Users Feel Special By Creating New Role Centers For Their Unique Roles

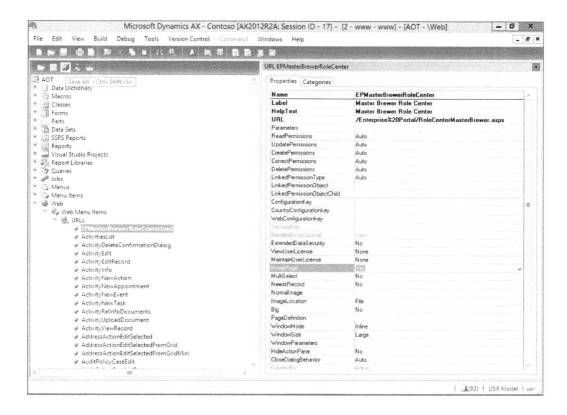

Once you have done that, then click the Save button in the tool bar to save the change.

Make Users Feel Special By Creating New Role Centers For Their Unique Roles

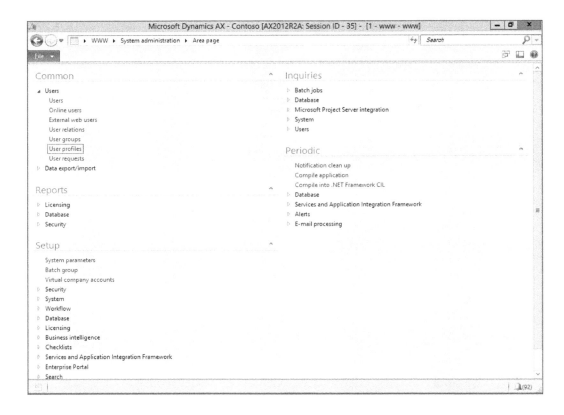

Now we need to create a new User Profile. To do this, click on the User Profiles menu item within the Users folder of the Common group within the System Administration area page.

Make Users Feel Special By Creating New Role Centers For Their Unique Roles

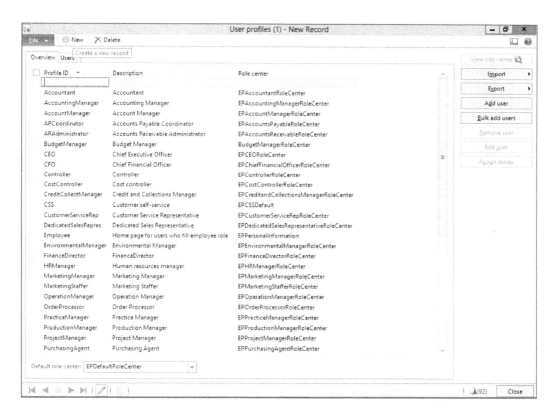

This will open up a list of all the User profiles in the system. Click on the New button within the menu bar to create a new record.

Make Users Feel Special By Creating New Role Centers For Their Unique Roles

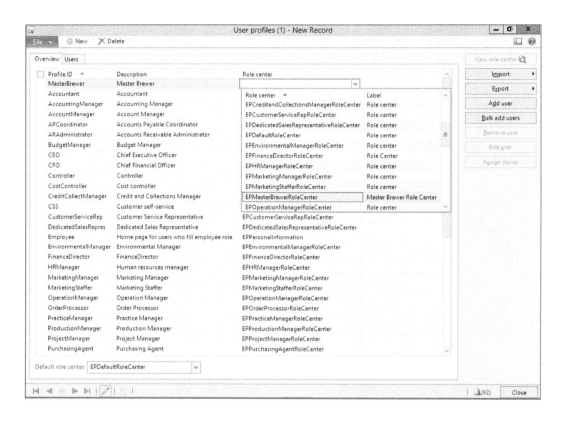

You can give your new profile a Name and a Description and from the drop down box on the Role Center field, you should be able to find the new Role Center menu that you just created.

Make Users Feel Special By Creating New Role Centers For Their Unique Roles

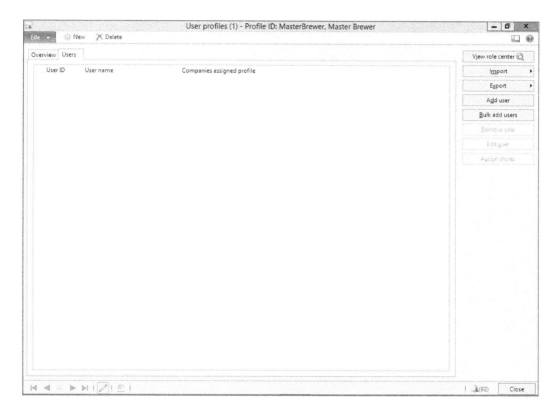

Then click on the Users tab. To assign your users Profile click on the Add user button.

Make Users Feel Special By Creating New Role Centers For Their Unique Roles

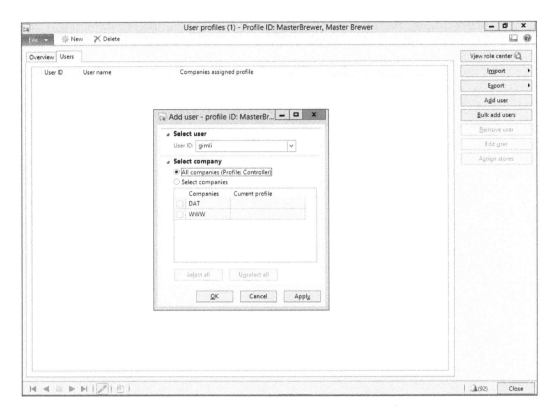

Now you can select the users that you want to assign to the role, and then click on the OK button.

Make Users Feel Special By Creating New Role Centers For Their Unique Roles

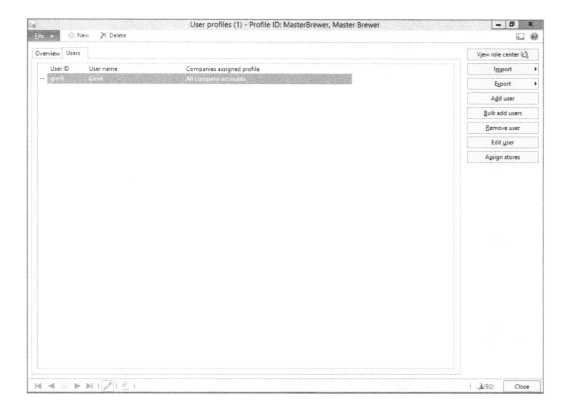

Now you are done.

Make Users Feel Special By Creating New Role Centers For Their Unique Roles

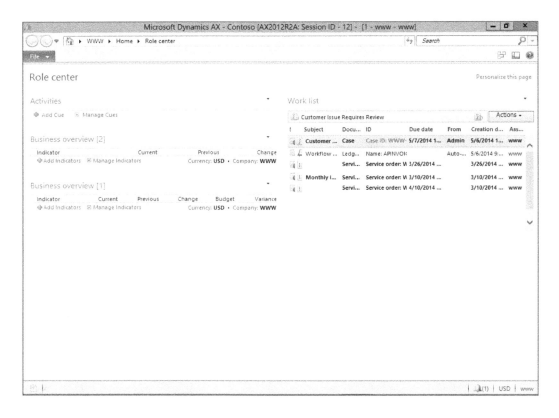

The next time your user logs in, their Role Center will be the new template that you created.

Make Users Feel Special By Creating New Role Centers For Their Unique Roles

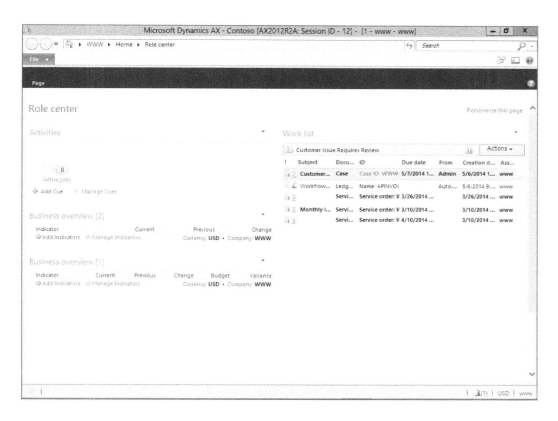

And your user is able to personalize their own custom custom role center.

Very cool.

Add Flair To Your Forms With Achievements

Achievements are everywhere you look. You can get them for checking into your favorite restaurant through Foursquare, you can get them for writing code within Visual Studio, and you can definitely get them on any game that you play on your phone. So why not add them to your Dynamics AX forms so that you can add a little pizazz to day.

In the immortal words of Stan... I need to talk about your flair.

Add Flair To Your Forms With Achievements

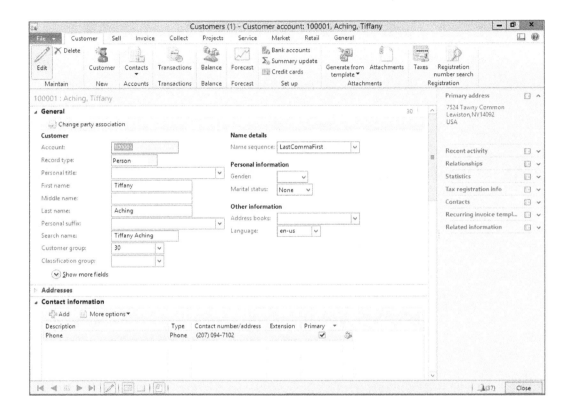

Start off by finding the form that you want to add your achievements to.

Add Flair To Your Forms With Achievements

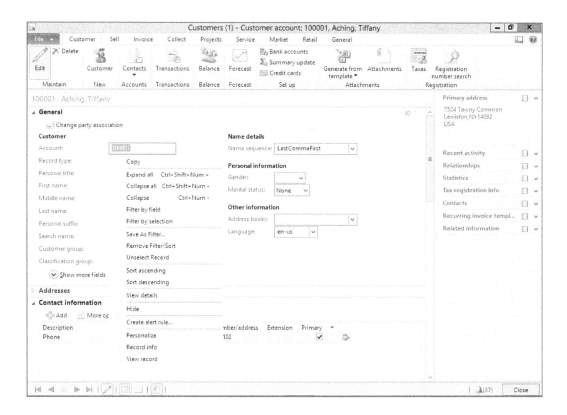

Then right-mouse-click on the form, and select the Personalize option from the pop-up menu.

Add Flair To Your Forms With Achievements

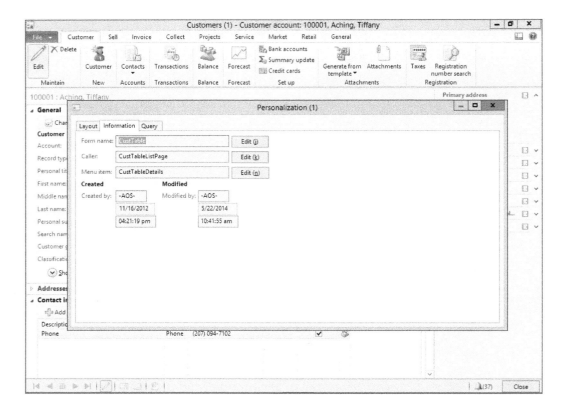

When the Personalization form is displayed, switch to the Information tab, and click on the Edit button to the right of the Form Name field.

Add Flair To Your Forms With Achievements

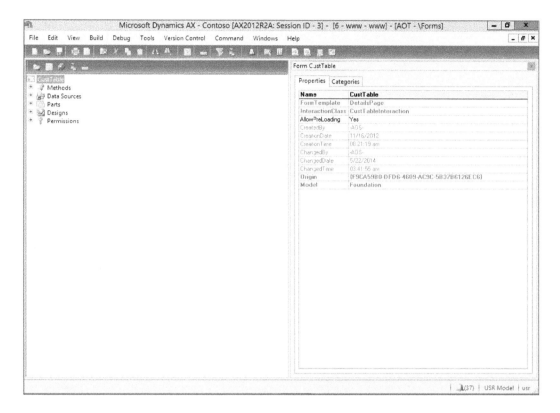

This will open up AOT and with just the form that we selected showing in the explorer.

Add Flair To Your Forms With Achievements

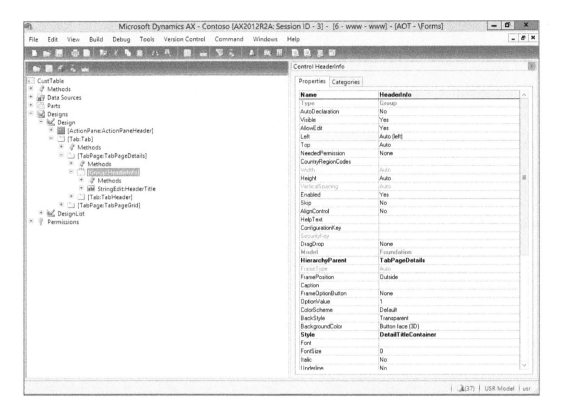

Expand out the Design section to the spot that you want to add your flair. In this case we will add it below the title on the form details.

Add Flair To Your Forms With Achievements

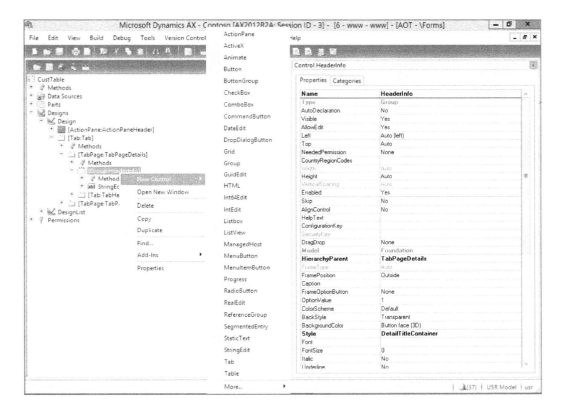

Then right-mouse-click on the group form and select the New Control option from the pop-up-menu, and then choose the Button control.

Add Flair To Your Forms With Achievements

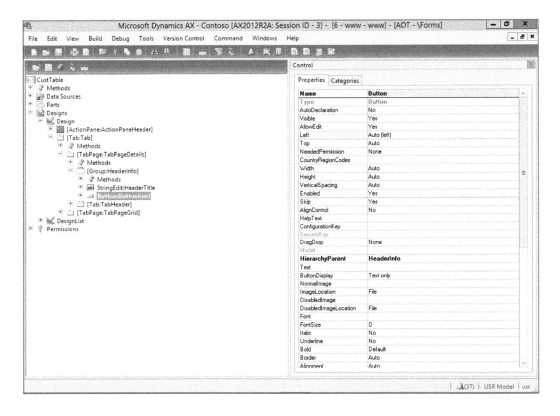

This will add a new Button control to the group.

Add Flair To Your Forms With Achievements

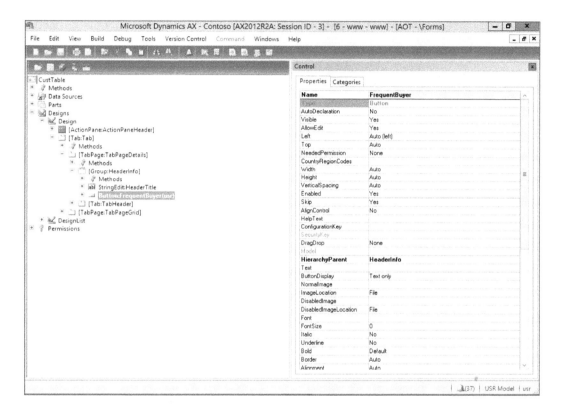

Within the Properties panel, update the Name.

Add Flair To Your Forms With Achievements

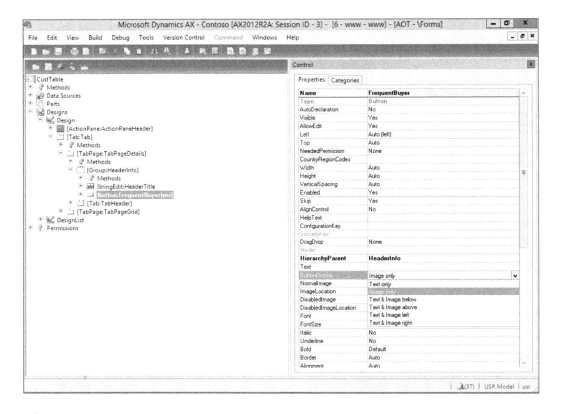

Set the Button Display property to Image Only.

Add Flair To Your Forms With Achievements

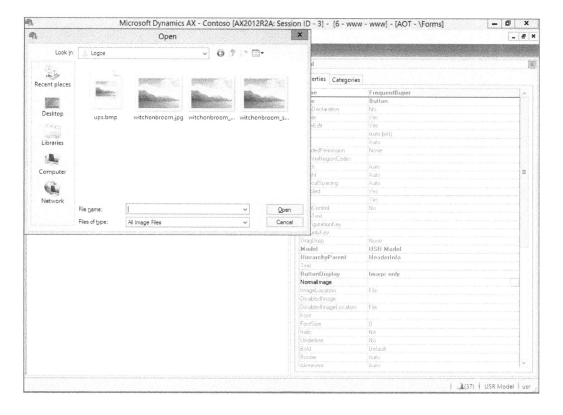

Then click on the ... to the right of the Image URL property so that you can browse and select an image to show for the button.

Add Flair To Your Forms With Achievements

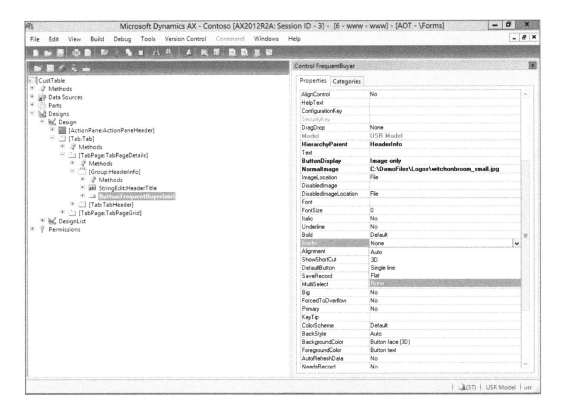

Set the Border to None so that the button shows up as a flat image... which looks nicer.

Add Flair To Your Forms With Achievements

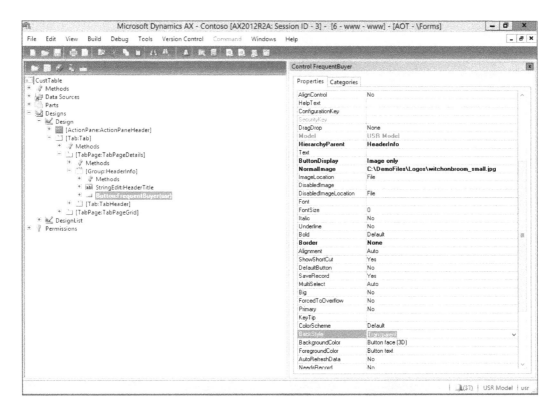

And finally, set the Back Style to Transparent so that it doesn't look like a button ☺

Add Flair To Your Forms With Achievements

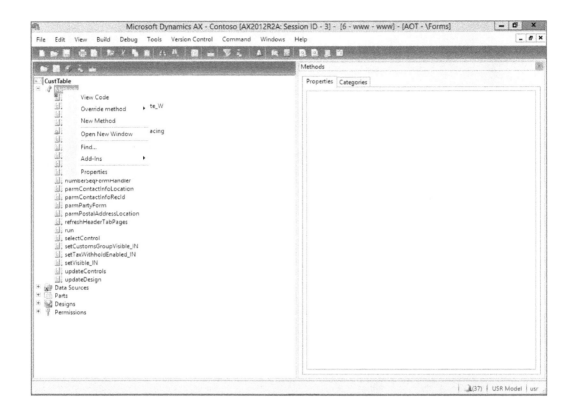

Now we need to create a method that we will use to tell Dynamics AX if we want to show the achievement button or not. To do this right-mouse-click on the Methods folder within the AOT and select the New Method menu item.

Add Flair To Your Forms With Achievements

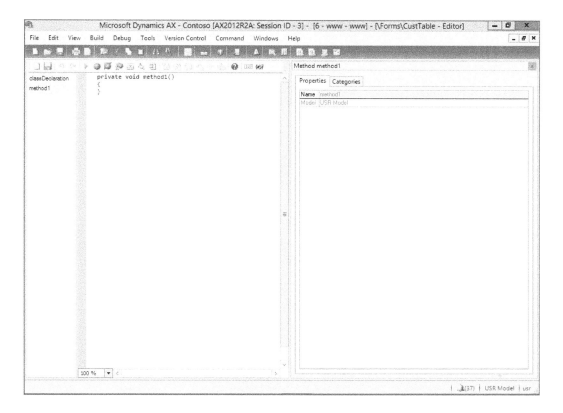

This will open up a new X++ editor window.

Add Flair To Your Forms With Achievements

```
private void updateAchievements()
{
    int recCount;
    SalesTable salesTable;
    ;
    Select count(RecId) From salesTable
        where salesTable.CustAccount == CustTable.AccountNum;
    recCount = salesTable.RecId;

    if (recCount > 1)
    {
    element.design().controlName("FrequentBuyer").visible(true);
    }
    else
    {
    element.design().controlName("FrequentBuyer ").visible(false);
    }
}
```

Replace the code within the method with the following code.

Add Flair To Your Forms With Achievements

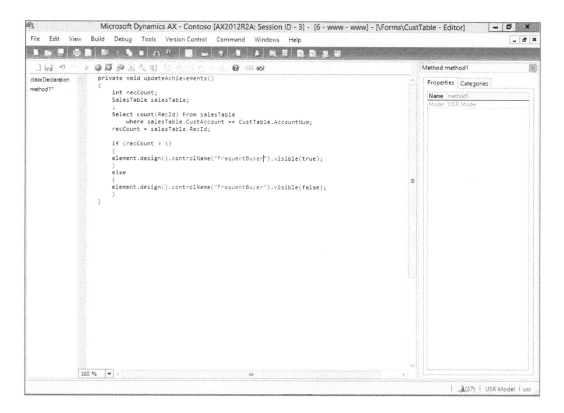

Once you have updated the code, you can close the editor.

Add Flair To Your Forms With Achievements

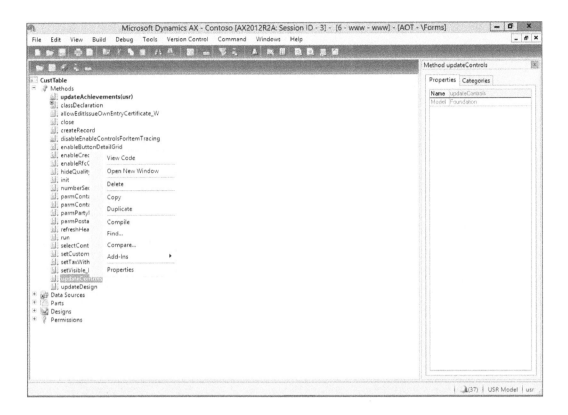

Now we have all of the framework for our achievement. We just need to update the form to tell it to refresh for each record. To do this, expand out the Methods folder and double click on the UpdateControls method.

Add Flair To Your Forms With Achievements

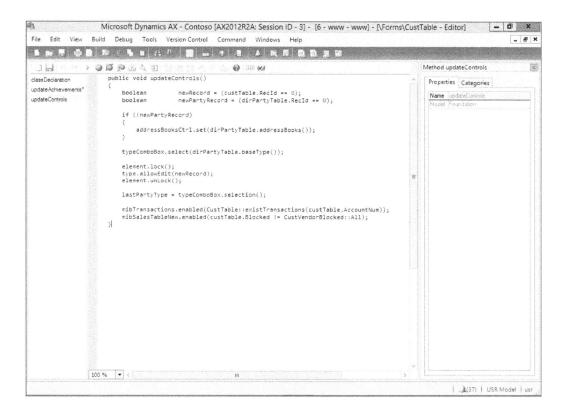

This will open up the X++ editor with the code that is ran every time the record is refreshed or changed.

Add Flair To Your Forms With Achievements

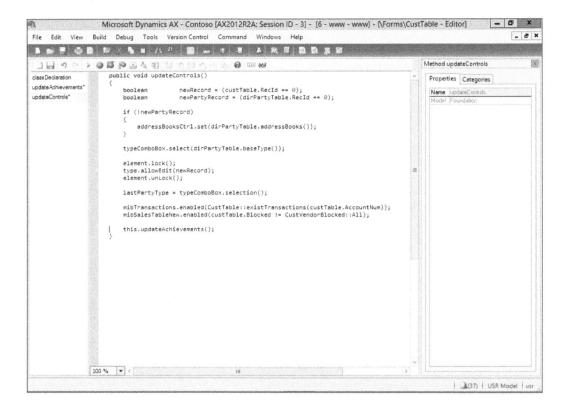

Add the following code to the bottom of the method:

This.updateAchievements();

Once you have done that, save the updates and then close out of AOT.

Add Flair To Your Forms With Achievements

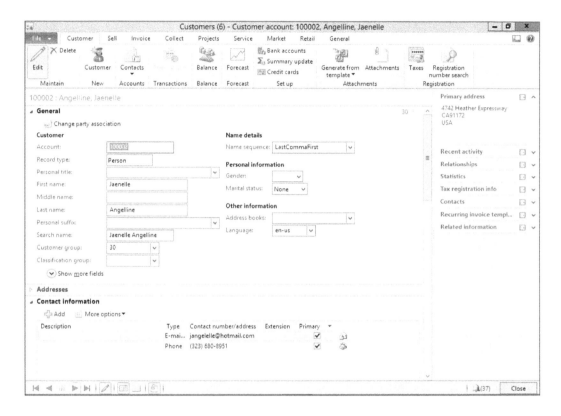

Now when we open up the form, if the condition is met (in our case more than one order being placed for the customer) then everything looks normal.

Add Flair To Your Forms With Achievements

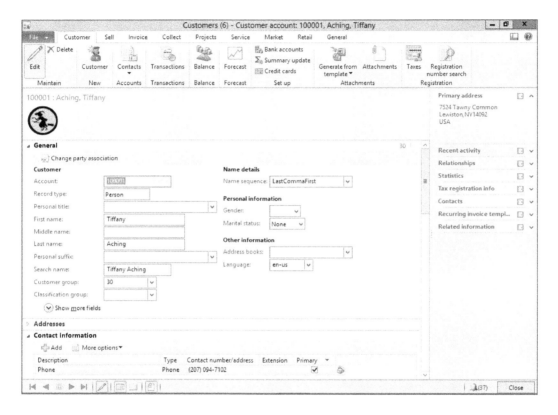

But if they have met the criteria then it shows up.

How cool is that.

Choose Where To Go When You Click On Pop-Up Notifications

Pop-up notifications are great because it's like Dynamics AX is sending you a personalized gift every time they show up. You could be getting a personalized alert that you have set up, or being invited to help with workflow task to streamline the business. You can tweak what happens when you click on the link though to fit your personality. If you are more of an cautious person, then you have the link take you to the alert details where you can contemplate what you want to do. If you are more of a impulsive person, then you can throw all caution to the wind and just go straight to the transaction from the link and get things done right away.

Either way I am sure you will still be excited to see what the notification is...

Choose Where To Go When You Click On Pop-Up Notifications

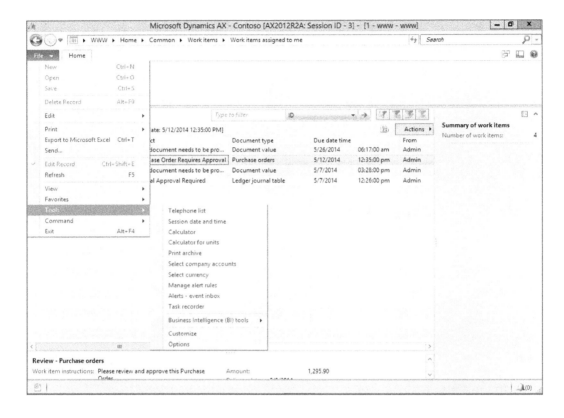

To select what happens when you click on a notification from Dynamics AX, click on the Files menu, then select the Tools sub-menu, and then select the Options menu item.

Choose Where To Go When You Click On Pop-Up Notifications

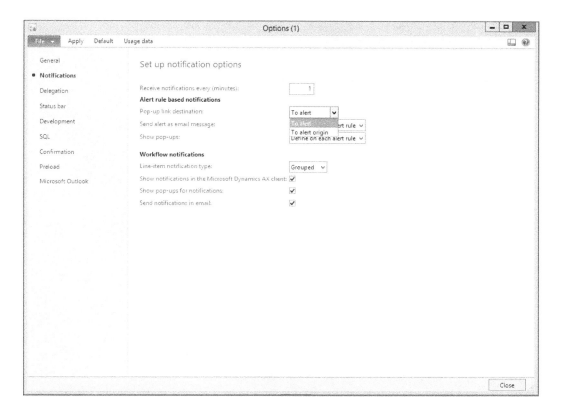

When the Options dialog box is displayed, switch to the Notifications page and you will see a Pop-Up Link Destination field within the Alert Based Notifications field group. To go to the alert detail from the pop-ups, select the To Alert option and then click the Close button to exit from the form.

Choose Where To Go When You Click On Pop-Up Notifications

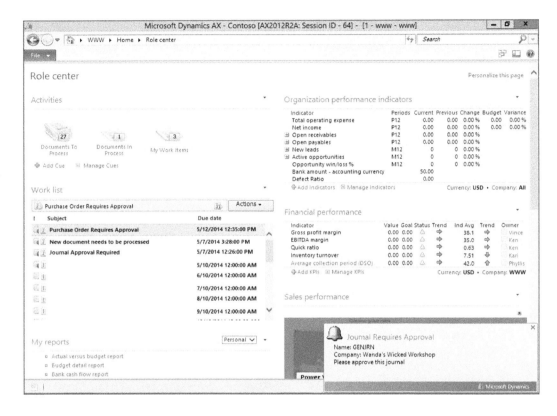

Now, wait for an alert to come through, and then click on it.

Choose Where To Go When You Click On Pop-Up Notifications

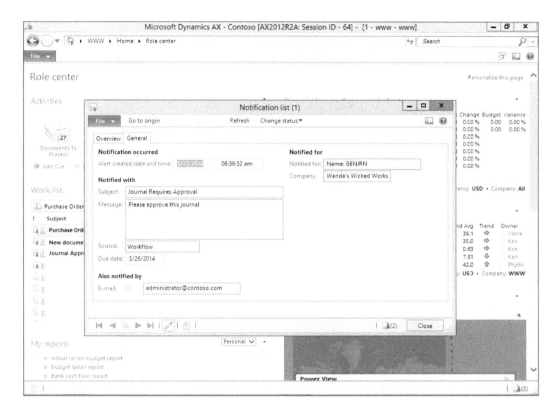

Clicking on the pop-up alert will take you to the alert details with the message information, and from here you can click on the Go To Origin button in the menu bar to navigate to the original transaction.

Choose Where To Go When You Click On Pop-Up Notifications

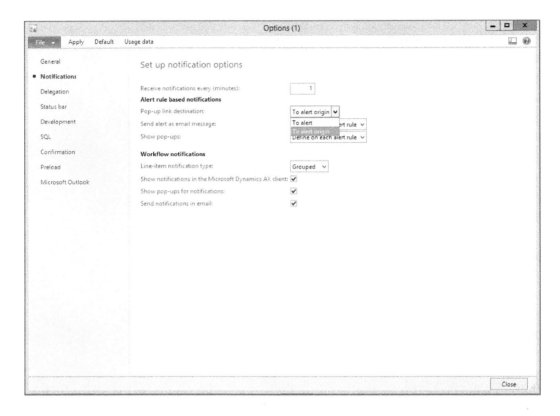

If you want to skip the alert screen and go straight to the transaction, the return to the Options page and change the Pop-Up Link Destination to To Alert Origin.

Choose Where To Go When You Click On Pop-Up Notifications

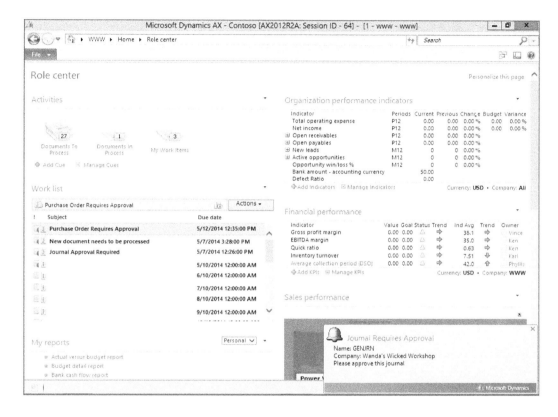

Now wait for an alert to come through and click it.

Choose Where To Go When You Click On Pop-Up Notifications

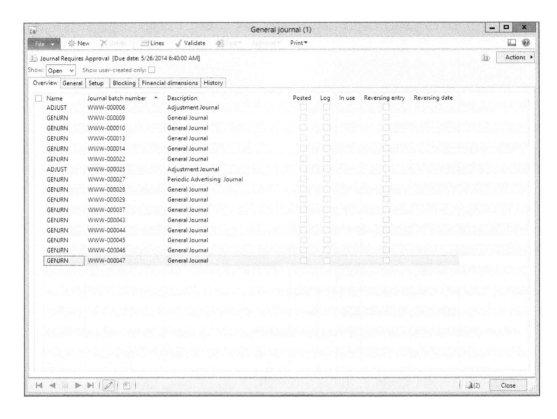

Now you will go straight to the transaction that initiated the alert.

Ripping wrapping paper off presents is much more fun.

Declutter Your System By Turning Off License Features You Don't Use

Dynamics AX is chock full of useful features, but you probably don't need to use it all right away, and in some cases even through other people will need a particular feature you may never consider using it. Rather than having everything enabled within the system, you can use the license configuration tool to deactivate is so that it's not showing up on the forms, and the menus. Later on if you find that you want to use the feature then you can always just turn it back on again.

Don't be an extreme hoarder when it comes to ERP features.

Declutter Your System By Turning Off License Features You Don't Use

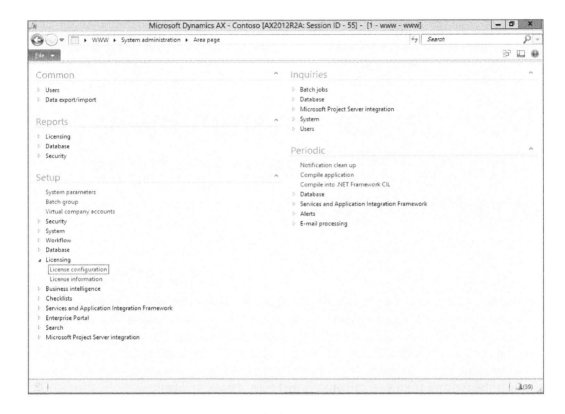

To do this, click on the License Configuration menu item within the Licensing folder of the Setup group within the System Administration area page.

Declutter Your System By Turning Off License Features You Don't Use

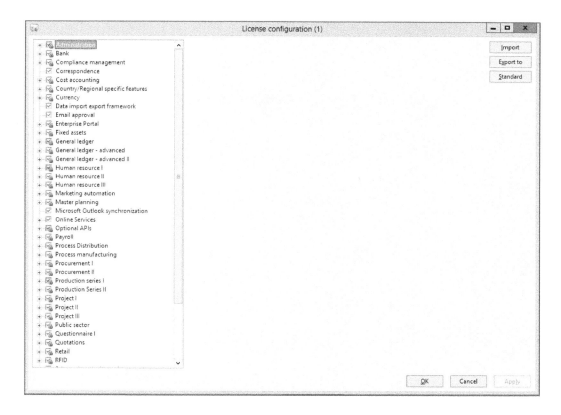

When the License Configuration maintenance form is displayed, you will be able to see all of the different configuration options that are available within the system.

Declutter Your System By Turning Off License Features You Don't Use

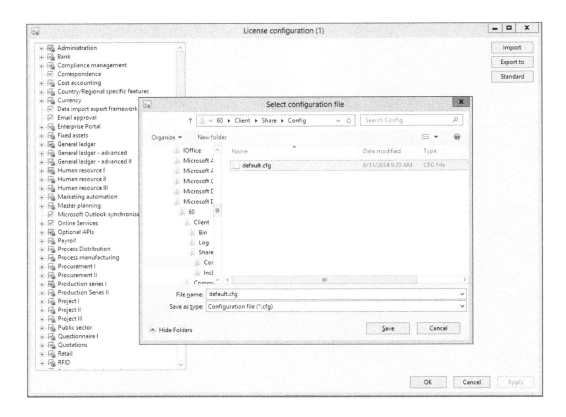

Tip: Before you continue on, just click on the Export To button and save your current configuration just in case you want to restore all of the features back to the same state that you currently have them in.

Declutter Your System By Turning Off License Features You Don't Use

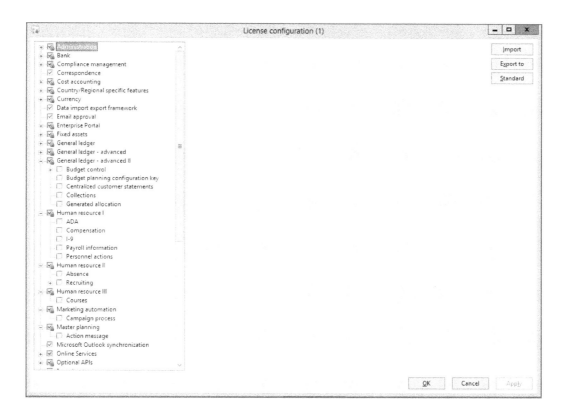

Now you can go through all of the different options, and turn off the features that you don't need. If you want to be super simple, then just click on the Standard button to turn off all but the bare necessities.

Declutter Your System By Turning Off License Features You Don't Use

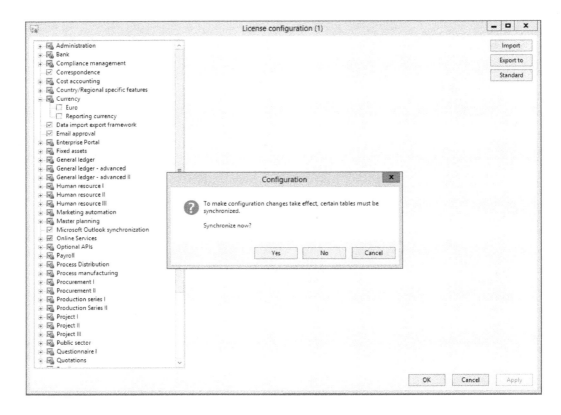

After you have tidied up the license options, click on the OK button, and you will be asked to synchronize the database with the license files. This will go through all of the tables, and make any necessary adjustments for you.

Declutter Your System By Turning Off License Features You Don't Use

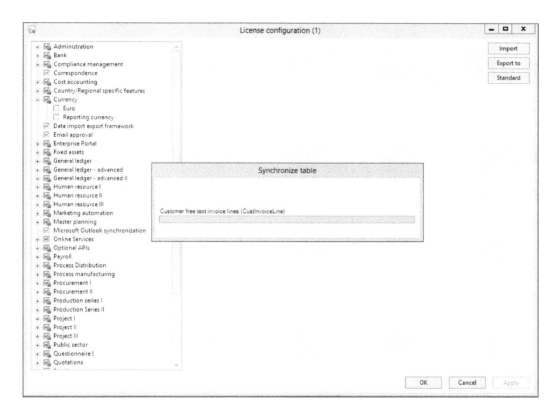

You may want to get a coffee while this is running.

Declutter Your System By Turning Off License Features You Don't Use

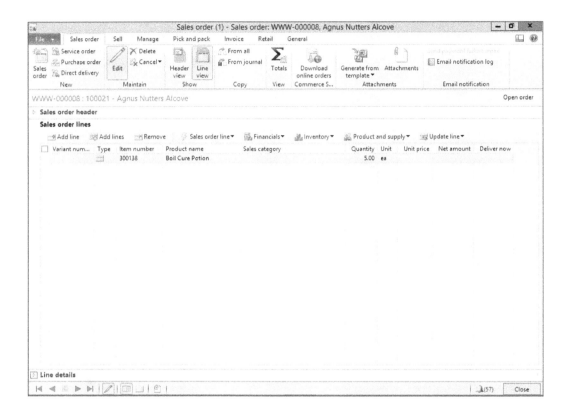

After the synchronization has completed, you will notice that there are not as many bells and whistles configured in the system. For example, by turning off the Catch Weight options, the sales order screen looks a lot more compact.

Declutter Your System By Turning Off License Features You Don't Use

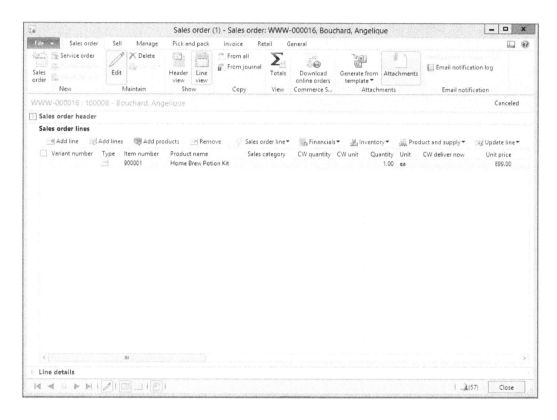

With all of the options turned on, there is a lot more columns available for you to hide.

Declutter Your System By Turning Off License Features You Don't Use

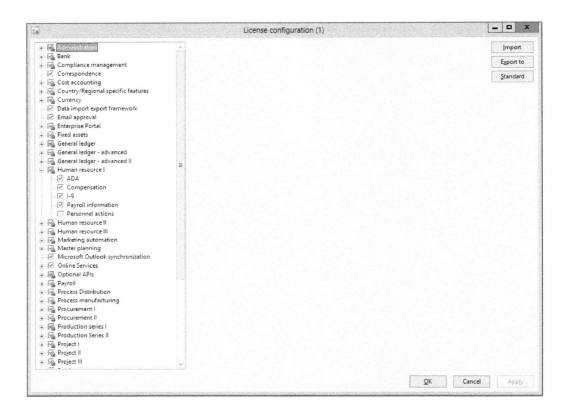

Just as a side note, if you can't kick the habit of turning on all of the features, then you can also feed your compulsive disorder by looking through the licensing file to see what options you are missing.

Declutter Your System By Turning Off License Features You Don't Use

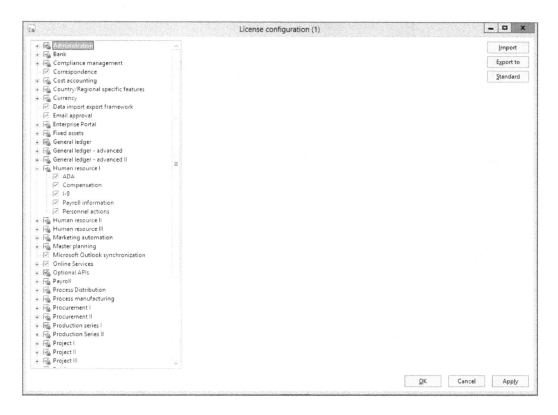

To make sure that you're not missing out, you can enable some more features.

Declutter Your System By Turning Off License Features You Don't Use

And like magic, you now have new features that you may not have known that you can take advantage of.

Add Menu Items To The Tools Menu

You probably know already that you can create your own menu items and menus within Dynamics AX, but in addition to being able to update the navigation menus for the area pages, you can also update the Tools menu as well to add any utilities and forms that you may want users to access. This way the users don't have to have access to AOT in order to open up those common hidden utilities.

If you really want to be clever, you can even add Tetris.

Add Menu Items To The Tools Menu

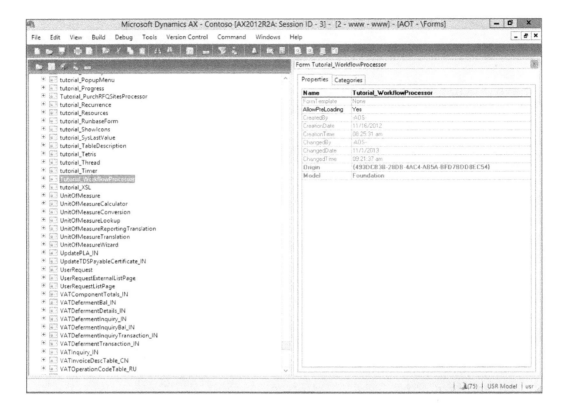

Start off by opening up AOT and finding the menu item that you want to add to the Tool menu.

Add Menu Items To The Tools Menu

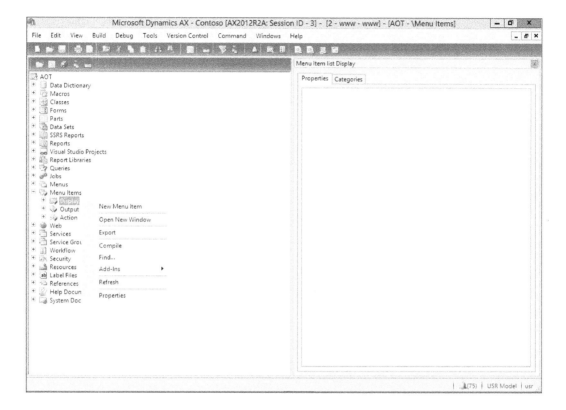

Now we will want to create a menu item for the form. To do this navigate to the Menu Items folder within AOT, right-mouse-click on the Display node, and then select the New Menu Item menu item.

Add Menu Items To The Tools Menu

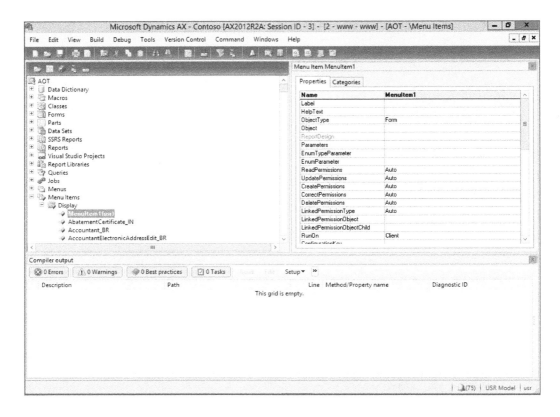

This will create a new menu item element for you.

Add Menu Items To The Tools Menu

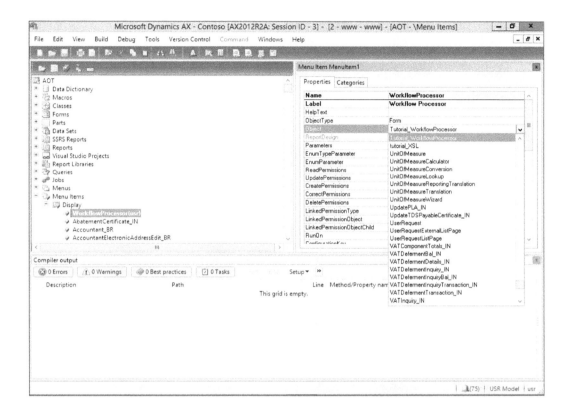

Give the new menu item a Name and a Label and then from the Object dropdown list, select the form that you want to add to the menu.

Add Menu Items To The Tools Menu

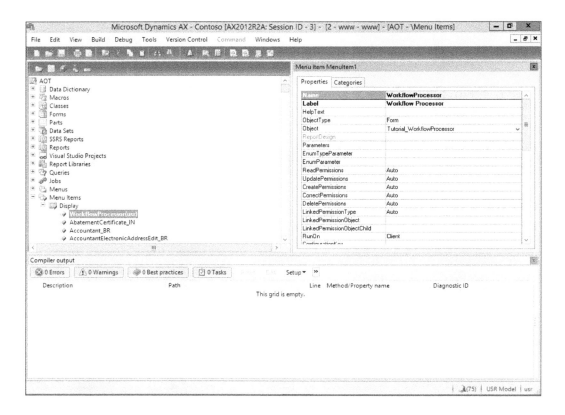

You don't have to make any more changes to the Menu Item control.

Add Menu Items To The Tools Menu

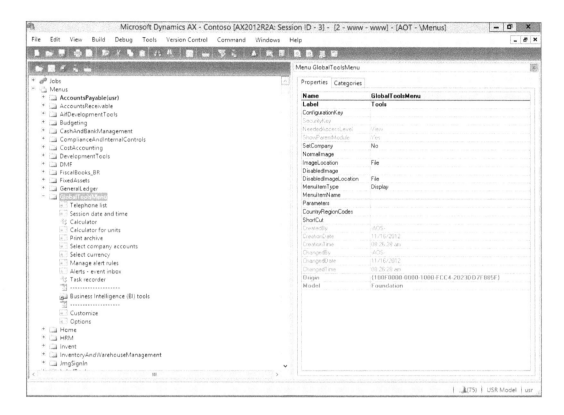

Now we want to add the menu item to the Tools menu. To do this, expand the
Menus folder within AOT and find the GlobalToolsMenu item within the menus.

Add Menu Items To The Tools Menu

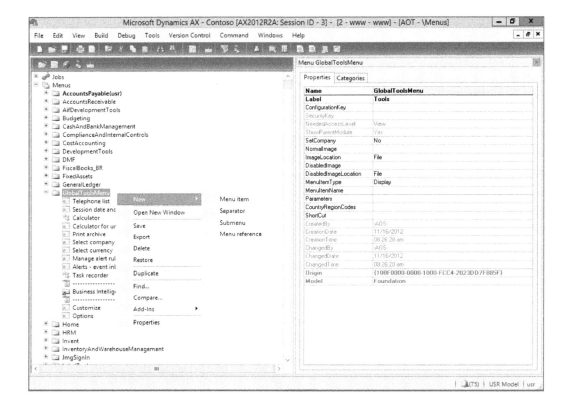

Right-mouse-click on the GlobalToolsMenu item, select the New menu item and then click on the Menu Item menu item.

Add Menu Items To The Tools Menu

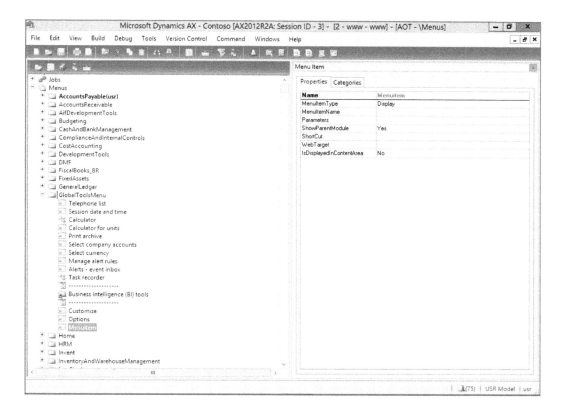

This will create a new menu item node within the GlobalToolsMenu.

Add Menu Items To The Tools Menu

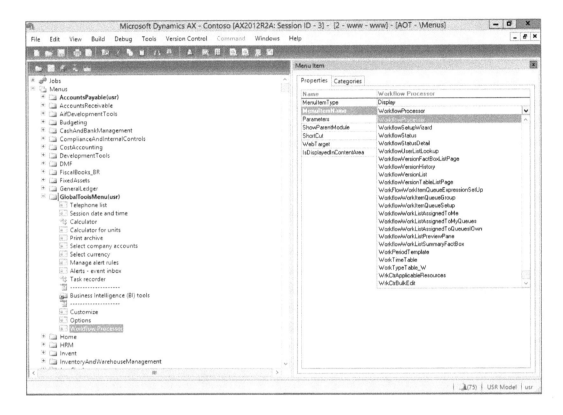

From the MenuItemName dropdown box in the Properties panel, find the new menu item that you just created.

Add Menu Items To The Tools Menu

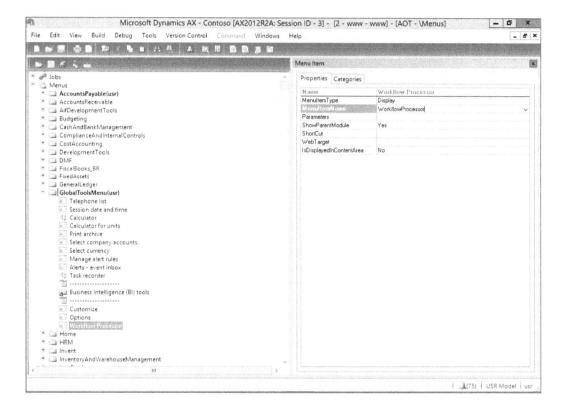

This will automatically populate the Name property for you from the Menu Item details.

Add Menu Items To The Tools Menu

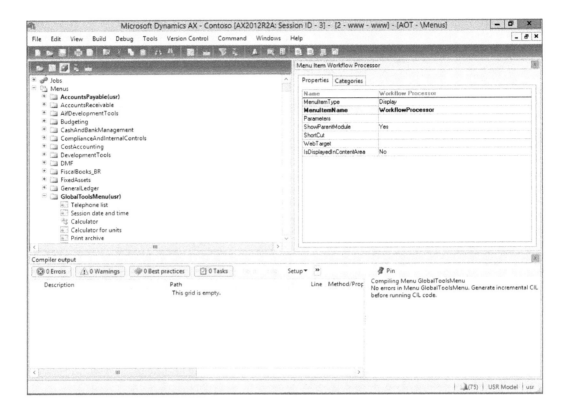

All you need to do now is click on the Save button to update the code.

Add Menu Items To The Tools Menu

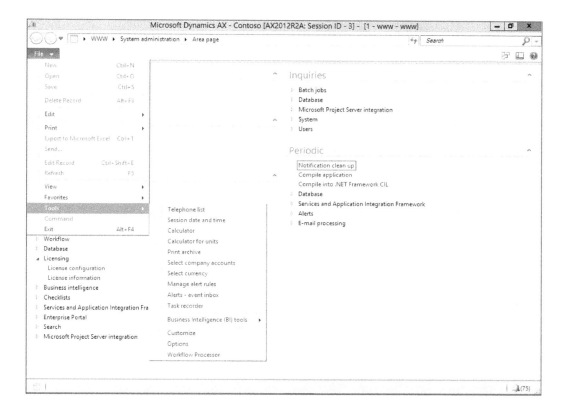

Now when you open up the Tools submenu menu you will see your new menu item there.

Add Menu Items To The Tools Menu

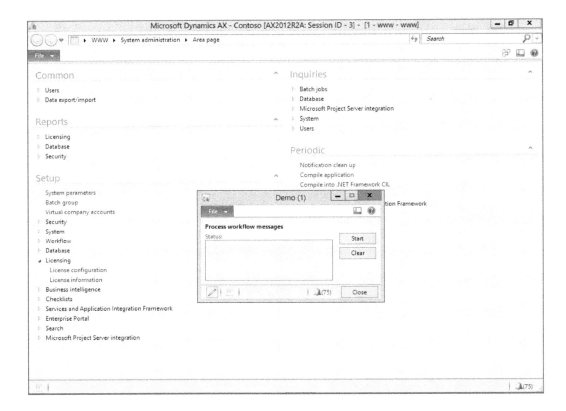

Clicking on it will open up the menu item.

That's too simple.

Create Composite Menus That Combine Functions From Multiple Areas

As you use Dynamics AX more and more, you will find that you are sometimes using some functions from one area of the system, and then other features from another area in order to complete a task. Although everything is in the logical place, you may want to have a way to access everything at once from one menu. That's not a problem though, you can easily create your own menu groups that meld multiple areas into one single location to make it easier to find everything that you want.

And you don't even have to wait for lightening in order to make it come alive.

Create Composite Menus That Combine Functions From Multiple Areas

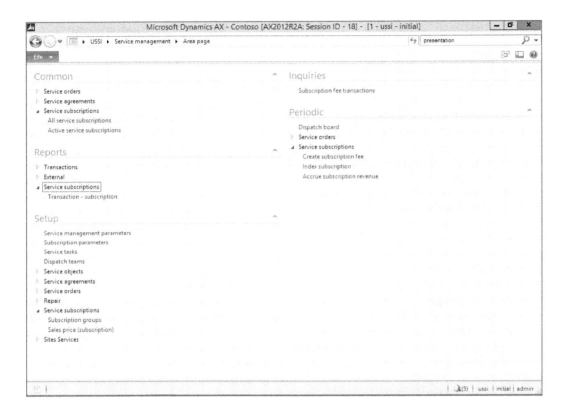

In this example we want to create a menu that is joins two areas into a single menu. The first is the Service Management menu.

Create Composite Menus That Combine Functions From Multiple Areas

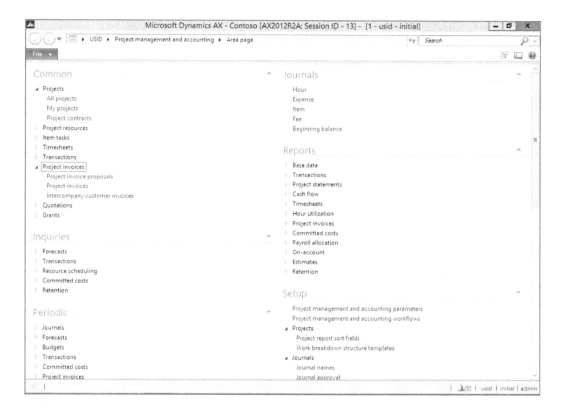

And the second is the Project Management and Accounting menu.

Create Composite Menus That Combine Functions From Multiple Areas

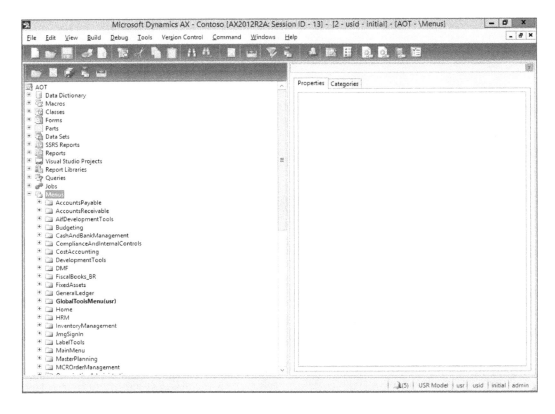

To start off, open up AOT and expand the Menus node in the tree.

Create Composite Menus That Combine Functions From Multiple Areas

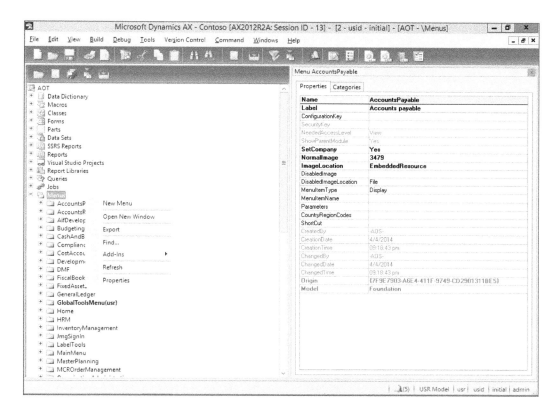

Right-mouse-click on the Menus node and select the New Menu menu item.

Create Composite Menus That Combine Functions From Multiple Areas

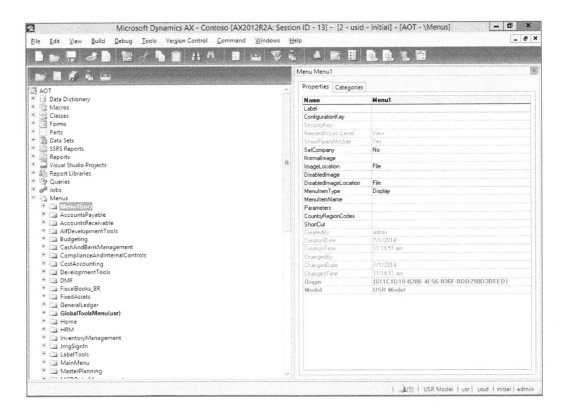

This will create a new Menu for you.

Create Composite Menus That Combine Functions From Multiple Areas

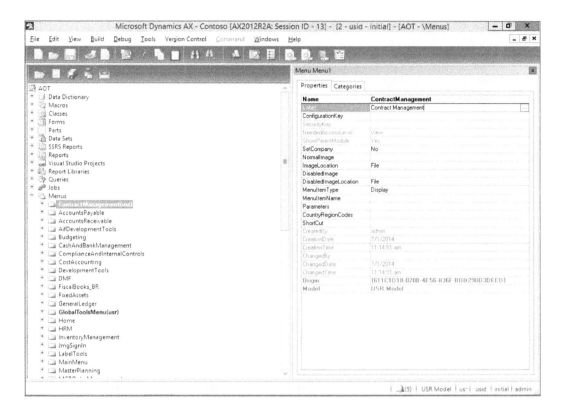

In the Properties panel, assign the menu a Name and also a Label.

Create Composite Menus That Combine Functions From Multiple Areas

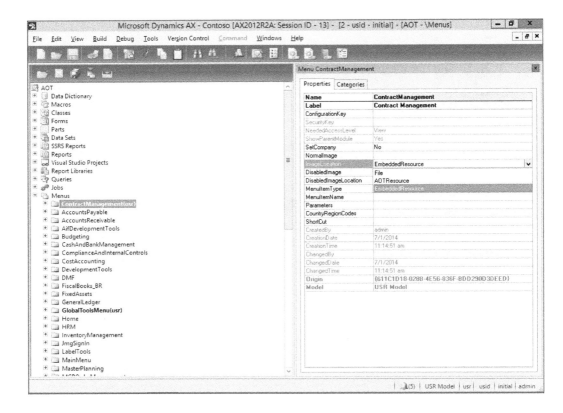

To make this menu look like the other ones we will assign it an icon. To do this, change the ImageLocation field to EmbeddedResource so that we can use the existing icons within the system.

Create Composite Menus That Combine Functions From Multiple Areas

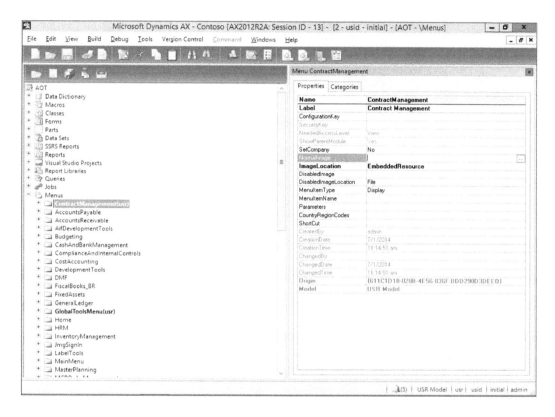

Then select the NormalImage field and click on the ... icon to the right of the field.

Create Composite Menus That Combine Functions From Multiple Areas

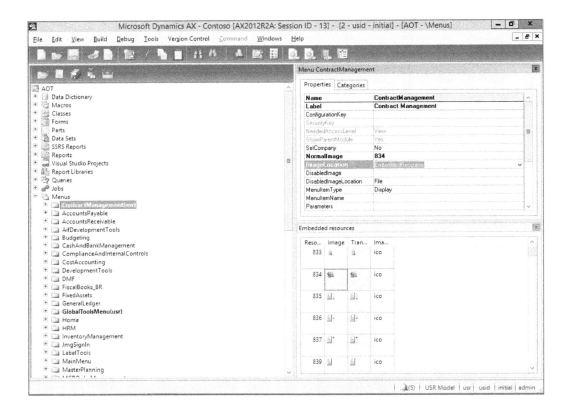

This will open up the Embedded Resources browser and you can scroll through to find the icon that you want to use and then just copy the resource id into the NormalImage property field.

Create Composite Menus That Combine Functions From Multiple Areas

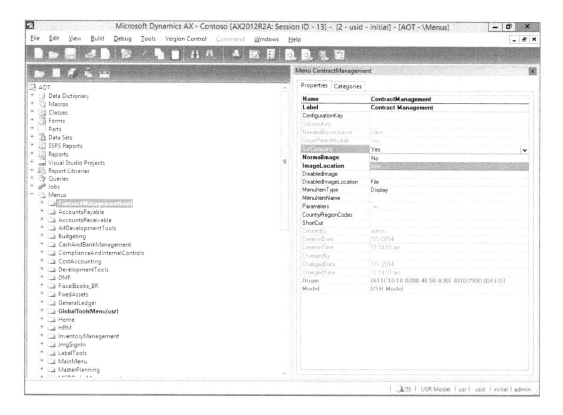

Also, change the SetCompany field to Yes.

Create Composite Menus That Combine Functions From Multiple Areas

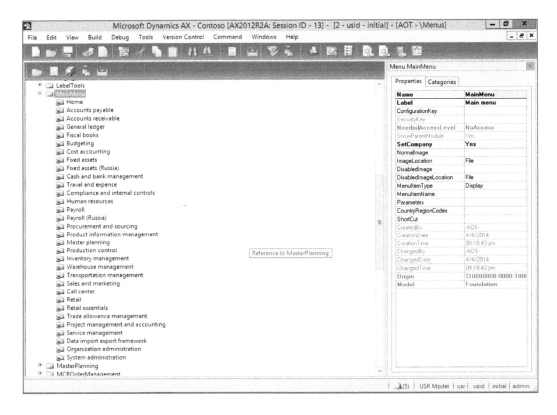

Now we want to add our new menu to the main menu. To do this scroll down within the Menu group and expand the MainMenu menu.

Create Composite Menus That Combine Functions From Multiple Areas

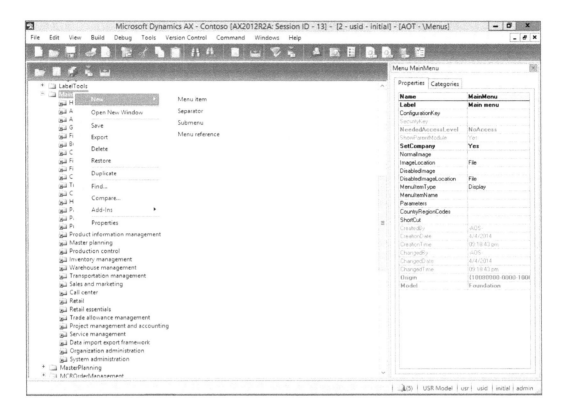

Right-mouse-click on the MainMenu node and select the New and then the Menu Reference menu item.

Create Composite Menus That Combine Functions From Multiple Areas

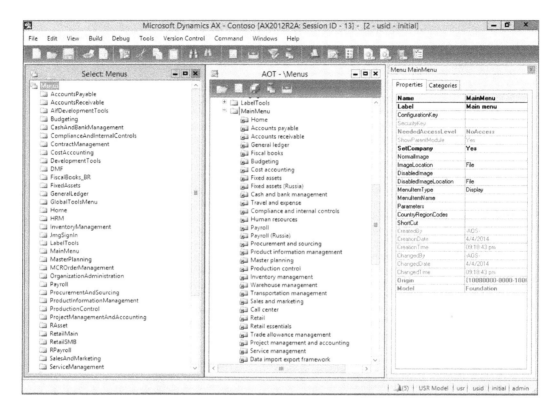

This will open up a Select Menus panel.

Create Composite Menus That Combine Functions From Multiple Areas

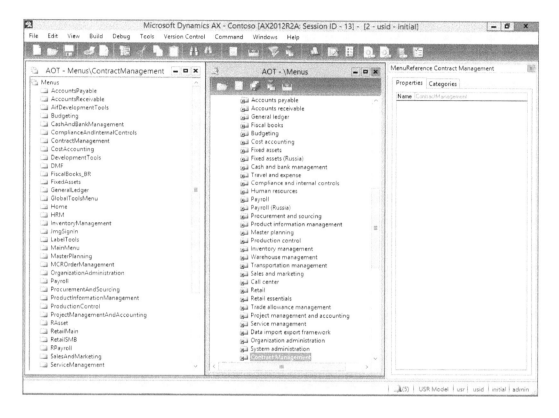

All you need to do is drag the new menu that you just created over to the MainMenu.

Create Composite Menus That Combine Functions From Multiple Areas

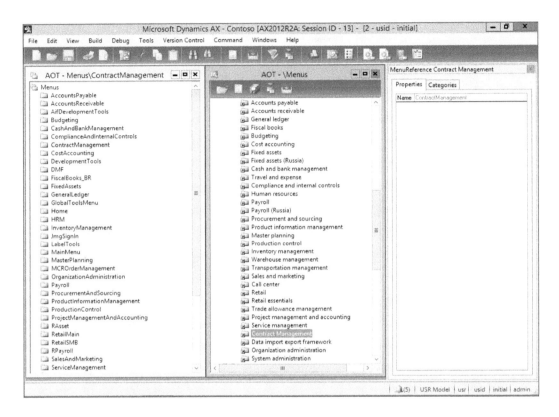

The menu will be added to the bottom of the menu. To rearrange it, just select the menu reference and then use the ALT+UPARROW to move the menu up in the list.

Create Composite Menus That Combine Functions From Multiple Areas

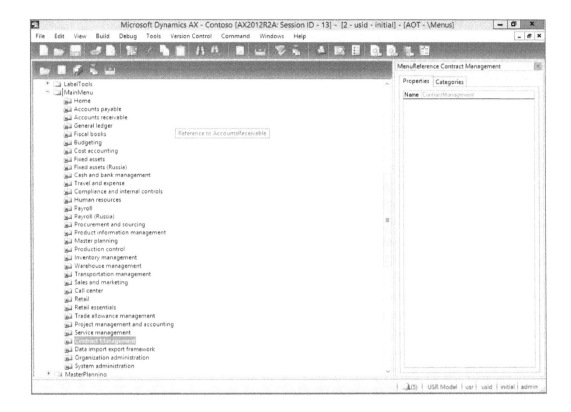

Then close down the Select Menu pane.

Create Composite Menus That Combine Functions From Multiple Areas

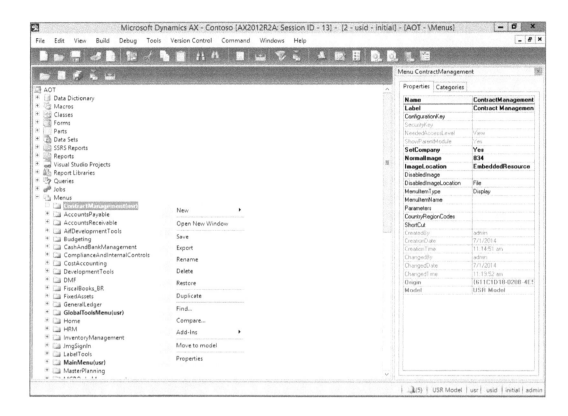

Next we want to add the sub-menus to our menu. To do this, right=mouse-click on the new menu that you created and select the Open New Window menu item.

Create Composite Menus That Combine Functions From Multiple Areas

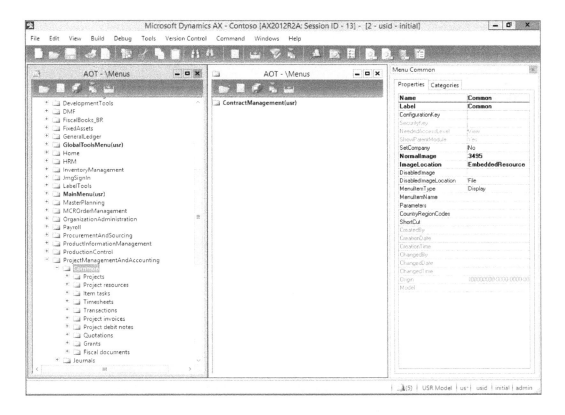

This will create a new window with just that menu it it and you can then tile the windows so that you see the original AOT explorer, and then the menu that you are creating.

Create Composite Menus That Combine Functions From Multiple Areas

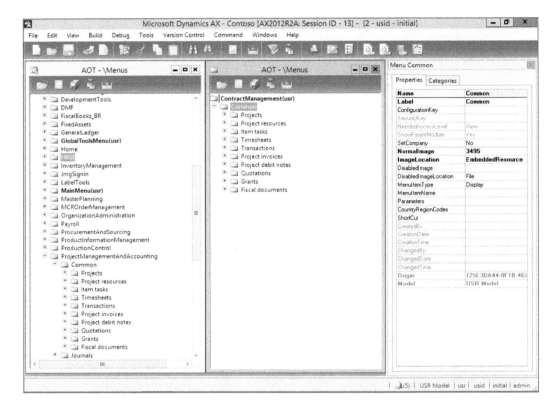

Expand out the menu that you want to copy the menu items from, and then while holding down the CTRL key (so that you copy and not move) drag the sub-menu that you want within the new menu over into the mew menu's window.

Create Composite Menus That Combine Functions From Multiple Areas

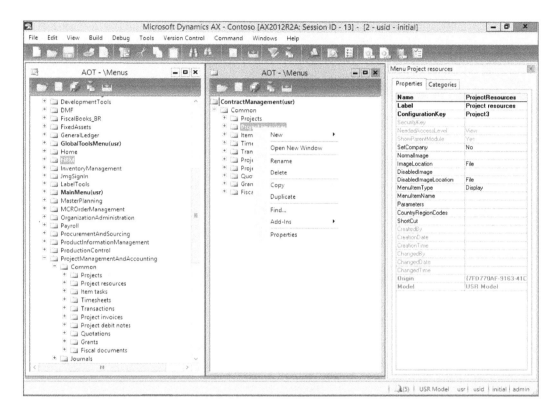

In this case I don't want all of the sub-folders within that group, so just delete all of the ones that are not necessary. This is easier than copying the menu items one by one.

Create Composite Menus That Combine Functions From Multiple Areas

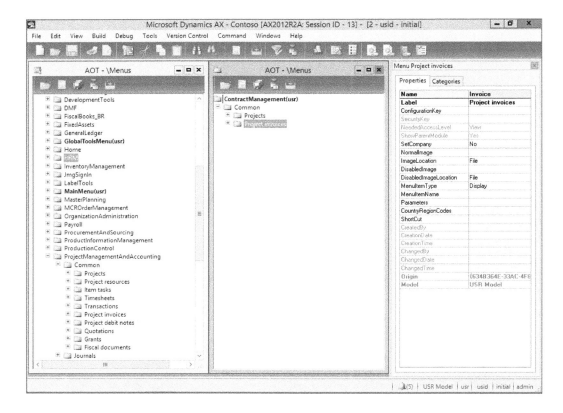

After you have deleted all of the items that you don't need then your menu should look a little simpler.

Create Composite Menus That Combine Functions From Multiple Areas

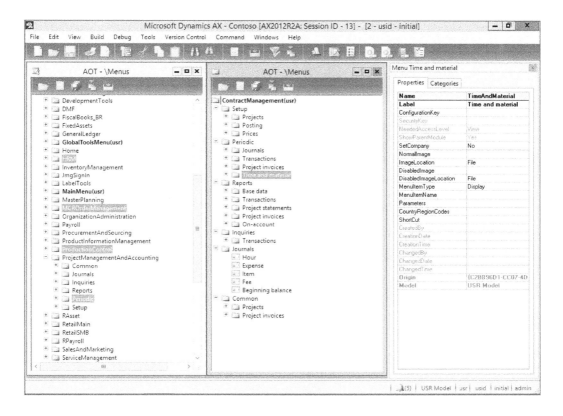

Repeat the process for all of the other sub-folders of the menu.

Create Composite Menus That Combine Functions From Multiple Areas

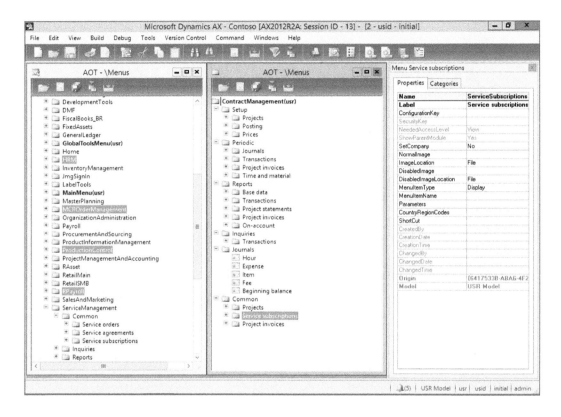

Now expand out the second menu that you want to combine together with the first one and repeat the process.

Create Composite Menus That Combine Functions From Multiple Areas

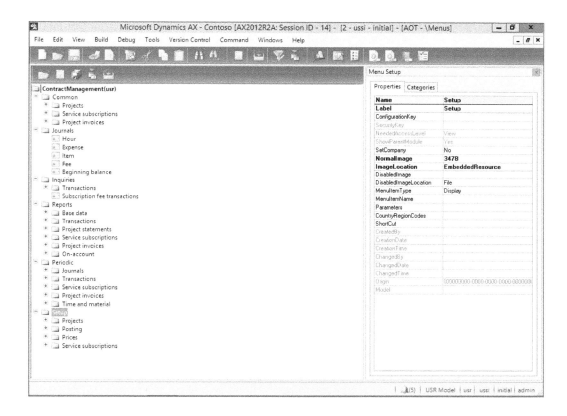

After a few minutes you should have a new composite menu. After rearranging the main menu groups, just save the menu by pressing CTRL+S.

Create Composite Menus That Combine Functions From Multiple Areas

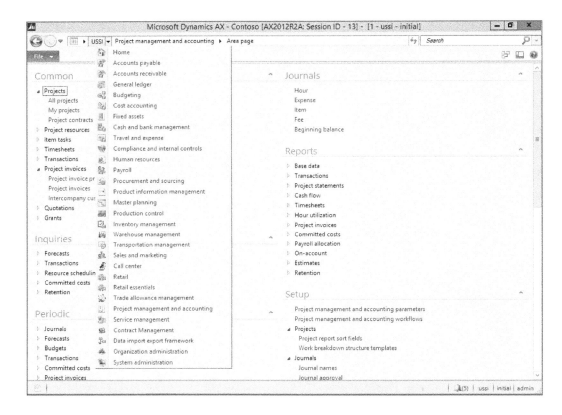

The next time that you log into Dynamics AX you will now see your new menu.

Create Composite Menus That Combine Functions From Multiple Areas

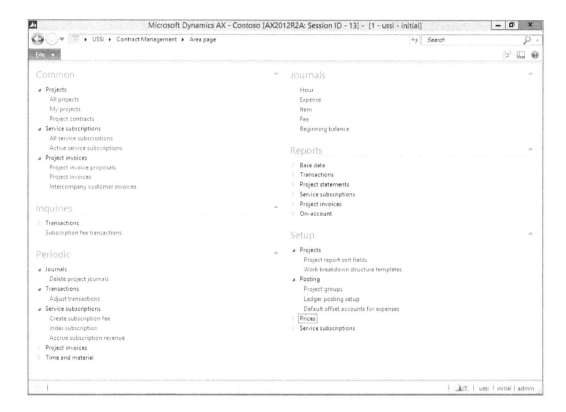

And when you open up the menu you will see all of the menu items that you want and just the menu items that you want.

Now I have a Contracts Management menu item.

SUMMARY

There are so many tricks and tips that you can take advantage of within Dynamics AX, that we cannot possibly inventory them all, but the ones that we have shown throughout this book are a good start.

About the Author

Murray Fife is a Microsoft Dynamics AX MVP, and Author with over 20 years of experience in the software industry.

Like most people in this industry he has paid his dues as a developer, an implementation consultant, a trainer, and now spend most of his days working with companies solving their problems with the Microsoft suite of products, specializing in the Dynamics® AX solutions.

EMAIL	murray@dynamicsaxcompanions.com
TWITTER	@murrayfife
SKYPE	murrayfife
AMAZON	www.amazon.com/author/murrayfife
WEB	www.dynamicsaxcompanions.com

www.ingramcontent.com/pod-product-compliance
Lightning Source LLC
Chambersburg PA
CBHW080128060326
40689CB00018B/3718